A Judge Too Far

His Honour Judge Keith Matthewman, QC
of the
Nottingham Crown Court

A Biography

by

Narvel S Annable

Belper 2001

Note!
The original quality of some of the
newspaper cuttings and letters is poor
but every effort has been made to achieve a
legible reproduction

Copyright © 2001 Narvel Annable

British Library Cataloguing in Publication Data.
A catalogue record for this book is available
from the British Library

ISBN 0 9530419 9 9

Published by
Narvel S. Annable
44 Dovedale Crescent
Belper
Derbyshire DE56 1HJ.

Produced in England by:

MOORLEY'S Print & Publishing
23 Park Rd., Ilkeston, Derbys DE7 5DA
Tel/Fax: (0115) 932 0643
using typesetting supplied on disk

To

Paul Sharpley

For enthusiastic encouragement together with inspiration and the laughs, especially the laughs, down the long journey of our friendship - albeit a bumpy ride!

Keith Matthewman, a law student at University College London aged 19.

FOREWORD

by

The Rt. Hon. Geoffrey Hoon MP

The Secretary of State for Defence

The landscape of this book is almost wholly familiar to me. Long Eaton's West Park, where Jane Matthewman first took an interest in Keith, separates my childhood home from that of my wife. My wife also attended Long Eaton Grammar School, as did many of our closest friends.

The Bull's Head at Breaston, where Keith was invited to think about applying to the Nottingham Bar, was a regular Friday night venue - as was the local fish and chip shop where many years later I found myself standing behind His Honour Judge Keith Matthewman QC. I wonder how many of Her Majesty's judges can be found queuing for their fish and chips wrapped in a local newspaper?

The Nottingham Bar treated us both well - Keith for far longer - because twenty years apart we both had a significant interview with the all-powerful Clerk to The Ropewalk Chambers, Michael Churm.

In Keith's case, in what Judge Richard Benson describes as a 'cross-roads' in his life, he accepted his clerk's injunction against 'political barristers' and turned down an open opportunity to stand for Labour for Parliament in a safe Labour seat. With the support of the local miners' union branch he would almost certainly have been propelled to a successful Parliamentary career, supporting, and then no doubt participating in, Harold Wilson's Government elected in 1964.

My interview in 1981 was my first meeting with Keith, who was at the time in charge of interviewing potential tenants for places at the Ropewalk Chambers in Nottingham. I had applied there for a difficult-to-obtain pupillage, and my nerves were not much helped by Keith's kindly, but persistent, cross-examination of my background, which soon revealed that I had been the Junior Common Room President of my Cambridge College. From this meagre information Keith extracted the admission that I had a practical interest in politics.

My recollection of the interview differs in one significant particular from that of Keith's therefore. Far from volunteering an ambition to go into politics, I recall a good deal of nervous prevarication on my part - not least as the early 1980's was not a good time to be confessing to membership of the Labour Party, as it tore itself apart under Michael Foot. My assumption was that a deeply conservative profession was not likely to welcome a practising member of the Labour Party. Keith's penetrating cross-examination left me with a clear choice - I could join his Chambers and give up all idea of politics or take myself off elsewhere.

Keith never resented or complained about my rejection of his offer when our paths later crossed in East Midlands robing rooms. I was right in those days to be cautious about revealing my political leanings. No-one then could have imagined a Labour Barrister as Prime Minister - indeed there was at that time only one other East Midlands Barrister I knew to be a member of the Labour Party - Willy Bach, now Baron Bach of Lutterworth, and coincidentally currently a fellow Minister in the Ministry of Defence.

Keith was a robing-room star - witty, irreverent and thoroughly entertaining, not least when describing a visiting judge suffering from too much judicial pomposity. As a Judge himself he set out to, and succeeded in, imposing his authority on the local criminal population.

There can be no doubt that the House of Commons lost the prospect of an extremely effective parliamentary performer when Keith decided to concentrate on the practice of the law. The country gained the services of a first-class Barrister, Queen's Counsel and high profile Judge.

Above all, it retained a man true to his East Midlands' roots, widely respected and admired for his plainly-spoken fairness. That is what this book is about. It could easily be called 'An East Midlands Man and Judge'.

G. W-Moon

FOREWORD
by
Lord Bach of Lutterworth
Minister for Defence Procurement

I became a pupil at 24 The Ropewalk in July 1972. Keith Matthewman, although still a young man, was already a star with a large criminal practice. One of my earliest memories is sitting in that same Shire Hall, to which young Keith had been taken 21 years earlier by his father, hearing that same Keith prosecuting case after case of unlawful sexual intercourse, all guilty pleas, before a distinguished but elderly High Court Judge who took an extremely dim view of 16 year old boys taking advantage of their all too willing 15 year old girlfriends, which was what normally happened.

Finally the exasperated judge turned to Prosecution Counsel and asked the immortal question:
> *"What are we going to do about sex in Nottingham, Mr Matthewman?"*

I knew already that Keith was a skilful advocate used to answering Judges' awkward questions, but surely this was too much for our hero! Not a bit of it: Keith replied at once:
> *"Yes indeed, My Lord."*

This immediately took the heat out of the situation and Keith went on to make sure, as good prosecutors always have, that the judge didn't go 'over the top' when it came to sentence the young men concerned.

I have always thought there was something of 'Matthewman the politician' in that reply. I have never doubted that if Keith had chosen politics instead of the law, he would have been a success. He had many of the necessary attributes, and would certainly have illuminated any front Bench! However, he would have missed out on a great career in the law - and a career he clearly loved.

Young barristers over many years owe a lot to Keith Matthewman's kindness and encouragement. I was lucky enough to be one of them, and nearly 30 years later I am grateful for the opportunity to thank him in this way.

WILLY BACH

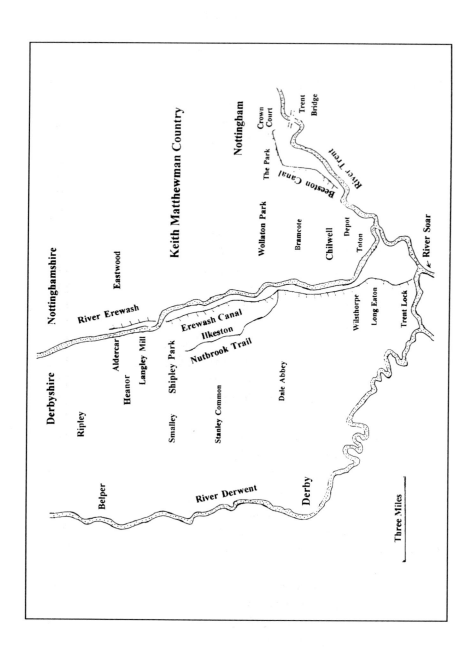

CONTENTS

Introduction

It was a rather miserable, rainy day in March 1996 when I went to interview my former teacher Peter Crofts at his house in Smalley. He and his wife Joyce Crofts had kindly offered to provide me with some information I needed for my second book - "Heanor Schooldays" - A Social History, ISBN 0 9530419 1 3.

In retrospect, it turned out to be a poignant first and last visit because, shortly afterwards, Mr Crofts was informed that he was terminally ill. He died, almost to the day, one year later. However, at that time in March we were blissfully ignorant of this appalling fact. In the friendly atmosphere of their comfortable home, with a big cuddly ginger tom nuzzling at my foot, I was busy making notes whilst various old photographs were fondly examined and discussed with enthusiasm.

Opposite is a photograph taken in 1960 of the full staff of William Howitt Secondary Modern School in Heanor where I had been extremely happy.

Top row standing from left to right - Mrs Winifred Molly Smith (widow of Mr Leonard Smith the long serving Headmaster of Mundy Street Boys School). Mr Peter Crofts, Miss Anne Henshaw, Mr Alan Priestley, Mrs Nancy Carswell, Mr Jim Ferraby, Mrs Dorothy Cullen (Secretary) and Mr Keith Matthewman.

Seated - Mrs Evelyn Mitchell, Miss Freda Brentnall, Mr Maurice Brentnall (Deputy Head), Miss Mary McLening (Headmistress), Mr John Rigby, Mrs Maud Buxcey and Mrs Doris Cook.

We exchanged nostalgic and informative comments about these fifteen teachers, who were frozen in a moment of time, as they smiled at us over the years from 36 summers and 36 winters back. Having retired from a career as a teacher the year before, I regarded these good people with considerable respect and affection and eventually, in the finished book, gave it the following caption -

"Look long and hard. These are the people who taught me how to teach. These are the people who taught me how to live."

The finger of Mr Crofts hovered over a good looking young man, top right, who was probably the youngest person in the picture.

"That man ..." I took advantage of his hesitation and said -

"Yes? Mr Matthewman. He once gave us a history lesson."

11

A 'one off' memorable lesson on medieval and Victorian morality to which I will refer later. Mr Crofts continued -

"He's a judge now!"

At that moment, after the initial rather pleasant surprise, I must confess that my thoughts were rather selfish! A teacher, who nearly four decades before had come into our class on one single, clearly remembered occasion, to speak on a very interesting subject, now, was at the end of the century - a judge! Surely here was the embryo of an entertaining anecdote.

Should I dare to approach The Bench? He would hardly recall the occasion, let alone a scruffy, pimply teenager out of many in the distant past. Decidedly this was indeed 'a judge too far'. Just for the record, the title of this book was suggested by Mrs Jane Matthewman.

I wrote to my ex-teacher at the Nottingham Crown Court asking for permission to describe and publish the notable occasion when I 'first came before him' to hear all about chastity belts and the attitudes of a lost world. I hoped for co-operation, but braced myself for a formal reply from a plain, sour sounding court clerk, along the lines of -

"His Honour thanks you for your recent letter but regrets that he has no memory of the lesson you describe. Accordingly His Honour, who incidentally specialises in libel actions, would very much appreciate it if you did not link his name with lessons concerning devices used upon wives by medieval husbands away at war."

What **actually** happened took me by surprise. I received a letter from Judge Matthewman in his own hand -

"I don't remember the lesson, but don't deny it!"

He invited me to telephone him at his home and discuss the matter more fully. He was immediately enthusiastic about "Heanor Schooldays", very keen to help and delighted to hear that I was writing about a school and a period of time in which he too had been very happy. He shared my affection for the staff and pupils of William Howitt Secondary Modern School -

"People knew how to be courteous and how to be kind."

It was during that introductory conversation that I had my first glimpse of the real Keith Matthewman. The man sitting high, in his robes under the judicial wig, the real man behind the very strict respected schoolmaster, who was received in silence as he entered to teach the class of Mrs Doris Cook all those years ago.

I come from a time when convention required that the pupil showed respect for his teachers by addressing them as 'Sir' or 'Miss', unlike today where some schools allow children to call staff by their forenames. In spite of having a university degree, being past my half century and having behind me a career in teaching, out of a habitual deference, I would always address one of my former teachers as Mr, Mrs or Miss, until such time as I was invited to be on first name terms. If that same teacher had been elevated to the level of a judge in the Crown Court of a major city and have an entry in 'Who's Who' and 'Debrett's People of Today', it seemed to me that my form of address should convey a higher esteem.
Keith Matthewman took a different view -
> *"Narvel! What's all this 'Sir'? My name is Keith!"*

This was the very first step in my beginning to untangle a complex and interesting character; a jocular character who could be high, mighty and ruthless, but in his personal life was also patient, modest, generous, diplomatic and very kind. Be not mistaken reader, this last does not signal the start of a hagiography. This book is not a schmaltzy whitewash nor a complimentary catalogue of endless congratulation. In this biography I have worked closely with the eponymous Judge, but what follows is an honest objective account, as accurate as time and money has allowed. Many have been spoken to, and as you will see in the following pages, most have spoken well of Keith Matthewman - but not all.

The popular image of a judge in court is of a high, remote, powerful figure; respected and learned, yet not quite in touch with everyday reality; but here follows a story over the last six decades of the previous millennium which takes many surprising twists and turns. From a modest start in life and then on to the classroom, on to the Bar and then the Bench; the following pages will also see Keith Matthewman working in films, holding political office, speaking on the radio and helping to breath life into one of Britain's most exciting and innovative museums - The Galleries of Justice in Nottingham.

He was appointed to the Council of HM's Circuit Judges 1984-1989, a member of the Nottinghamshire Probation Committee in 1986, the Parole Board in 1996, served on the Mental Health Review Tribunal 1993 to 1999 and is also an external examiner for the Bar Vocational Course at Nottingham Trent University.

Eventually he appeared on television, as Rosalind English put it in the 1994 July edition of BBC Worldwide, to -

"... rescue the public image of those who sit in judgement on the rest of humanity and defend his profession against the growing barrage of adverse media coverage."

In the foreword to 'Heanor Schooldays', Judge Matthewman said it was '*... a thoroughly enjoyable read*'. My aim is to have the same said of the following pages which, speaking personally, have been an enjoyable and enlightening experience. Accordingly, employing the skills of my former profession, I set out to reduce complexity, inform and clarify the legal language along the path of this interesting life story. Over two thousand years ago, the Latin poet Horace put it very well -

"He has won every vote who mingles profit with pleasure, by delighting and instructing the reader at the same time."

Chapter 1
The Red Judge

The cover story of The Nottingham Evening Post 'WEEKEND' Magazine of March 11th 2000 was entitled 'Judge for Yourself'. In the large type opening paragraph which preceded several full pages, Mark Patterson introduced Judge Keith Matthewman as -

"One of the most senior, longest serving and outspoken judges at Nottingham Crown Court."

Mr Patterson went on to describe one of the most influential experiences in the life of his subject -

"One day in 1951, Lieutenant Frank Matthewman took his 15 year old son Keith to the old Shire Hall [today the Galleries of Justice Museum] *in Nottingham to watch some Assize Court cases in action. From the Sheriff's Gallery, young Keith saw the sober High Court Judge, the 'Red Judge', in the pomp and finery of robe and wig, a ceremonial but potent representation of judicial authority and state power. He was also impressed by the showmanship and one-upmanship of the barristers as they pressed their legal arguments. Clerks, ushers, police officers and witnesses completed the cast of dramatis personae in the theatre of justice.*

He was hooked. 'I thought: That's for me, that's what I want to do.'"

This momentous and decisive day would not have been possible without the kind permission of another potentate in the small world of adolescence; second only to the Red Judge - 'Drac'! Drac was short for Dracula. Contrary to appearances, this was an affectionate name given to Mr FE Roberts, the esteemed headmaster of the Long Eaton Grammar School, whose long and intriguing jet black Oxford MA gown would rise and billow behind him as he silently glided through the venerable corridors of learning. This sophisticated, intellectual and slightly distant gentleman had to be consulted personally by any pupil who needed to be absent from school.

Soon after the above defining, judicial adventure, Bill Shaw, a scouting friend, tells us that their scout leader George Pembleton (Skip) had started to notice in Keith, certain attributes and mannerisms which suggested a budding lawyer. Jokingly, Skip started to refer to him as

'KC' which sounded to Bill and the other scouts as 'Casey'. Under a male monarch, the elite of the Bar were '**His** Majesty's Counsel, Learned in the Law', that is King's Counsel - KC. King George VI died on February 6th in 1952.

Bill Shaw said -

"Keith was expressing an ambition to become a barrister when he grew up while the rest of us were aiming to be cowboys, engine drivers, sea captains or space explorers."

Mark Patterson drew attention to the 'pomp and finery of robe and wig' and the 'judicial authority and state power' which were making a deep impression on the young Keith Matthewman. I will go further and suggest that a deeper and more subtle influence from that court scene affected the psyche of the young man. What Keith saw before him on that day was quintessentially a traditional English scene which held something of the ineffable unique charm and un-hurried courtesy which is so typical of the British courtroom; a room in which affable colleagues may well disagree, yet, can gallantly still refer to each other as 'my learn-ed friend'; a room in which an all powerful, yet avuncular, courtly, diplomat, seated high on his Bench, may, typically with iron hand in velvet glove, ever so gently remind counsel that -

"It would be helpful to these proceedings, Mr X, if perhaps you would kindly re-phrase the question."

It could be said that the Shire Hall court room was a microcosm of all that was best in the society which Keith Matthewman (young as he was) had come to know and love.

In April 1965, at the age of 19, I was thrilled to be sailing on the Empress of England returning home on an extended holiday after having emigrated to the United States 18 months before. Unlike the rest of the family, I had been miserably homesick for all things familiar and all things British. On the four available TV stations in Detroit, a British film was very rarely seen, and, if seen at all, almost always in the small hours after midnight and vandalised by numerous, irritating, low quality commercial breaks.

So it was with eager anticipation that I sat down in the darkened ship's cinema to view an all English, Agatha Christie film called 'Murder Most Foul' starring that personification of a 'blithe spirit', the whimsical and picturesque Dame Margaret Rutherford who played Miss Marple.

16

We see a dignified court room of oak panelling, similar to the old Shire Hall in Nottingham. The camera pans to an elderly judge who is summing up in careful, measured and cultured, sonorous tones.

"...and, furthermore, members of the jury, you will need to give consideration to ..."

His unquestioned wisdom and authority is integral to the total scene before us, reflected in the respectful faces of the film jury. Over these erudite and genteel judicial inflections, gradually we become aware of a small clicking and clacking sound. The judge stops speaking. At this unexpected silence, Miss Marple looks up to the Bench. The distinguished looking gentleman, grand in his wig and robes, leans forward -

*"Madam. Either **you** will have to stop knitting, or **I** will have to stop judging! Which shall it be?"*

"I'm sorry, My Lord, it helps me to concentrate."

This fondly remembered fragment of magical and quintessential British theatre with its gentle undertones of subtle and delicate understatement, was a sheer joy to behold in sharp contrast to the brash practicalities of a harsher, gavel banging, louder, more quarrelsome American court of law, whose plainly dressed leading players function in a functional, more modern, younger, utilitarian country.

As Keith was deeply affected in 1951, so I, now the confirmed anglophile, was deeply affected on the high seas on that day, fourteen years later, by a similar scene after being starved of the familiar, the droll and the eccentric for nearly two years out of an already short life.

Tradition, continuity and dignity are important themes in the life span of Keith Matthewman. In October 1999 he was interviewed by Jeremy Evans on Radio Nottingham for the series 'The Century Speaks'. Extracts have been compiled by Julie McGuinness and published in 'Voices of Nottinghamshire' ISBN 0 7524 1843 2. Mr Evans asked why wigs and gowns should be worn in court. Judge Matthewman responded -

"I know the Lord Chancellor is floating the view that we shouldn't wear them but it gives the court an air of something important and serious happening. I've always thought that wig and gown is appropriate and I think that most barristers would agree. It gives the court a more solemn feeling, not that all courts are always solemn - my court is certainly not always solemn! I gather that

prisoners coming into court have expressed alarm and little confidence in a bare-headed advocate - 'Is he the real thing? Are you sure? He's not wearing a wig! I want to be defended by one of those blokes wearing a wig!'

An example of totally unfounded fears from defendants, because in my experience I've heard some very effective solicitor advocates who do not wear a wig."

In these days of child-centred progressive education where fear of authority is eradicated by the 'let them do what they like' brigade, we should not overlook the healthy aspect of judicial intimidation which lends support to Keith's point about the importance and solemnity of the occasion. Charles Dickens wrote -

"Life in a wig is to a large class of people much more terrifying and impressive than life with its own head of hair."

One judge gave me an example of modern disrespect when a child was giving her evidence in a case of abuse. His Honour, speaking very gently to her, suggested he might look a little frightening and therefore would remove his wig to make her feel more comfortable. Head on one side, she considered the wigless judge for a moment before responding -

"Put it back on! You look silly!"

With regard to the possible intimidation of children and the suggested removal of robes and wig, Keith expressed to me a more forthright and trenchant view -

*"A load of rubbish! Absolute rubbish! Take the Bulger case; they should be made to feel the weight and seriousness of their horrific crime. It's these idiotic edicts from the European Court of Human Rights which have more concern for the criminal than the victim! If it ever comes about that wig and robes disappear - then I'm glad I'm going! If any Lord Chancellor ever tells me to remove my wig and orders the removal of wig and gowns in my court, I would say - 'Sorry, but **NO!** This is **my** court and **I** will decide.' Nobody tells me how to run my court."*

Very rarely is there animosity from a sentenced prisoner, but His Honour Judge Richard Benson made an interesting point about the value of the regalia in respect of anonymity and security -

"Very important in a small place like Nottingham. Grandly attired under the wig, wing collar and bands, nobody sees an individual; we all look the same and there is little risk of being recognised in the street. A judge is a judge. Apart from practical considerations, it dignifies the profession and lends a touch of history."

Former Executive Producer for Central Television, Mike Morley has his own views about regalia, but vigorously commends the real man under the robes who helped him to achieve the Royal Television Society Documentary Award for his 1992 programme 'Caution - Our Hands Are Tied'. Mr Morley told me that -

"We've all read examples of out-of-touch judges asking 'Who are the Spice Girls?' or 'What is a DVD player' (This out-of-touch author had to check on that one!) *and frankly few of us are surprised. Being gowned-up like Santa Claus every day and having people bow every time you enter a room is likely to loosen most people's grip on reality!*

Keith Matthewman is one of the few figures who restore public faith in the judicial system. Here is a judge who actually says what the man or woman in the street wants them to say and who hands out the kind of sentences they would like to be handed out."

Dignity and decorum have always been important to the Matthewmans. On the Sunday of the Queen's Official Birthday, the Lord Lieutenant, the High Sheriff and all the Nottingham judges and their wives are invited to attend a colourful display of judicial pageantry, a procession of judges which takes place at Southwell followed by a service at The Minster.

In one particular year it was an exceptionally beautiful warm day when a cheerful Keith packed the usual suitcase which contained the usual items including the 18th century horsehair ceremonial wig, potent and principal image of all judges, it is 'full bottomed' which comes right down to the shoulders. Before departure Jane said lightly -

"Do you have everything Keith?"

"Yes, don't worry. It's all there. I've packed it."

In the dressing room before the procession it was a difficult task for each judge to put on his full regalia so, by custom and practice, Jane would help before assisting her husband. The wig was in place, but, to her horror, she found that Keith's robe was missing -

19

"The robe! Of all things! I couldn't believe it!"

The procession was about to start! Keith could not possibly appear with just wig and cape. After a moment of self annoyance they were still determined to enjoy what was left of the day, therefore they quietly slipped away and headed back home to Nottingham. As it was a pleasant sunny afternoon, they relaxed in their well stocked and carefully tended colourful garden. Keith cradled his drink and shook his head ruefully -

*"My robe. How the hell did it happen? My bloody **robe** of all things!"*

At this point his eyes travelled slowly beyond the glass of gin and tonic and further down to his feet, where, somewhat startled, they re-focused -

*"**Bloody hell!** Just look at that! I've got odd socks on!"*

They both fell about laughing.

Three judges at the annual Southwell procession.
On the left is His Honour Judge Tom Kellock QC now deceased. In the centre His Honour Judge Ian Davidson QC and on the right, complete with robe - His Honour Judge Keith Matthewman QC.

Just before his retirement, Judge Matthewman received a letter from a Nottingham barrister called Michael Auty -

"Legal luminaries as well as junior members of the Nottingham Bar will mourn your leaving. You treated the latter with kindness and courtesy not only in Court, but at social functions as well where you always took time to talk to the most junior barristers and, more importantly, spoke to them in a way that made them feel valued.

When Shaun Smith and I said to you recently that you were held in extremely high regard by the local Bar and that there was much competition to conduct trials before you, neither of us were being sycophantic, simply truthful.

It is a curiosity, though you may think an interesting one, that your most enthusiastic support has, in recent times, been from my generation. Some of your most vehement supporters from the local Bar are those that are young enough to be your children. Whilst we are supposed to be the great modernises, it is interesting that we take great comfort in a Court that is run as Courts always used to be, with dignity and respect. Barristers are, to use Judge Benson's expression 'the fancy dress wing of the DSS' and, as we lurch ever closer to extinction, this old dinosaur cannot help but feel that we are losing something extremely precious and that, once lost, it can never be recaptured."

At the same time, Michael Auty will be the first to agree that the Matthewman Court was far from solemn. On one occasion, mindful that the defence counsel had recently barked *'Don't lead!'*, Mr Auty, prosecuting, was questioning a Police Officer -

"What happened after the collision?"

"A person ran from the vehicle, sir."

"What sex was he? I'm sorry, let me ask that question in a non-leading way. What can you tell me about sex?"

"Absolutely nothing, sir."

At this point, somewhat intrigued, Judge Matthewman intervened -

"Is that right, Officer?"

"Yes, Your Honour."

"Let me get this straight. 'I can tell you absolutely nothing about sex.' Is that right Officer?"

"Yes, Your Honour."

"Well! All I can say, Officer, is that you must have had a singularly unrewarding life thus far and you have my sympathy!"

Michael Auty tells of another occasion at Leicester Crown Court when Judge Matthewman was dismayed to see in the dock, seven exotic looking Rastafarians, each sporting a weird coiffure. Long locks wrapped in assorted colours of material enhanced the strange spectacle. As it was not April 1st, the judge was prompted to ask -

> *"Why have these people come into my court dressed in this way?"*

Michael could hear -

> *"Rumblings from my Learned Friends in London about Human Rights Act violations and all sorts of other nonsense!"*

He calmed the affronted judge with superb and courtly diplomacy giving the assurance that -

> *"May it please Your Honour; the defendants in this case have already been advised that they are in possession of a hair style* [here a tactful clearing of the throat] *not entirely commensurate with the dignity of Your Honour's Court."*

Former Crown Court reporter for The Nottingham Evening Post, Judy Cullimore, told me about another light moment when, with some alarm, an unsavoury character was once discovered lurking at the back of Judge Matthewman's Court. He was the late Paul Scarrott, nicknamed 'Britain's number one hooligan' due to his violent behaviour at football matches. When asked to leave by an usher, Scarrott begged Judge Matthewman to let him stay! He explained that he was 'seeking sanctuary' because rival fans on the streets of Nottingham were looking for him. His Honour, with dead pan face, responded -

> *"In that case, I suggest you find your 'sanctuary' in the nearest church."*

To his credit Mr Scarrott was polite and compliant. For further clarification of my subject's personality and courtroom management, let us now see how this judge deals with a another young man. A young man who has been shaped by a 'brave new' code of conduct ...

Chapter 2
A Judge of the Old School

On Wednesday February 22nd in 1995 a 23 year old man came into the public gallery during a fraud trial. He had matted shoulder length hair and was wearing dirty, hippie-style clothing. It soon became apparent that this individual had not entered Nottingham Crown Court to improve his knowledge of the judicial process. The ongoing case of fraud did not seem to hold his attention but **did** have the effect of sending him to sleep! Normally this may not have been noticed, since the judge was pre-occupied and conscientiously attending to his job, concentrating on the evidence and correct procedure ensuring a fair trial.

The visitor started to snore and his snores were loud, too loud, distracting for counsel, jurors and judge. Accordingly, His Honour Judge Matthewman asked the usher to wake the sleeper with a polite request that he should not sleep. Alas, minutes later, once again he slipped back into the arms of Morpheus and the snores were louder than ever, disrupting the court. The jury were sent out and then the young snorer was reprimanded by the judge -

"I have no objection to anyone coming into court if they were interested in the case or court procedure, but I am not having my court used as a dosshouse."

"Are you asking me to leave?"

*"No, I am **telling** you to leave."*

It should be pointed out here that this judge was at one time a schoolmaster; a schoolmaster who once taught me; a schoolmaster at a time when schoolmasters and schoolmistresses were usually obeyed without question; a time when pupils may have been politely **asked** to comply with an instruction in the first instance but were definitely **told** in the second instance and, if it ever got that far, were punished in the third instance. However this minor drama was being enacted in the 1990's when pupils were, and, alas, are still, encouraged to assert their rights and insist on politically correct terms of reference.

To fully understand the next move, the reader should be aware that this youth, a youth of the 'New School', is likely to have attended a modern school with progressive tendencies. For six years, casual young trendy teachers, probably addressed by first names, would encourage him to have 'free expression' and challenge authority whenever it 'comes on strong'. For six years he may well have been taught to despise what he sees. In his waking moments he has seen a room full of obsequious wigs representing a dictatorship of command from a man in 18th century garb. He sees what he does not like; an orderly structure, power and courteous obedience; this at variance with his comprehensive school experience where he has very likely spent his six years, not sitting in traditional rows, but idly lolling in friendship groups, chatting about subjects which need have little to do with the subject taught, without accountability, since formal marks were probably abolished years before. He has learned, many times, over and over that if he annoys a member of staff nothing much is going to happen to him - beyond a slightly uncomfortable meeting chaired by a head of year when he is persuaded to be more co-operative to 'John' or 'Mary' who -

>"......*after all is only trying to do her job! Please go back to class and do try to be more reasonable.*"

What happened next is likely to be the very first time that he has had any effective discipline, from one who once taught at the William Howitt Secondary Modern School in Heanor, where there was always effective discipline.

The youth, angry at not getting his way, rose to his feet, made an obscene remark to the judge followed by a rude gesture. The judge ordered his arrest! Sergeant Andrew Widdowson said his charge was argumentative, foul-mouthed, not violent but (no doubt recalling the advice of his left-wing teachers) refused to give his name or address. Difficult pupils take advantage of the anonymity offered by the crowds of a large comprehensive school and frequently will not give their correct names to a teacher.

A whole new experience followed: he was forcibly detained for the next three and a half hours in a court cell. Should detention have ever been mooted at his comprehensive school he could just laugh at the law and refuse, or quite simply not turn up - and, too often, that would be the end of the matter.

Bewildered by this new reality out in the big world, the enraged young prisoner is brought before the judge he had previously offended with his coarse, pornographic invitation and is about to suffer another new experience. He is to suffer a reprimand from a judge, who, still familiar with the high standards of a 1960 classroom, will not compromise with the permissive, loose, indecent standards of the late 20th century.

"When you were in court this morning I gave you the chance to go. If you had gone properly and quietly none of this would have happened. You and others have got to learn that in a court of law nobody is entitled to disrupt the court, or to make it difficult for the jury to concentrate on the case. The result of your conduct is that I ordered you to leave. You refused, you were offensive and you were in contempt of court. As a result of that I had you arrested and taken to the cells. Counsel has been asked to assist, but as I understand it, you have refused to be represented?"

Jim McNamara, a Nottingham barrister replied -
"Your Honour, in the cells the defendant said the same thing to me as to Your Honour! In those circumstances it is impossible to represent him today since that is all he would say."

The judge looked sternly at the silent young man before him. Far from being remote and out of touch with popular culture, this 59 year old judge knew and clearly understood the changes of attitudes in society over the last 35 years.

"There are, I know, some courts which seem to take the view that nothing should happen, it all ought to go away and there should be no fuss. I am afraid I do not take that view. Courts of law are places where serious matters are dealt with. I am therefore sending you to prison for 28 days. Take him away."

The sullen silence was broken. He raised his arm and said *"Peace man"*. As the dock officer was leading him out, yet again, this offensive man who had just been jailed for a month, shouted out his original, disgusting, coarse remark! In this situation a modern schoolmaster is likely to be at the mercy of his assailant to be sadistically re-attacked many times.

Perhaps the young man, even now, is unable to believe that his customary conduct is going to deprive him of his freedom beyond the lost three and a half hours. Unlike the poor schoolmaster, the judge had proper professional power and reacted quickly -

"For that you will serve another 28 days to make a total of 56 days in prison ...."

The disobedient youth opened his mouth .... but then closed it ... as His Honour continued -

*"....and **before** you say anything else ..... I can go on increasing the sentence up to a maximum of two years!"*

The culprit's mouth is now firmly and finally shut as he skulks away to be processed for his two months of punishment.

When the news of this relatively minor incident broke in the local and national press, a great cheer went up from the populous which was long, loud and heart-warming to this writer. I know, because I have read the letters of commendation sent directly to Judge Matthewman and the published correspondence to the newspapers concerned. The Nottingham Evening Post led with "NO DOZING MAN ENDS UP IN JAIL" - 23.2.95 and The Times misled with "SNORING SPECTATOR JAILED BY JUDGE" - 23.2.95 and on 7.4.95 - "A TALE OF TWO KINDS OF JUSTICE" by Bernard Levin.

Within this national applause (apart from Mr Levin, whose article by his own standards was almost pro-judge) there was just one other single note of dissension from a London woman who is definitely not on Judge Matthewman's Christmas card list -

"I read with incredulity that you imprisoned a person for being rude to you. You are an arrogant fool! I have written to the Lord Chancellor to ask for your removal from the bench which is too much infested with buffoons of your type.

Yours sincerely, Rose Kearns (Miss)."

> Churchfield. Nursing Home
> Knighton. Avenue
> Radford
> Nottingham NG7. 5QD. February 1'95
>
> Dear Sir / I take an interest in local News,
> under the heading of the Nottingham
> Evening Post, and the artical published in
> Thursday's edition (Feb: 23ʳ) has promoted me
> To write and thank you, for your self
> control, and verdict.

Not wishing to draw attention to myself I am in my eventide years of 88, and the lack of court manners is appalling, indeed this attitude is subject in all walks of todays society, and makes a mockery of law and order, and the common bond of respect.

May you continually experience a wisdom beyond your own, as you balance justice, now, and point to the future

Yours. Faithfully
Constance. A. Mason Miss.

On the occasion of Judge Matthewman's retirement in January 2001, the former Chief Constable of Nottinghamshire [1995-2000] Colin F. Bailey QPM (Queen's Police Medal) made the following comment which inspired the title of this chapter.

"It is intended to be a compliment to state that Keith Matthewman was a Judge of 'the old school' who sought to preserve the traditions of his profession and will be sorely missed from the Judiciary. I was always impressed by his common-sense approach, particularly with regard to sentencing, having the victims in the forefront of his mind and was never concerned at later possible interference by the Court of Appeal!"

In a personal letter to Judge Matthewman, Mr Bailey said -

"You were always admired by police officers who were always grateful for your support - when of course it was earned: we did not always get it right."

A judge of the old school? We shall see.

Making an ass of the law

THE magistrate who has resigned in protest over "soft" court sentences will find a lot of support and sympathy in Nottinghamshire.

Judge Matthewman has on a number of occasions in Nottingham courts expressed his frustration at the leniency of some of the maximum sentences he is empowered to impose ... particularly on driving offences and crimes of violence.

"Don't blame me — blame the politicians," the judge said at the end of one case.

On another occasion he told a meeting: "Offenders know that if they are caught and convicted of assaults the result will be a small inconsequential fine. They are leaving the court laughing."

JUDGE Matthewman pulls no punches on the subject. Too many times, he has said, we hear of the loss of dignity of the prisoner.

But what, he asked, about the 87-year-old widow who is assaulted and robbed and left bleeding on the pavement or the girl who is raped and strangled in an alleyway?

Only this month, the judge complained that the maximum sentence he was able to impose in a local case of dangerous driving was "wholly and ludicrously inadequate."

The convicted defendant had driven at and ran over a man after a row over a woman in a city nightclub.

He could easily have killed the other man, said Judge Matthewman. But the maximum prison sentence the law allowed was two years.

It is a deeply disturbing situation when against a background of ever increasing crime so many people involved in administering the law feel so angry and helpless.

Yet this government, which claims to be the party of law and order, does nothing about it.

On the contrary, attempts to solve the problems of our antiquated and overcrowded prisons by reducing the prison population could make things even worse.

There is now a generation of offenders who expect to be able to commit crime and never be punished for it.

And too often that expectation is met.

The vociferous anti-prison lobby which wails that prisons are merely "universities of crime", while ignoring the plight of the victims, also contributes to the current absurdity.

"Pseudo-sociological claptrap" is how Judge Matthewman lucidly describes the view of that lobby.

And the vast majority of members of the public would agree wholeheartedly with him.

So when is the Government going to react to this huge weight of public feeling and do something about it?

Judge warns over respect

NEP JUNE 1990

A NOTTINGHAM judge has warned that anyone who shows disrespect to his court can expect jail.

Judge Keith Matthewman QC issued the warning as he released 19, of Beechdale Road, Aspley.

spent a night in custody after saying "cheers" to the judge on his way out of Nottingham Crown Court.

After his night in a cell he apologised to the judge, who said: "All who come into a court of law are to show proper respect."

Chapter 3
Laughing at the Law

Former Crown Court reporter, Judy Cullimore of The Nottingham Evening Post, once told me that Keith Matthewman was the most quoted of the Nottingham judges. On television, radio, or in the newspapers, when commenting on youngsters and others, a frequent refrain is 'laughing at the law'.

A judge is seen as a reassuring figure, a powerful man, in his regalia, sitting high up on the bench. But Judge Matthewman is becoming just as frustrated as the former colleagues in education he left behind 40 years ago. It should come as no surprise to us that he appeared on a disturbing, prime-time television programme in 1992 and said -

"As a nation, we are in danger of bringing up a generation of young people who expect to be able to commit crime and never be punished for it."

This was the very start of an award winning documentary by Central Television in their 'Tuesday Special' series, produced by Mike Morley, called - **"Juveniles - Caution, Our Hands Are Tied"**.

It made for sad and depressing viewing. We were told that 100,000 children are breaking the law each year and two thirds of all offenders between the ages of 10 and 17 are released with no more that a telling off, what the police call 'a caution' -

"By cautioning you today I'm giving you another chance. OK? So get out there and put this behind you, and leave it at that, and stay away from it - it's just not worth it."

At this point we get the impression that the teenager (whose face is partly obliterated) seems to develop a slight smirk. The senior police officer continues, but briefly stumbles over his words -

"It doesn't matter what others .... other criminals say, at the end of the day you will eventually be found out."

We then learn that this youth has little to fear from this procedure having been 'found out' many times before and is very familiar with 'the caution', having had many 'cautions' before. Caught red-handed, he readily confessed to breaking into BMW cars, causing many hundreds of pounds worth of damage, inflicting an un-measurable degree of human distress and stealing hundreds of pounds worth of radios. On this occasion, as on many previous occasions, he does not pay any fine or compensation. He is simply warned that if he is caught again he may be taken to court - or, indeed, he may receive another 'caution'! We then see the youth walking out of the police station. The camera cuts back to the police officer who admits that -

"Half the cautions are a total and complete waste of time."

Albert Pacey, Chairman of the Assistant Chief Police Officers Crime Committee, puts the blame on the Government of the day -

"Through the Home Office and their circulars, we are required to caution juveniles in ever increasing numbers. Two hundred and fifty thousand juveniles are now cautioned each year."

As an experienced schoolmaster, I was by necessity skilled and well practised in the art of reprimand at its various levels of severity: very often the only punishment which could be given in some cases. Looking back 40 years into the William Howitt Secondary Modern School at Heanor, no one appears to have any memory of the type or severity of a 'Mr Matthewman style reprimand'. It is said he never raised his voice, but then again, who, in those days, would have dared put it to the test?

Detective Chief Superintendent Mike Woodhouse, Head of Nottinghamshire, CID (at that time) tells us that up to 70% of all crime is committed by juveniles. He shows us a long computer print-out sheet, fairly typical of a persistent offender with many 'cautions' on his record.

"Started stealing cars, placed in care, absconded and steals more cars. Then goes on to robbery, wounding, then burglary...."

We go on to hear that magistrates are also restricted by government orders: that is the Conservative Government of John Major as it was in 1992.

Senior Magistrate Jasmine Kendall -

"I feel I was appointed to the magistracy to protect the law-abiding citizen. This is now very difficult to do because our hands are tied. We can't deal with the offenders who come before us as we would wish to do. Some come to us after the fourth caution. We know

nothing of these cautions and it appears to us as their very first appearance in court, which explains the lack of a custodial sentence."

Judge Matthewman responds -
> *"They are almost encouraged to commit crime if that is all that is going to happen to them when they are cautioned over and over again. It's common sense that there's no incentive not to commit crime if nothing nasty is going to happen to you and you're not going to be punished."*

We see a group of pre-teens who have been arrested for shoplifting from Boots. They appear cocky and give false names and addresses to the store detective. Later, at the police station, an officer politely asks for their real names. They respond by demanding a solicitor. Superintendent Mike Woodhouse says this is not unusual -
> *"They often exercise their right of silence and refuse to answer any questions during an interview with the police. A marked change from when I was a young constable interviewing juveniles. It would have been unthinkable for me not to establish the facts. I would only need to say one thing to the youngster - 'tell me the truth'. I was **supported by the parent** and invariably we **got** the truth."*

In the presence of parents, the pre-teens are given a caution. One boy is on his own because his father chose to be absent attending a football match.

Even if juveniles are charged they are released on bail before appearing before magistrates. Many bailed offenders carry on and continue to commit crimes. Inspector Mike Smith of the Gloucestershire Police cites examples -
> *"One offender has been bailed 20 times in six months, one 16 times and another 24 times! Juveniles have to be bailed unless they are currently on bail in which case we can put them before the court. But the courts hands are tied and in the majority of cases they are bailed yet again!"*

Keith Matthewman -
> *"They don't get the impression that crime is important enough to stop. They go to court on some serious matters such as violence and they come away, having been fined a small inconsequential amount. They come out laughing. Their friends accompany them and they all come out*

on to the court steps laughing together! It gets around that it doesn't matter what you do, it's highly unlikely you will be punished for it!"

Eight years later the author Frederick Forsyth CBE made a similar point writing in The Daily Mail, 27.4.2000 -

"Insidiously, inexorably, our liberal establishment inverted centuries of morality by sympathising with the criminal rather than the victim. We entered the age of the can't-touch-me-thug when they leave court with ill-concealed contempt and swagger out grinning and smirking."

Albert Pacey -

"The public are suffering an enormous increase in attacks on themselves and their property and the police feel greatly frustrated in the way in which the Criminal Justice System generally is inept at dealing with this difficult problem."

A jaunty seventeen year old, no stranger to court with seven convictions, has re-offended regularly but **never** been jailed -

"I've done burglary, first one when I was eight. (He laughs) *A few ABH's* (actual bodily harm) *drugs, shoplifting, theft - loads o' theft, criminal damage, fraud and deception ...."*

In 1974 the Government scrapped the old borstal system. In 1988 Detention Centres and Youth Custody were abolished. In 1992, 32 Young Offender Institutions held just 2,400 juveniles. New laws mean even fewer will end up behind bars. It's a move a certain seventeen year old agrees with. He's carried out more than 300 burglaries, and like 80% of juveniles he re-offended after his first stretch inside.

"Puttin' someone in 'ere is a waste a time. Ya learn more about crime. Ya bored, ya talk to ya mates about burglaries, about safes an' stuff."

Judge Matthewman does not agree with this lad -

*"People don't **learn** how to commit crime in prison. You don't learn how to rape. You don't learn how to rob. You don't learn how to set a house on fire. It may be that people in prison discuss how to break into a motorcar, but no more than they do in the local pub or on the street corner, or for that matter, in a group on community service."*

Much has been said about prisons being 'Universities of Crime'. In October 1990, Keith Matthewman addressed the Northern and Midland Licensing Forum at Keyworth in which he referred to this view as - *"pseudo-sociological claptrap"* and added -

"The public are being seduced by a small but highly vocal anti-prison lobby. We are being led down a very dangerous road which can only lead to escalating crime. City centres at night are becoming 'no-go areas' because of gangs of youths looking for a fight - not the case 20 years ago. Violent thugs are leaving the court laughing and the police are justified in feeling let down by the courts."

Keith Matthewman went on to make a vital point which I feel is pivotal and crucial in today's society which (in my opinion) has been fashioned, shaped and damaged by the trendy teacher who has been trained by left-wing, modern progressive colleges of education.

"Anyone who tries to remonstrate with groups of young people will know the response; not one of embarrassment or apology but abuse and threats."

Up until the mid 1960's the very presence of adults on the public streets was a deterrent to bad behaviour. Bad language and loutish conduct would always attract reprimand - or worse. Boys and girls were well aware of this and acted accordingly. In "Heanor Schooldays" the example of Mrs Maud Buxcey is cited on page 157. A strict traditional teacher who back in 1960 was able to walk the streets of the old mining hill town, meeting pupils in complete confidence, safe from any embarrassment or verbal abuse. Eighteen years later as a starting teacher I was told to find a home - 'at least five miles away from the school'. It was very good advice.

Judge Matthewman's Keyworth speech was reported in a front page headline 'THUGS ARE LAUGHING AT THE LAW' - The Nottingham Evening Post, October 27th 1990. Also in The Daily Telegraph, October 29th 1990 - 'THUGS LAUGH AT LENIENCY CLAIMS JUDGE'.

Ten years later in a new century with a new Labour Government a depressing, screaming front page headline in The Nottingham Evening Post (22.02.00) gives evidence of little improvement - 'NAME, BLAME AND SHAME' - 'Law shelters teenager with shocking catalogue of crime' - by Ian Dury.

A familiar story of a 14 year old who has been arrested more than 100 times and convicted of 60 offences. He is the first teenager in England to breach new laws brought in by the Home Secretary Jack Straw as part of the 1998 Crime and Disorder Act, which is an (apparently failed) attempt to stop anti-social behaviour. Police and councils can now apply for an order against any person aged ten or older who persistently harasses, alarms or distresses neighbours. Hold tight! The following is mind-boggling -

The young malefactor broke curfews and admitted more crimes including threatening and insulting his neighbours, trespassing on other properties and finally deliberately ramming a stolen car into a police car after a reckless drive!! Other charges - threatening to set fire to a woman's house, threatening a shopper with a four inch blade, stealing £850 in cash, breaching bail, damaging a lottery ticket machine, aggravated car theft, dangerous driving, driving without insurance, then driving whilst disqualified by reason of age.

Magistrates argued that he could not be named because of his age. Rightly appalled and horrified by this protective decision, the Nottingham Evening Post on a front page 'Opinion' sought a comment from one who is well known for his empathy with the pain, suffering and distress this single yob has unleashed upon (at least) hundreds of honest law abiding citizens of Nottinghamshire -

"We think the public has a right to know the identity of this young criminal who has been arrested more than 100 times and convicted of 60 offences. Our view is shared by a top judge. Senior Nottingham Crown Court judge, His Honour Judge Keith Matthewman, QC said -

'I think people have a right to know. If someone is running wild and committing crimes left, right and centre then the general public and particularly the people he lives around, have a right to know who he is and what he's doing. I'm not saying the magistrates are wrong, all I'm saying is that's what I would do in the circumstances. They may have different views.'"

Keith Matthewman made a similar point three years before when he wrote a full page article in the Daily Express on August 31st, 1997 -

"A useful deterrent for youngsters would be for newspapers to print the names of offenders under the age of 16. Some text-book theorists worry about the psychological effect of exposure on those named. Perhaps, if they spent a couple of weeks in court they would approach this issue with more of an open mind."

34

At his next court appearance this troublesome teenager was in fact named and photographed in The Nottingham Evening Post and Councillor Graham Chapman, leader of the city council said -

"I hope the magistrates take a tough line but we've got to remember that this lad is only 14, he's got the rest of his life before him and we've got to look at how to stop him behaving this way."

Albert Pacey spoke the last ominous words at the end of the documentary on the same subject which was made eight years before Mr Chapman's comment -

"I don't think that anyone is satisfied with the Criminal Justice System. There is enormous scope for improvement. It is too long winded. It takes months and months to bring cases before the court. In my view it is on the verge of breakdown and the public are losing confidence in it."

It was this very lack of public confidence about judges and sentences which brought Judge Matthewman to be interviewed by Sue MacGregor on the BBC Radio 4 Today Programme on August 30th 1997. Ms MacGregor asked Keith about the problem of statutory maximum sentences being at odds with the flexibility needed by judges to impose an appropriate punishment in individual cases. Keith responded by drawing attention to violent teenagers who (at that time) could not be sentenced to more than two years in custody in contrast to the five year sentence for an adult -

" ... in general the public don't think that justice is being done and I have some sympathy with them."

Sue MacGregor bounced back with -

"But once Parliament decides on sentencing, a lot of judges say it is taken out of their hands and, in fact, it leads to far fuller jails, or in your case, fewer ... fuller young offender institutions!"

In between interruptions and Ms MacGregor shifting her ground, Keith managed to keep the discussion well focused making it clear that he was not speaking for all judges and added that the building of new prisons and new offenders institutions was a matter of politics, the responsibility of Government - not judges.

NOTTINGHAM JUSTICES' JOURNAL

MARCH 1991

JUDGE KEITH MATTHEWMAN Q.C.

How do clubs fare in maintaining standards inside the establishments? Generally speaking very well indeed. Management and staff maintain control. They are treated with tolerance, enough respect for everyone to have a pleasant time and no doubt some with courtesy and friendliness.. Acts of bad behaviour and violence appear to be decreasing in number and severity inside clubs. The reason is that patrons know they will not be allowed to get away with bad behaviour. Management and staff know they will not be allowed to let their patrons get away with bad behaviour. They have a licence to consider. There is incentive to behave acceptably.

How does this compare with standards maintained by society outside the clubs? Unfortunately there, violence and bad behaviour is increasing rather than decreasing. Decent law-abiding citizens of this country do not need statistics on crime, nor any arguments and counter arguments on those statistics, to know that 20 years ago they could walk safely down many a city street at half past eleven at night, whereas today they would not dream of doing so for fear of being assaulted by gangs of drunken youths and girls, looking for a fight. Anybody who has ever tried to remonstrate with a group of young people behaving badly will know the response; not of apology, not of embarrassed silence, but of abuse, hostility, threats and always, spoken or unspoken the riposte "Nobody can do anything to me," and they really mean it!!

It is appalling, but as a nation we are in danger of bringing up a generation of young people which expects to be able to commit crime and never be punished for it. They expect that, because that is the message they are getting from certain sections of society; sections which are gaining in influence; sections which openly say "Do not punish wrongdoers."They are an undesirable influence. The only result of constantly forgiving sin is to create more sinners. If more people recognized that, we would have a more law-abiding community. So it must be said the general level of behaviour in society is worse than that inside the clubs. The reason is the lack of sanctions being brought into operation in society in general.

What of those who undertake the task of keeping order in society generally, i.e. the police? Far from being treated with restraint or co-operation when doing their duty they are frequently subjected to attack by violent, aggressive youths aching to have a fight.

THE VICTIMS

I now come to the last comparison before we move on to consider the future of the clubs. The last comparison concerns the treatment of the victims of wrong doing. Nightclubs may have their own rough and ready justice for dealing with victims of wrong doing but I have never heard any complaints that victims feel ignored by the management. My information is that generally everything possible is done to help victims of any sort in the clubs. Almost the reverse occurs in society outside.

Too many people seem to have forgotten that behind every criminal there is a victim. Time and time again we hear complaints about the loss of dignity suffered by criminals kept in custody. How often do we hear about the loss of dignity of their victims? What of the 87 year old widow who has been assaulted and robbed, left on the pavement bleeding, so shocked and terrified that she loses control of her bodily functions. What of her dignity? What of the young girl raped and half strangled, left bruised and frightened in an alleyway? What of her dignity? There are dozens of examples, whom I see and hear about. Why is it that associations and societies rant and rave about criminals "slopping out" for a few months and yet give no thought to the fact that their victims may have the rest of their lives ruined — some physically, some emotionally, some both. The victims cannot get away with a few months "slopping out" and then forget about it as criminals can.

Let me say I am not a hanger or a flogger and if "slopping out" can be done away with then so much better. But let us not forget the old saying "If you can't do the time, don't do the crime." i.e. If you don't want to go to prison don't commit crime! Let me further say I do not forget the sterling work done by Victim Support nor the Home Office Victim's Charter. But the fact is, and everybody seems to be afraid to say it, that as compared with their victims, and I repeat, as compared with their victims, criminals are cosseted and feather-bedded from the time of their arrest to the end of their after-care on release from prison, if they go there. Victims do not get free advice from expensive lawyers from the start of their trauma. They do not get a vast Probation Service network helping them and their families to cope with the shock of being a victim and the emotional stress they have to live with thereafter.

Chapter 4
A Judge for the Victim

If we scan newspaper cuttings about Judge Matthewman over the last ten years we will see a reoccurring theme of concern for the victims of crime. In 1990 he said in The Nottingham Evening Post - 27.10.90

*"Too many times we hear of the loss of dignity of the prisoner. But what about the 87 year old widow who is assaulted and robbed and left bleeding on the pavement - or the girl who is raped and left bleeding in an alleyway? What of **their** loss of dignity?"*

Fourteen months later in the public gallery of Judge Matthewman's court, Barbara Roberts interrupted the proceedings by screaming out -

"She can afford to go to the pub and run a car!"

Moments later she was led out of court sobbing.

The judge said *"Her outburst was entirely understandable"*, and readily forgave Mrs Roberts because she was one of the many victims he so cares about. In October 1990, her 22 year old son Dale Roberts had been killed on his motorcycle by a 37 year old drunk driver, (the subject of Mrs Robert's outburst) who was found to be twice over the limit. Her punishment was a conditional discharge, three year driving ban and an order to pay £50 costs. Judge Matthewman apologised for this *'paltry punishment'* which was due to the drunk driver living on state benefits, hence the angry response above. He went on to tell the jurors that he was *'stumped by Parliament'* -

"If you think my decision is unfair and distressing - I'll be the first to agree with you! Courts are constantly asking for more powers to punish people properly ... but Parliament is making sure on many occasions that it becomes more and more difficult. Don't complain to the court if you want something done about it, write to your MP."

The above made a front page headline in The Nottingham Evening Post, 12.12.91 - 'NO JAIL STORM ON DEATH DRIVER' by Marian Bryson.

A similar and even more serious case involved a victim who survived after being deliberately driven at and run over! The maximum sentence allowed to Judge Matthewman was two years, which he described as *'wholly and ludicrously inadequate'*. In the August of 1998 he wrote to the Home Secretary, Jack Straw, demanding more power to punish dangerous drivers such as a 20 year old who put her foot down, saying *'Go baby go!'* She went, with three passengers, one of whom was eleven years of age, at 75 mph with no insurance or licence, pursued by the police, through the Bestwood Estate, Nottingham, before crashing head on into another car. Judge Matthewman said it was -

" *... ridiculous that I can only impose a maximum sentence of two years on a dangerous driver who may inflict desperately serious injuries on innocent parties. But we are not Parliament, we just carry out the will of Parliament.* "

Judge Matthewman never did received any acknowledgement, let alone a reply from Mr Straw.

"In many ways Jack Straw is a good Home Secretary, but obviously his civil servants are not as efficient as Michael Howard's used to be."

However we have now moved on. Today there is an offence of Causing Death by Driving while under the influence of drink or drugs which could attract a maximum prison sentence of up to ten years.

Judge Keith Matthewman Q.C.,
Crown Court,
Nottingham.

Bourne, Lincs.
23rd. February, 1996.

Dear Sir,

It was very encouraging to read your complaint that the maximum sentence for aggravated vehicle taking was lamentably low.   Unfortunately the same complaint can very justifiably be laid against sentences for so many offences.   It is even more deplorable when some judges will not impose a maximum sentence when it is available.
The Daily Telegraph on the 16th. February reported that a sentence of 5 years was imposed on a youth who killed two people by dangerous driving.   This in spite of the fact that the judge could, and should, have imposed the maximum sentence of 10 years.   One can only guess at the feelings of the parents of the 15 year old girl , and the relatives of the elderly man also killed.

One reads almost daily of the most trivial sentences for the most horrendous crimes committed not infrequently by someone with a previous conviction for a similar offence.   A life sentence no longer means life now.   A man sentenced to life for murder in 1989 and released after only 4 years has just been sentenced to life again for the murder of a second woman.   Will he be released again in 4 years time ?
It is not surprising that the law , the legal profession and, presumably, the Home Office, are now held in such low esteem.   Whatever happened to the principle that Justice should not only be done but should also be seen to be done ?   It seems we need more Judges like you prepared to do something about it .

Yours faithfully.

Richard Culpin
Richard Culpin.

Keith is prepared to admit his mistakes. I suspect he was thinking about the victim on the one unique occasion he walked out of court at the end of a trial without the customary courtesy of thanking the jury for their time and effort before the final and formal dismissal. A somewhat embarrassed and mystified clerk said later -

"After you rose, Your Honour, I told the jury that they were now free to go ... I do hope that was in order?"

Keith confided that his unthinking conduct was due to annoyance with the jury who had just acquitted a defendant he believed to be guilty -

"It was plain rude but it was early in my time on the Bench and shouldn't have happened. It certainly never happened again."

Keith Matthewman was also concerned about another victim of crime, a Mr Geoffrey Thibeault. After Mr Thibeault took over Cherry Tree Stores on the 'troubled' Bestwood Estate in 1994, he, Thibeault, suffered regular attacks from hooligans which included verbal abuse and throwing stones causing broken windows, each of which cost him £200 and an increase in his insurance premium. It was reaching a point where he had to consider giving up the business. Others had done just that, resulting in many shops being boarded up due to vandalism and arson.

In October 1995 a gang of youths were throwing mud balls at his shop. Twice he asked them to stop which resulted in a predictable disrespectful chorus of cheek from boys who had been taught over and over again that they were not accountable for their actions. They would have learned this lesson at home, at school and in society at large. Why should they stop having their fun?

Geoffrey Thibeault decided to make a citizen's arrest and to put his trust in the law. Sadly the law failed him. His grabbed one 11 year old yob and dragged him into the shop whilst his wife telephoned the police. Quite naturally, after a year of this type of harassment, Mr Thibeault was furious and slapped the culprit after further taunting. The little hooligan complained bitterly to his father about this unwelcome, unexpected (but much needed) discipline. Normally one might have thought the parent would have felt some responsibility or shame regarding the appalling conduct of his tearaway son, but this appears not to be so in this case. He went to see Mr Thibeault and punched him!

What happened next is difficult to believe. This already much wronged shopkeeper is wronged yet again. He is charged by the police for assaulting the youth and hauled up before the magistrates court who convict him of assault. Mr Thibeault, a man who is trying to earn an honest living in peace, is given a 12 month conditional discharge and ordered to pay his young persecutor £100 compensation. The law has been stood in its head! The public boil with rage.

On November 14th, 1995 the Nottingham Evening Post leads with -
'FURIOUS SHOPMAN FIGHTS ORDER' - 'I can't believe this ruling'.
Neither could Judge Matthewman when, sitting on appeal with two magistrates, he revoked the £100 compensation order.
"This case should never have been brought. We are mystified why the appellant was charged in the first place. The most sensible and appropriate action would have been a police caution."

It is interesting to note that Geoffrey Thibeault, a law abiding man providing a valuable service to the public, is not even once extended the generosity of a 'caution' given many times over to persistent, destructive young offenders. This supports the growing view that the compliant, respectable citizen is a 'sitting duck' whenever some police forces wish to bring upon him / her the full force of the law.

In a BBC Radio Nottingham interview [The Century Speaks, October 1999] Keith Matthewman at his home made a similar point in a hypothetical scenario put to interviewer Jeremy Evans -
"If, right now, a gang of youths started to shout abuse and throw stones at my car which you see outside, and - just supposing that I went out to tackle them, grabbed one and hit him! My God! I would be the one to end up in court - not them!"

The mind boggles. I can just see the headlines in the 'News of the World' - SENIOR JUDGE ARRESTED AND CHARGED FOR VIOLENT ATTACK ON YOB - 'I'd do it again' said unrepentant Judge Matthewman.

Back to the reality of the Thibeault appeal. Judge Matthewman -
"How can anyone be expected to put up with the continuous and deliberate misbehaviour of a gang of unruly youths? Eventually,

and in understandable frustration, he went out to try to deal with the situation himself. A situation which is unfortunately all too common these days.

We do not want to encourage people to take the law into their own hands but unfortunately sometimes these days that may be a necessity. One can imagine the scene - no doubt they were swearing and being abusive. Mr Thibeault knew that the law is powerless to discipline these juveniles who were making people's lives a misery.

In our judgement, entirely the wrong message is given to youths who act in that way if they think they are above the law and think they can get compensation for themselves as a result of their original wrong doing. We are of the clear and unanimous view that the juvenile complainant was the basic author of his own misfortune - if a couple of red marks can be described as a 'misfortune'."

For the original sentence of conditional discharge, Judge Matthewman substituted an absolute discharge. Mr Thibeault said -

"It might not discourage yobs from pelting my shop but at least the judge was trying to do something about it. When I was ordered to pay compensation I knew the kids around here were just going to think it was a joke. I want to thank people for all their support. It's marvellous. I am overwhelmed by the response and congratulations from my customers."

Mr Thibeault's comment made together with smiling photographs under the headline of 'JOY AS SLAP ORDER GETS OVERTURNED' in The Nottingham Evening Post 21.12.95 by Lynette Pinchess and Simon Harrison, was well justified but does not take account of the cost of money, time and mental stress the shopkeeper had to endure before he arrived at this victorious position.

Keith Matthewman's wise words were reported nationally in The Daily Express, on the same day under 'WHEN IT'S RIGHT TO GIVE THUGS A CLIP AROUND THE EAR' - 'Attack case trader backed by judge' - by Ian Cobain.

The Nottingham Evening Post also said -

"Well done Judge Keith Matthewman. We think the judge's ruling is a victory for common sense. What do YOU think?"

The results of the telephone poll were published on 23.12.95 and an overwhelming 668 supported Keith Matthewman and just 33 disagreed with his decision. On 22.12.95, a letter of fulsome support (a typical example of several) travelled to the Nottingham Crown Court from Wick, Littlehampton in Sussex -

"Dear Judge Matthewman, I would like to thank you for your comments regarding Mr Thibeault ... what a pity there are not more judges with your common sense! As for the Crown Prosecution Service, I sometimes wonder what kind of people make up this organisation ... I wanted to let you know how I, and thousands of other members of the public, appreciate your sensible outlook ... P.W. Watson.

VIRGINIA WATSON
SURREY GU25 4JT

DEC 1995

Sir

Allow me to wish you and your family the happiest of christmases.

To say that I am delighted to read that you quashed the verdict against Mr Thibeault would be an understatement.

I was born in the blitz in Jan 41 and many's the time I had a clip "around the ear" from a P.C. when I had been caught scrumping ect. If I had told my dad he would have clipped the other one.

I have 3 grown up sons one works in the Bank of England, One for the Police in London and one for BT doing Desk Top Publishing They were taught from the beginning what was right from wrong and being brought up in Army Schools gave them the experience of disapline. IF other Judges were like you England would be a much better place. Well done Sir Happy Xmas.

Edward Smith

42

The Nottingham Evening Post also reminded readers about related 'victims' such as the time a 15 year old refused to give his name to, and swore at, police officer PC Nicholas Godber. He was fined £300, ordered to pay £300 costs and £50 compensation to his victim. That is, the **policeman** paid the compensation to the yob - the 'victim'. Again common-sense is stood on its head. Mr Godber, who grabbed the lad by the ear, nearly lost his job for trying to uphold the co-operation and respect which is due to an officer of the law. Respect which was commonplace when Keith Matthewman and Narvel Annable were teenagers.

In the November of 1995, Judge Matthewman had cause to refer to another appalling case of twisted justice. Remember Ilkeston pensioner Ted Newberry? He was the victim of persistent damage and theft from his garden allotment shed and decided to do something about it. In March 1988 he lay in wait and blasted the criminal with a 12 bore shotgun. The result being that Mr Newberry, who was 76 at the time, had to pay the burglar £4,000 compensation.

Seven years later that same burglar, now 28 years old is standing in court number five at Nottingham Crown Court, having been convicted of an attempted burglary from another frightened elderly pensioner, this time 78 year old Cyril Clifford. Before passing sentence Judge Matthewman referred to the previous Ilkeston allotment incident -
"Obviously it has not taught you a lesson."
He then imposed a two year jail sentence. This took account of the terror suffered by Mr Clifford who was now very frightened in his own home.
This story was fully reported in The Nottingham Evening Post 21.11.95 under a front page headline - 'SHOT, AWARDED £4,000 .... NOW HE'S IN JAIL - JUSTICE' and on page three 'YOU DIDN'T LEARN said JUDGE MATTHEWMAN'.

During April 2000 we had screaming headlines of indignation and outrage over the conviction of Tony Martin who shot and killed 16 year old Fred Barras who was in the act of burgling Mr Martin's farm. In the Daily Mail [17.04.00] Frederick Forsyth had no doubt where the true blame lay -
"The real villains of Bleak House are not the panicky farmer Tony Martin, nor yet the constables of West Norfolk. They are the

magistrates and judges who allowed the three burglars to still be at large after a total of 114 convictions."

Earlier in Nottingham, under the headline of 'JUDGE COMMENDS BATTLING STEPHANIE', Judy Cullimore wrote the following dramatic and disturbing lines in the edition of The Nottingham Evening Post on 10.6.92 -

"Stephanie Richmond was terrified when she woke to find a burglar in her bedroom. Yet she tackled him as he ran off."

The twenty year old broke into the Bulwell home and stole property worth more than £2,000 when Mr Richmond was in hospital and Mrs Richmond was alone with her two young children. She grappled with the intruder pulling off his jumper when he broke free. Meanwhile her nine year old daughter Jennifer called the police.

After sentencing the thief to four years in a young offender institution, Judge Matthewman awarded Mrs Richmond £200 for her bravery and £25 to Jennifer.

"In these days when so much help and attention is focused on the criminal and very little on the victim, I want you and others to know that I do not forget the victim or those who assist the police to bring criminals to justice. You fit into those categories. Your life may be permanently scarred by your distressing experience. All I can do is to make a token gesture but I do it on behalf of all decent, law-abiding citizens. We know from your evidence that it was a terrifying experience. However, you acted with the greatest of courage to make sure that no harm came to your children by tackling the burglar and trying to prevent his escape."

Thirteen months later the Appeal Court in London rebuked Judge Keith Matthewman for those generous words. The criminal had appealed to Lord Justice Farquharson who sat with Mr Justice Alliott and Mr Justice Rougier. The latter took exception to Judge Matthewman's comments on victims -

"He has probably forgot that two thirds of Appeal Court judges regularly preside over criminal trials and were well aware of the effects of crime on victims. Judge Matthewman's sentence of four years is demonstrably out of line. The Appeal courts guidelines on sentencing were issued for the express purpose of providing uniformity in sentencing which is not a matter for judicial whim."

Judge Matthewman gives a robust response to this criticism -

"Although there are tariffs and guidelines intended to be helpful to judges, the Court of Appeal have repeatedly said that every judge should look at each case on its own merits. Therefore whatever the tariffs or guidelines may say, there are bound to be some cases where the sentences are going to be higher or lower depending on the particular circumstances.

The comments of Mr Justice Rougier were inappropriate. I was not stuck with the tariff and never have been. I always sentenced on the basis of what I considered to be the correct and fair sentence - fair to the criminal, the victim and to society. The views of Their Lordships never affected me in the slightest! Fortunately for decent people, my views now carry the day and the tariff for house burglary was increased some time ago and not before time. It is still too low and many judges are still too soft when it comes to sentencing for dwelling house burglary. However, things are better than they were.

The fact that a mere - 'two thirds of Appeal Court judges regularly preside over criminal trials and are well aware of the effect of crime on victims' - must give precious little comfort to victims whose tormentors appear before the 'other third' of Appeal Court judges!"

When Stephanie Richmond heard the appellate criticism of Judge Matthewman and that the original four year sentence was reduced to three, she was furious -

"I just can't believe it! These judges just can't have their heads screwed on. They have no idea what the victim goes through. It was a terrifying experience and I still don't sleep properly at night. I lie awake if I hear the slightest noise. What would they think if this had happened in their homes, to their wives? It seems the law is weighted in favour of the criminal. Cutting the sentence is wrong. He should serve the time he was given."

This report came under the front page headline 'TOUGH LINE CITY JUDGE RAPPED' - 'Mum slams appeal ruling' - in The Nottingham Evening Post - 4.8.93.

Mrs Roberts also supported Judge Matthewman on Radio Nottingham and invited him to attend a rally at Theatre Square in Nottingham in an attempt to change the law. Such attendance for a sitting judge would have been inappropriate.

POST Comment

Judge's tough line sets a good example

A NOTTINGHAM judge's knuckles are smarting today after being rapped by his superiors in the Appeal Court in London.

It wasn't just a normal swat either.

There was more than a modicum of muscle-flexing in it, too. Definitely a no-nonsense rebuke.

Judge Keith Matthewman, in doling out a four-year sentence to a burglar, said judges in higher courts tended to forget the victims of crime. What that really means, of course, is that some judges are not in touch with the public as much as they should be.

Judge Matthewman certainly isn't a member of that group.

He knows what's going down on the streets. He sees the effects every day in his court.

He has a streetwise feel for the balance of the law.

But the Appeal Court judges have reduced the burglar's sentence to three years, saying the original was out of line and that Judge Matthewman "had probably forgotten" that two-thirds of Appeal Court judges regularly presided over criminal trials and were "well aware" of the effects of crime and victims.

Sentencing, it was said, was not a matter of individual judicial whim.

One person who won't support their view is Mrs Stephanie Richmond, who still has sleepless nights after she fought off the man who was burgling her home.

"It was a terrifying experience," she says. "I think cutting his sentence is wrong. He should serve the time he was given."

Here was a woman alone in her home, trying to protect her two young children as well as her property. And after taking brave — some might say foolhardy — action against the intruder she feels devastated that the break-in seems less serious than it was previously.

"What would they think if this had happened in their homes, to their wives?" queries Mrs Richmond.

She has a fair point.

AS so many victims know only too well, a crime statistic suddenly takes on a whole new meaning when you're smashed in the teeth by a fist or a boot.

Or when you find your car window's been shattered, the radio taken and the contents of the boot swiped.

Or, as in Mrs Richmond's case, your home is messed up and thousands of pounds of your possessions are cleared out by some callous individual.

That's the point that Judge Matthewman picked up.

And he's right.

It's all very well for Mr Justice Rougier in London to refer to the guidelines given to judges to provide uniformity of sentences, but no guidelines can cover the fact that some crimes just *seem* to be particularly bad.

To Mrs Richmond it was a nightmare experience.

To Judge Matthewman it *seemed* to warrant an extra severity in the sentence.

There are some judges who, especially in rape cases for example, have allowed personal viewpoints to affect the soft sentencing and nothing has been retracted or altered. Quite rightly there has been a public outcry.

The only difference in this case is that Judge Matthewman has allowed his frankness to be part of his harder sentencing and he's to be applauded for that.

Those who uphold the law should be concerned when people like Mrs Richmond claim it's weighted in favour of the criminal.

One small step was taken by Judge Matthewman.

Others should copy.

The document above shows strong support from The Nottingham Evening Post, but in the August of 1999, Judge Matthewman had an opportunity to return the compliment under the headline - PRAISE FOR POST EFFORT ON CRIME by Judy Cullimore. He said -

"The Nottingham Evening Post is to be commended for the continuous effort to fight cowardly crime in this county."

He was particularly referring to the newspaper raising awareness about the danger of sneak thieves who prey on the elderly. The vulnerable victim in this instance was an 81 year old woman who had left her handbag on a kitchen unit while she went out to bring in washing from the garden line. A 19 year old Worksop youth would have got away with the crime, but for the quick action of five good neighbours who gave chase across several gardens until he was cornered. They were commended by Keith Matthewman and awarded £50 each for acting with -

"....speed and courage. Offences like this on elderly people are becoming more and more prevalent in Nottinghamshire. One reads about it daily in The Nottingham Evening Post. It has got to be stopped."

Pat Morgan, a man who lived in Mansfield as a teenager, was telling me that Judge Matthewman had the following of a popular local hero protecting the innocent and punishing the wicked -

"Eagerly we'd seize the paper and enjoy reading accounts of the 'no nonsense' Judge Matthewman - sending down the yobs!"

This reminded me of a comment made by my friend Terry Durand when we paid a visit to Nottingham Crown Court during December 1999 to observe Keith at work -

"An extraordinary experience rather like a visit to an actor friend at the theatre just before he gives a performance. It started in Keith's chambers when we were sipping coffee enjoying a pleasant, relaxing informal chat, laughing and delighting in the comfortable company of the friend we'd come to know very well during the previous year.

When it was time to move, an usher came to escort us into the court through the public entrance. We said goodbye to Keith 'the friend', who was about to undergo a personality change by donning his robes before using his own private entrance into the courtroom.

There we sat with all the others in the 'theatre of justice' when an authoritative voice rang out and commanded us - 'All rise'. It reminded me of 'Superman', but this was 'Super-Keith'. The warm, friendly, familiar, kind man we knew of one minute before had gone! Here, now, with stern countenance and empowered by all the force of

47

The State, he appeared: a be-wigged, impressive, different, strong figure who was ready to do battle with the forces of evil!"

Concern for the victims of crime was never very far away from Court Five, the court of His Honour Judge Keith Matthewman, QC One of them was once actually working in it. Mr Matthewman the schoolmaster of 1959 was an excellent classroom manager, keeping a quiet room with good control. It comes as no surprise that forty years on he keeps good order in his court room and loyal ushers react quickly and politely to stop distracting private conversations in the public gallery.

In February 1994 a 35 year old Corby man was pleading not guilty to charges of deception when an usher called Margaret Taft noticed a woman talking. This distracting chatterbox later turned out to be the common law wife of the defendant. Mrs Taft asked her to be quiet, but as she turned away the prisoner waved his arm in a threatening manner and was heard to say -

"I'll give that xxxxxxx old cow a slapping."

As a schoolmaster from the 'old school' who always insisted upon full attention in the classroom, it was with no small amount of glee and gloating that I read in the Nottingham Evening Post 3.2.94 that Judge Matthewman gave this particular naughty boy, clearly un-accustomed to discipline, an effective detention which lasted for six months! The judge said -

"The accused has committed a serious contempt of court. Those of us who have to deal with these matters have to make sure that court officials are protected when doing their duty. Ushers have a difficult task in helping to control the court."

Keith Matthewman may be a tough judge but when he made his famous speech at Keyworth in March 1991 he said -

"I am not a hanger or a flogger."

This was well illustrated in a case, widely reported in the national press, of a difficult 15 year old boy whose chronic bad behaviour for the previous ten years, had driven his parents to desperate measures. As a younger boy he would excrete on the floor and rub it on the furniture and walls. Just to annoy his parents he would urinate in his toy box. As a teenager he tried to set fire to their garage in Warsop. He stole £400 from his mum and dad, who were described in court as

48

'good caring and respectable parents'. He stole from his grandmother and had beaten up his eight year old brother. He was facing charges of aggravated vehicle taking and burglary.

Judge Matthewman did not punish the youth. Judge Matthewman sent the father to jail for three years and gave the mother a suspended 15 month sentence! A victory for the progressives? No, in this case it was the **son** who was seen as 'the victim'.

In his sentencing remarks, Judge Matthewman said -
"I have no doubt that your son was a very difficult person to deal with and might very well have tested your patience over the years. Nevertheless you used methods of discipline and punishment not merely inappropriate but cruel, degrading and criminal. Your actions were brutal and sadistic."

The father had strung up his troublesome son to a hook, with chains attached to his wrists, dowsed his T- shirt in paint thinners and held a cigarette lighter next to him. In an attempt to stop him smoking he was forced to eat two cigarettes before being left in the padlocked garage which was guarded by a rottweiler. The boy was rescued later when his friends alerted the police.

Judge Matthewman's sentence was described in a letter (dated 11.6.96) as *"a national scandal"* by J.L. Tilleray, a retired secondary headmaster from Whitby - .
"Have you taken leave of your senses? No wonder today's youth are like they are. I am not condoning the parents action but a suspended sentence would have been just."

Kenneth Creffield of Weston-Super-Mare on the same date was just as critical but took a more lenient view towards the whole family -
"Your decision to jail the father of this boy was grotesquely unjust and an expense society simply can't afford. This is a family crying out for help. Why can't the father be put on probation?"

Moving through this book, the reader will note that letters of praise far outweigh letters of censure.

Lancaster Way
Nottingham

1 September 96

Dear Sir,
　　You may remember sentencing
　　　　　　to one year in a
young offenders institution for
burglary about two weeks ago.
　As the victim of her crime and
also on behalf of my son, Dominic,
I wish to thank you for giving
her a custodial sentence.
　The burglary has had a devastating
effect on both my son and I
and even after a year there isn't
a day goes by without either
one of us thinking or speaking
of it. My son had terrible
nightmares for quite some time
and we are still very nervous
and suspecting.
　A few days after the crime
was committed I put our house
on the market, hopefully we
will be able to move away
very soon.
　Again, I thank you for removing
her from the streets for a while
and for restoring my faith in
the courts. We were very happy
that the offender may at least
experience some of the distress
and unhappiness she has caused
us.

Yours faithfully
Julie K
Dominic.

Dear Judge Matthewman

Thank you for your letter of 19 October about the reforms to the criminal
justice system which I announced at the Conservative Party Conference in
Blackpool. I am sorry for the delay in replying.

I am pleased to note your approval and support for my approach to law and
order, and the reforms I am taking forward in the Criminal Justice Bill. I
share your concern that the interests of the victims of crime should be taken
seriously and that criminals should be appropriately punished. It is
encouraging to hear that a large number of your fellow Circuit Judges also
support the measures I am taking.

I know that you have written separately to David Maclean about the level of
financial support that my Department provides to Victim Support. He will be
replying in detail. I believe that the substantial increase in support - from
£286,000 in 1986-87 to £10.016 million in 1994-95 - demonstrates clearly our
commitment to the work of Victim Support.

Thank you again for taking the trouble to write.

QUEEN ANNE'S GATE LONDON SWIH 9AT

25 JAN 1994

Yours sincerely
Michael Howard.

MICHAEL HOWARD

Chapter 5
A Judge Ever at War

From the headline below it can be see that it was not only Judge Matthewman who was annoyed about the course of events which hit the headlines at the very end of the year 2000. Geoffrey Brown of Warwick Street, Dunkirk, spoke for many people when he was moved to write to The Nottingham Evening Post.

ANGER AS FIREBOMBERS' SENTENCES CUT

Saturday December 30, 2000 **Evening Post**

CRIME SCENE: The house in Newcastle Avenue.

Our judge got it right

WHEN will judges in this country develop a modicum of common sense. I agree entirely with Judge Matthewman on his remarks about sentencing.

How anyone throwing a petrol bomb through a window can claim they didn't intend setting fire to the property with intent to harm the occupants beggars belief.

This country is going downhill fast as regards crime. And decisions by appeal court judges plus the vociferous minority of so-called do-gooders imposing their views on a silent majority ensures a downward trend.

G. BROWN
Warwick Street
Dunkirk

Mum's fury at judges

EXCLUSIVE
By BRENDAN McGRATH

This was the most recent and high profile example of Judge Matthewman's dispute with the Court of Appeal Criminal Division which came to public attention in the dark mid-winter days following Christmas 2000, just two weeks before his retirement. Readers of The Nottingham Evening Post were appalled with the story which followed the headline - 'FIREBOMB CASE SENTENCES CUT' on December 28th also written by Brendan McGrath.

This tragic story started 18 months before when 19 year old Rachel Davey, already in bed at 11.00pm, received a late evening and unwelcome visit from two friends who had come to remonstrate with her in regard to a 'trivial disagreement over the debt of a third person'. Since the callers were refused admission, this tense conversation of July 14th 1999, took place through the bedroom window of her terraced house in Newcastle Avenue, Gedling, Nottingham. The visitors were a man of 22 and his girlfriend.

Enraged, the same man returned home, and together with his 17 year old brother, planned a revenge attack using a milk bottle filled with petrol - a fire bomb, sometimes called a Molotov cocktail. To help commit this crime, a 16 year old accomplice stole a car which he later set on fire in a Tesco car park. The brothers had previously been in the house and knew that Rachel slept in the ground floor bedroom. Although both brothers were involved, the younger brother hurled the bomb through the window, laughed loudly, and was heard to say *"We done it. I chucked it."* The bed caught fire. Rachel caught fire and her hair burst into flames. As the fire spread very quickly, Rachel panicked and rushed upstairs, crying, to her father, Barry Davey. Father and daughter (who had now been burned on her head and neck) managed to survive the suffocating, choking smoke and poisonous fumes by getting down on their hands and knees and crawling down the stairs. Mr Davey was able to save two of the three family dogs. Rachel's particular pet 'Sweep', died in the fire. The Fire Brigade arrived very quickly, but it took ten fire fighters to extinguish the flames which completely gutted the interior. A photograph of the appalling damage appeared in The Nottingham Evening Post. Rachel's mother, Carol Davey, who was at work at the time, told Mr McGrath -

"It was everything I ever possessed, including photographs of my daughters growing up. I can't replace those. It's been 18 months now and we're still receiving counselling."

The defendants faced an original indictment charging them on the first count 'with arson with intent to endanger life'. However, when the matter came before Judge Matthewman on February 29th, 2000, their counsel had advised them to plead guilty to the lesser charge of 'arson being reckless as to whether life would be endangered'. The prosecution accepted that plea to the lesser count and did not proceed on the first count. In other words the brothers admitted deliberately causing the fire but denied that they intended to endanger Rachel's life. A plea of guilty saves time and avoids the necessity and expense of a jury trial.

Judge Matthewman sentenced the brothers to ten years in custody. In his 'Sentencing Remarks', he told them -

> *"It is highly likely that you have destroyed that family's future life. If they had been asleep maybe they could have been killed. It was obvious the flat was occupied when you launched your deliberate and malicious attack."*

Determinate sentences of four years or more (as opposed to life sentences) are subject to a review by the Parole Board when half the time has been served, which means that the brothers could stay inside for at least five years, but, at the earliest, **could** be free shortly afterwards. So for example a prisoner sentenced to ten years could be released after five years; five years if they do not appeal. These two **did** appeal.

It has been an interesting and educational experience for me to read and study a full transcript of a formal Judgement handed down from the Court of Appeal Criminal Division - Royal Courts of Justice, The Strand, London WC2. A formidable array of judicial might formed the appellate court on the front cover - one Lord Justice, one High Court Judge and one Circuit Judge. Keith tells me that the inclusion of a circuit judge on the panel is an attempt to broaden the range of experience. We shall see! Next it said - REGINA -v- the full names of the two defendants now referred to as 'the appellants'.

The Judgement concluded by reducing Judge Matthewman's sentence of ten years to seven years.

It starts by giving a detailed account of the original crime and refers to Judge Matthewman's sentencing comments in the following terms -

"We can see absolutely no criticism in that comment made by the learned Judge and the approach to sentencing in that context."

However, the appellate circuit judge went on to contrast Judge Matthewman's ten year sentence with an earlier eight year sentence given by a different judge for a similar but contested case, described by the appellate judge as a much worse case, involving the permanent disfigurement of two children. The Appeal Court reasoned that ten years was therefore *'manifestly excessive'* since the earlier court assessed that 'the appropriate bracket' of the disfigurement case was eight to ten years. Judge Matthewman had referred to this precedent in his sentencing remarks at the Nottingham Crown Court -

*"I say straightaway, so that it is on the record, that I have listened with care to what has been said on your behalf and I have taken note of the authority that has been presented to me, but I take the view that in **this** court, I sentence on the basis of the facts of the particular case before me. If any court hereafter feels that my sentence is inappropriate, then, obviously, it will say so. At the moment, however, I regard the case that has been handed up to me as a case where the sentence was **very, very lenient indeed!**"*

In its Judgement on the sentence of Judge Matthewman, the Circuit Judge member of the Court of Appeal said -

"It is in our judgement, not open to a judge to disagree with a clear guideline given in the case to which we have referred and, of course, based on its particular facts which were, as we have said, very similar, really no less serious than the present case. [Rachel Davey] What we think may have happened is that Judge Matthewman was rightly appalled at the conduct of these two appellants [the brothers] and may subconsciously have passed a sentence which was more appropriate to a conviction on the first count."

Keith had heavily underlined the word 'subconsciously' and dashed out -

"Bloody cheek! Unwarranted personal attack on me! Quite unjustified by a Circuit Judge."

Above 'not open to disagree' he wrote -

"Dangerous dictatorial arrogance - very concerning."

The Appeal Court Circuit Judge refers to the suffering and injuries sustained by Rachel Davey in these terms -

"Her hair caught fire. It is apparent that she was quite unable to talk properly for a period of 12 hours after this attack. Obviously her nose and throat were sore and obviously she expressed herself as being very shocked and frightened by what had happened. She was distressed about her dog and her belongings. Since the incident she had not been able to sleep properly, has suffered nightmares and could not sleep in a room by herself. She has been prescribed sleeping tablets. She finds it difficult to go out alone."

Previously this Judge had said -

"Her injuries were quite modest, more psychological than physical."

Keith Matthewman had scribbled underneath -

*"**Modest!** Hair in a blaze of fire! Burns to the neck! Detained in hospital! Suffered after-effects of inhaling smoke! Modest? 'Modest' is quite beyond me and no doubt would cause disgust in the minds of decent, law-abiding people."*

We had a chat about this document and the reduction of sentence which had clearly annoyed Keith.

"It's not just a reduction for the defendants, but a reduction of the support for the victims, mother, father and daughter. I was approached by one woman who said to me -

*'Only a person **completely** out of touch with real life, in particular one whose house had never been fire-bombed and whose daughter had never been set on fire could reduce the sentence!'*

I told her that I could not summon up sufficient hypocrisy to disagree with her!"

Carol Davey was furious with the reduction from ten to seven years which could mean that the men who burned and traumatised her daughter may be free in four years time. She told The Nottingham Evening Post -

"I don't like it. I think Judge Matthewman was right in what he did in the first place. Rachel doesn't need this. They're going to be out sooner than she thought."

I steeled myself to invite further comment from Keith on the word 'subconsciously' -

"'Subconsciously'! Highly offensive! A suggestion that I was influenced by external considerations, particularly annoyed me. I've been passing sentences since 1977, which I guess is just as long as the three judges engaged on this appeal. I think I know a little bit about this part of a judge's function.

Guidelines are precisely that. They do not act as a cage in which judges are supposed to live like ciphers, leaving no independence of thought or action, prevented from exercising the very function for which they are appointed - that is, to use their independent judgement. I trust this aspect of the case is merely an example of rather sloppy thinking by one division of the Court of Appeal and not a move towards self aggrandisement restricting movement in sentencing brackets.

Most divisions of the Court of Appeal deal fairly with judge's decisions and if they think a judge is wrong, then their task is to say so. No one objects to that. However, judges of all categories have already lost a great deal of the trust of the public at large. Appeal judgements following the style of this one, concerning a horrific, deliberate fire bombing can only risk further erosion of the trust placed in the Court of Appeal by innocent victims of crime, by all the other decent, hard working, law abiding people."

Judge Matthewman was interviewed by former barrister Rosalind English in the BBC World Service programme - 'Who Are Our Judges?' In the 1994 July edition of 'BBC Worldwide' she wrote -

"Above the Crown Courts are the High Courts, above them the Court of Appeal with the House of Lords at the top. Many circuit judges at Crown Court level frequently feel the sting of humiliation when superior brethren in the Court of Appeal overturn their sentences. But Matthewman's irritation at having his sentences reduced comes not from personal embarrassment but from a sense of injustice. He said -

*'Circuit judges know about sentencing in their particular district. They know what is going to deter local criminals. They have seen the witness, the defendants and, most important of all - the victims. It is very important that the person who has seen both the victim and the defendant is the **same** person who gives the sentence.'*

Implicit in that comment is a bit of a swipe at the fastidious Criminal Appeal Division, where three Lords Justice of Appeal [sic] hear the learned arguments of counsel without being exposed to any of the raw evidence from the actual participants and victims of the burglary, rape, murder or violent assault."

In the retirement tribute to Judge Matthewman on December 22nd 2000, on the same subject of fire and judicial challenge, His Honour Judge Christopher Pitchers made a reference to an appeal which was reported in The Times 18.3.83, an appeal which turned out to be much less disappointing to Keith.

> *"Judge Matthewman began his career in a most distinguished way. Those of you familiar with the law of criminal damage will know that one of the leading authorities on liability for sitting back and doing nothing when a fire starts emanated with Mr Recorder Matthewman QC, whose pellucid direction to the jury was upheld in glowing terms by the House of Lords.*
>
> *That experience no doubt started the warm relationship of mutual trust and respect that has existed between Judge Matthewman and the appellate courts ever since!"*

To explain: in the August of 1980 a vagrant was living in an unoccupied house on Grantham Road in Sparkbrook, where he had been - *'kippin' for a couple of weeks'*. Returning to the property one night - *'at closing time after a few drinks'*, he lay down on a mattress in the room he was using, lit a cigarette and fell asleep. Later, he awoke to discover that -

> *"The mattress was on fire! I hadn't got anything to put it out so I just left it. I got up and went into the next room and went back to sleep. Next thing I remember, the police and fire people came."*

After £800.00 worth of fire damage and ten months later this same vagrant, now charged with arson, stood before Mr Recorder Matthewman QC at Leicester Crown Court.

> The year before in 1979, within a few weeks of becoming a Silk and after a reference from Mr Justice Nield, Keith had been asked if he would like to become a Recorder - a part time judge.

The accused pleaded 'not guilty' on the grounds that the fire was caused by an accident. Summing up, Mr Recorder Matthewman reminded the jury that the defendant (if not deliberately) **had** started the fire and therefore had a 'duty' to make some effort to put it out - or at least call the fire brigade. To simply leave the room to sleep elsewhere would allow the fire to spread and 'present an obvious risk' of serious damage to a house which, after all, was not even his property. After just 22 minutes of deliberation the jury convicted the man who was then sentenced to six months imprisonment.

Following this interesting saga in the 1983 April edition of 'The Weekly Law Reports', I was surprised to read that the trespassing arsonist appealed! His case was heard at the Court of Appeal on March 3rd 1982 and, on **this** occasion, Keith was upheld!

Surprise turned to astonishment when the Appellate Court gave leave to this squatter to submit his case to the highest court in the land, The House of Lords! Who was paying for this vagrant? - I asked Keith. Answer: I was - plus all the other tax payers. The vagrant was on legal aid, but Keith assured me the money was well spent on this particular case which would test the judicial system and produce a legal definition for future cases, thus in the long run, may be saving millions of pounds.

The defence argument turned on the Latin expression 'actus reus' which frequently cropped up in the Judgement (17.03.83) handed down by the noble and learned Lord Diplock who was sitting with four other Law Lords. 'Actus reus' was advanced to -

"... suggest that some positive act on the part of the accused is needed to make him guilty of a crime and that a failure or omission to act is insufficient to give rise to criminal liability."

In other words (to my lay mind) I assume the defence argued that Mr Recorder Matthewman should not have punished the vagrant because he did - precisely nothing! He lit his cigarette, **not** the bed, simply removed himself to another room away from the discomfort of the fire (which, after all, is much too hot) - and, why should he call the fire brigade to a house which was not his property? The mind boggles!

Lord Diplock drew a rough comparison between the inaction of the vagrant and the inaction of *'the deplorable conduct of the parabolic priest and the Levite on the road to Jericho'* who both passed by the prostrate victim of a violent robbery who was eventually helped by the pro-active Good Samaritan. This comparison becomes even rougher when you consider that at least these first two indifferent travellers had no direct responsibility for the condition of the victim.

Fortunately, in his complex Judgement, Lord Diplock said -

"My Lords, these alternative ways of analysing the legal theory that justifies a decision [the judgement of Mr Recorder

Matthewman] *which has received nothing but commendation for its accord with common-sense* [so good to see the first appearance of **common-sense**] *and justice."*

His Lordship went on to praise Mr Recorder Matthewman's 'lucid' summing up, especially in the way he focused on the word 'duty', which made the legal position easier for the jury to understand. One of the many qualities which made Keith a good judge was the ability to simplify and clarify but still deliver the accurate essence of the argument.

So, in this the highest court in the land, Keith Matthewman had won the argument. Out of some 80,000 appealed cases a year, only about 100 ever reach The House of Lords. Keith had set a new precedent made, new law and won the day when Lord Diplock spoke his final words -

"My Lords, while depreciating the use of the expression 'actus reus' in the certified question, I would answer that question 'Yes', and would dismiss the appeal."

Lord Keith of Kinkel, Lord Bridge of Harwick, Lord Brandon of Oakbrook and Lord Brightman all said -

"I too would dismiss this appeal."

Final score - Keith 2, Vagrant nil.

This case has become one of half a dozen judged by Keith (not all as successful) which have changed or clarified parts of English Law.

Elizabeth Matthewman with Raymond centre and Keith on the right

Chapter 6
Two Toy Soldiers

Judge Keith Matthewman retired in January 2001. From his Bench he looked out upon a technologically driven, fast changing world which to some people very often seemed dangerous, disturbing and confusing. Sixty five years before on Wednesday the 8th of January 1936, he came into a world which could have been described in the same way.

His parents would have been familiar with the reassuring gruff voice of King George V having gathered around the wireless set to listen to his previous four Christmas messages to the Empire. Thirteen days after Frank and Elizabeth Matthewman were safely delivered of a son, the 71 year old king died and a past age died with him. At the funeral, the Prince of Wales, now Edward VIII, walked with kings, princes and politicians from 47 countries which reflected the power and prestige of the one time Great Britain. The new monarch looked 'sad and forlorn', but not due to grief. Just before Christmas, with the rest of the nation once again gathered around the wireless, the Matthewmans found out that His Britannic Majesty -

 " ... *found it impossible to carry the heavy burden of responsibility and to discharge my duties as King as I would wish to do, without the help and support of the woman I love.*"

So inside of one year, the British Empire had its third king, the 'shy Bertie' of halting, nervous voice, the father of our present Queen, George VI.

Just months after his fourth birthday, Keith, the future politician, had already seen three very different prime ministers - the old fashioned and phlegmatic Stanley Baldwin, the peace seeking but failing Neville Chamberlain and then the fighting Winston Churchill who had - *"Nothing to offer but Blood, toil, tears and sweat."* At his retirement Judge Keith Matthewman had been governed by a total of 13 prime ministers, nine Conservative and four Labour.

Twelve days after the entrance of young Keith saw the exit of the writer Rudyard Kipling, another potent symbol of British power, prestige, pre-eminence and the glory of empire. Hitler had already been in power for three years and the ominous stomp of the goose-stepping jackboot sounded the forbidden arrival of German troops into the Rhineland on March 7th 1936. The eventual conclusion of these events would soon have a dramatic effect on the Matthewman family, but they probably felt confident and re-assured when the flickering cinema newsreels unveiled the new fighter aeroplane 'Supermarine Spitfire' and that other great symbol of British economic strength, speed, prestige and luxury - the eighty thousand ton super-liner, Queen Mary.

Elizabeth and Frank Matthewman would have visited the local cinema at least once a week together with nearly half the population. They may have just noticed the significant event in August that year at the Olympia Radio Exhibition when the refined and 'plumy' Leslie Mitchell made the first ever television announcement. It would be nearly two decades before the average working man could afford a set which in baby Keith's first year cost 100 guineas, or six months of his dad's wage packet.

Number 200 Sheffield Road, Birdwell, near Barnsley is still there. A fairly typical rented accommodation for a colliery electrician struggling to keep his family on five pounds a week - standard pay for a skilled man. Keith Matthewman was born into a rough working class world and decade, dubbed by Groucho Marx as the 'threadbare Thirties'. His first views were of a smoke-darkened, fume filled, bleak landscape of black pit hills and black pit head winding wheels. Rows and rows of monotonous terraces of small homes were kept spotlessly clean by dowdy hard working women, whilst their scruffy kids played in the near traffic free streets, probably teasing each other about 'Nitty Nora' the school nurse. Later in the day, cheerful men-folk with coal encrusted black faces, under cloth caps, clomped home in hob-nailed boots and once more, with care, crossed the well scrubbed stone door step.

October 1936 saw the start of the famous month long 'Jarrow March' from Newcastle upon Tyne to London in an attempt to publicise the humiliation and degradation of unemployment. Stanley Baldwin, the Conservative Prime Minister, refused to receive the weary and foot-sore protesters at Number 10. Returning home to the north they were received with a hero's welcome but their dole had been cut, a penalty for having made themselves unavailable for work.

On November 18th, King Edward VIII was moved by appalling living conditions in the Welsh Coal Fields to utter - *"Something must be done."* but nothing was done. At Worsbrough Dale Colliery, north-west of Wombwell in the Yorkshire coalfield, Frank Matthewman was fortunate to be working because just three years before, 40% of the nations coal miners were jobless. These considerations and the poverty of the time would eventually shape the politics of his baby son.

The Coronation of George VI took place on May 12th 1937 and Keith acquired a brother who was born the following August 8th, Raymond Matthewman. Alas, both lads were too young to appreciate the very first edition of 'The Dandy' which appeared just before Christmas.

The following year, the Matthewmans moved forty miles south to a place of cleaner industries. An area which had recently 'switched its focus from lace and net to bicycles, cigarettes and pharmaceuticals'. Frank Matthewman had obtained a position, just south west of Nottingham, at the Chilwell Central Ordnance Depot.

During the 1914-1918 'Great War', the National Shell Filling Factory was known for workers with yellow hands, yellow faces and yellow hair resulting from the curious reaction of handling chemicals. The local historian, Bill Shaw [Mayor of Broxtowe 1990-91] told me that the 'Chilwell Canaries', who were doing dangerous and patriotic work, far from being embarrassed by exotic colouring, were proud to be recognised. At the end of the First World War there was an inexplicable but totally devastating explosion killing over a hundred workers who were filling shells.

Bill Shaw has been a life long friend of Keith Matthewman -
"I remember Keith when he first moved into my neighbourhood, a few doors down at 17 Marton Road, Chilwell. Reasonably new semi-detached houses, all the same, not very grand - 'artisan class', I suppose, but very pleasant with gardens front and rear." [These houses were built by a man called Wit**ton** who had a daughter, **Mar**jorie - Mar + ton = Marton.]
"Living room, kitchen with bathroom off and three bedrooms upstairs. It was a fairly short cul-de-sac ending in a field on a hillside.

So in our childhood memories there are trees, hedgerows, grass, frogs and birds - even an ancient stone cattle trough."

Occasionally this field was used for training soldiers. They and the pleasant rural setting up the hill, fondly described by Bill and Keith, are now all gone to make way for the new homes on Redland Drive and Greenland Crescent.

One of Keith's earliest memories in his Chilwell back garden was of being teased about his broad Yorkshire accent. For novel entertainment, the neighbouring kids, with their south Nottinghamshire twang encouraged little Keith to repeat certain words such as the 'a' sounding like an 'e'.

A year later, on September 3rd 1939, the Matthewmans huddled around their wireless to hear the disappointed, weary and melancholic voice of Neville Chamberlain when he concluded *"...I have to tell you now that no such undertaking has been received, and consequently this country is at war with Germany."*

These words, not remembered by a small child in Chilwell, but spoken by a conscientious peace-maker with the anguished memory of a terrible war just two decades before, were to change everything for the next six years. Keith told me -

"The war destroyed so many people. It destroyed views about their parents. It destroyed parent's and children's relationships. The war was so destructive in that way. Therefore I don't blame my parents for their apparent indifference or lack of open affection. On the contrary they went through a very difficult time. I never needed to blame them because I've done well in life, made my own way, ploughed my own furrow."

Sometime after that broadcast, the three year old Keith has a memory of his dad making preparations against a new peril of death and destruction raining from the sky. The toddler watched with interest as his father and a family friend stacked sandbags up against the outside walls of the bathroom and lavatory. Huge wooden batons were installed to buttress walls and ceilings. The ominous significance of these mysterious exertions would have been lost on a small child, but the departure of Frank Matthewman to war in 1940 made a deep impact on his two sons. Keith has a clear memory of him and Raymond

Lieutenant Frank Matthewman in North Africa.

putting two toy soldiers in Mr Matthewman's kit bag just before he went many miles away to fight for King and Country.

At some point later in a sun scorched alien land Frank Matthewman found himself far away from the comfortable familiarity of 17 Marton Road, and far far away from the friendly touch of Elizabeth, Keith and Raymond. With the enemy nearby, in arid hostile conditions, he found these two little lead figures at the bottom of his kit bag. We can only guess at the emotional response to these tiny men symbolising the innocent good wishes and love of his two little boys. Frank must have been deeply touched as he gently examined these precious gifts, because they were referred to in his first letter written in North Africa which travelled the many miles back home to Nottinghamshire. His letters were infrequent during the following five years. Frank was a man of few words.

Lieutenant Frank Matthewman

On May 10th of that year, 1940, in an atmosphere of crisis and gloom, Chamberlain resigned to make way for Churchill. Private Frank Matthewman took note of the Prime Minister's famous words the following month and 'braced himself to his duty' to fight the might and fury of Nazi tyranny so the free world be able to 'move forward into broad, sunlit uplands' - at a personal cost.

From the age of four to nine, the war had deprived Keith of his father. Five years was more than half of his small life, an eternity for a child.

"When he finally returned I didn't know him. We were strangers. Basically thereafter, I'm afraid we remained strangers. You don't pick up those lost years - and we didn't."

Frank Matthewman is on the second row, seventh from the left

Jane Matthewman probably knows her husband better than anybody else and expressed the enormity and seriousness of this formative separation.

"I could cry when I think about this! This is where Keith had a big cut off somewhere along the line. After five years it had gone too far. How do you suddenly bond with your father? You just don't!"

Keith suggested that an absent father may have been, in part, beneficial.

"I don't feel damaged and don't resent it because I had to become my own person and think for myself. It may have helped to toughen me up. It does make one slightly harder. Perhaps it's an emotional setback because he's not there to discuss matters with. Perhaps."

Jane cross referenced with Melvyn Bragg's book, 'Soldier's Return' based on the absence of his father during similar tender years. I asked Keith if he felt his father had been changed by the horrors of war.

"It's difficult to say. He never spoke about his experiences of the war, most of them didn't. I don't know if he had a bad time or not. He was never taken a 'prisoner of war' or suffered any cruel treatment

67

at the hands of the enemy. He was not emotional at all and I can never remember him cuddling me, or, for that matter, hitting me. He was a taciturn man."

"Oh yes, you couldn't get much out of him." Responded Jane.

"Rather like myself, my father was very much his own man. If he wanted to do something, he'd do it come what may, no matter who got hurt, no matter what inconvenience he caused anybody. After those five long war years we were complete strangers. Totally unlike the close growing up relationship I've enjoyed with my own son, Adrian."

Private Frank Matthewman was commissioned in 1943 and promoted to Lieutenant Matthewman. Attached to the 50th Battalion Recce [reconnaissance] Corps and O.C. of a Recovery Section in the Royal Electrical and Mechanical Engineers; he saw service in Cyprus, Syria, Palestine, Egypt and the Western Desert. Under the encouraging and spirited command of General Montgomery, as part of the Eighth Army, he became one of the legendary 'Desert Rats' giving Erwin Rommel a very bad time in North Africa.

Keith Matthewman has a recollection of coming out of Meadow Lane School, Chilwell, one day to find his father, who had just arrived back from the army, waiting to take him back home. Bill Shaw supports this memory -

"What a surprise! There he was, in army officer's uniform, standing with the usual group of parents. Keith was overjoyed to see his dad."

After the war, Lt. Frank Matthewman became the Workshop Superintendent at the REME Workshops in Chilwell. A responsible position which enabled the family to enjoy the benefit of a second hand Austin 10 motorcar, at a time when car ownership was rare. Like his eldest son after him, it was becoming clear to me that Matthewman Senior had travelled a long way socially from a humble start in a Barnsley coal mine, distinguishing himself with an honourable and proud war record as an army officer and on forward to becoming a senior manager.

At one point I had an interesting discussion with Keith about what exactly we meant by the term 'working class'. My personal terms of reference, based on direct experience, included - poorly educated,

68

inarticulate, roughly-spoken, un-ambitious, un-polished - and so on. This caused Keith Matthewman, the one time left wing socialist, to reflect on the background and the progress of his father -

"I can't exactly define what it is to be 'working class'. As a collier working down the pit, I suppose my father was 'working class' as we generally understand the term, but he was a very intelligent man with a good brain and ended up in charge of many skilled men. From 1957 to retirement in 1964, he was a successful businessman managing our own general store in Aldercar. His hobbies were writing stories and listening to the plays of Shakespeare and Shaw - is that 'working class'?"

THE BRITISH BROADCASTING CORPORATION

BROADCASTING HOUSE, LONDON, W.1

TELEGRAMS: BROADCASTS LONDON TELEX • CABLES: BROADCASTS LONDON-W1 • TELEX: 22182
TELEPHONE: LANGHAM 4468

11th August 1966

Dear Mr. Matthewman,

Miss Crowther likes your story, "To Fittings and Labour", and will use it as the Morning Story on Thursday, 1st September from 11.00-11.15 a.m. in the Light Programme.

The reader will be Charles Hodgson.

Could you please let me know whether the story has been published at all?

Yours sincerely,

Judith Keay (Mrs.)

(Judith Keay)
Secretary to Barbara Crowther

F. Matthewman, Esq.,
16 Carlton Road,
Long Eaton, Notts.

I had some difficulty getting a fuller picture of the real Frank Matthewman from the recollections of his son and daughter - in - law, until the man himself spoke to me directly from half a century ago - out of old yellowing newsprint. Surely this is the miracle of the written word, to enable a man to reach out over decades and continue to communicate his thoughts and feelings with the living even after his own death. If Frank Matthewman was a man of few words to his immediate family, during the 1950's and 1960's he had plenty to say to local newspapers and national periodicals who published his numerous short stories.

The Author

Mr. Matthewman, expert —theoretically, of course—in murder, likes reading, writing and listening to Shakespeare's and Shaw's plays as a winter pastime, but in the summer, his thoughts turn to motoring and gardening.

He is a Yorkshireman, but has lived at Chilwell for almost 20 years. During the war he went overseas with the L.A.D. attached to the 50th Battalion Recce Corps, and saw service in Cyprus, Syria, Palestine, Egypt and the Western Desert. Commissioned in 1943, he was O.C. of a Recovery Section of R.E.M.E.

Married, he has a family of two boys.

Nottinghamshire Guardian
31.5.52

The first, a 3000 word story entitled 'COURAGE', was published by a magazine called 'Lucky Star' in March 1950. The editor paid him four pounds ten shillings which was in those days about half a week's wage. Nineteen hundred and fifty two was a particularly busy and successful year for the author. In February the 'Nottinghamshire Guardian' printed a surprising and clever mini whodunit - 'MURDER FOR A LIVING' by 'Fred' Matthewman.

In June, 'Reveille for the Weekend', a popular magazine of the day, paid ten guineas and published 'HEROES WITHOUT HONOUR' - a heart-rending tale which clearly drew upon Lt. Frank Matthewman's first hand geographical knowledge of the Sahara Desert together with the martial qualities of discipline and unquestioning obedience. In November 'Reveille' paid Frank ten guineas for the right to print 'THAT NIGHT **WAS** COLD' which demonstrated the writer's keen observations of the conduct, conversations and rivalry among drinking men gathered around the tap room fire on a winter's evening.

'RESPONSIBILITY' appeared in 'Punch' in January 1953. An interesting insight into the strengths and weaknesses of rank, teamwork and trust in a big organisation which may well be the REME Workshops at Chilwell.

'SECOND THOUGHTS' was published August 1954 in 'Labour's Northern Voice', a union newspaper - a graphic account written in dialect of two coal-miners descending into the bowels of the earth only to hear ominous sounds of 'creaking, rasping and splitting timber' just before a life threatening cave-in. Trapped and fearing the very worst in a black deadly silence, the younger man opens his heart to the other, in tearful, poignant admissions of wrong doing. In this story we get a taste of the social banter and chemistry between fellow colliers in the 1930's complete with the ever-present dangers, horrors and bleak atmosphere down the deep pits of Barnsley.

In 1955 'POOR OLD JOE' showed his ability to work a combination of humour and pathos and reproduces the nostalgic festive spirit of the Nottingham Saturday afternoon football match. Old Joe has spent his life trying to win 'the pools' and escape from his ever nagging wife. Eventually he is successful, but in the resulting excitement and euphoria, his bicycle collides with a motorcar on a busy Trent Bridge! Alas Joe is killed and his nagging widow cops the lot!

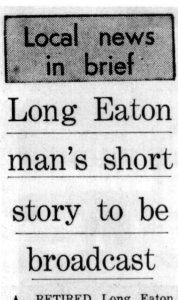

Local news in brief

Long Eaton man's short story to be broadcast

A RETIRED Long Eaton man, Mr. Frank Matthewman, of 16, Carlton-road, has by the BBC, and it will be broadcast as the "Morning Story" on September 1. had a short story accepted

The story, "To Fittings and Labour," is only one of a number written by Mr. Matthewman. Some of his other work has been published in the Nottinghamshire Guardian, and in national periodicals.

Mr. Matthewman began writing as a hobby when he was a workshop superintendent at the REME Workshops, Chilwell, but, when he and his wife took over a general store in Aldercar about ten years ago, the long hours he had to work left him little time for any leisure pursuits.

He retired two years ago and, after an initial period spent catching up on his reading, he recently turned again to writing.

Long Eaton Advertiser
11.8.66

71

We have all heard the expression - 'famous for fifteen minutes'. Lt. Frank Matthewman had his finest fifteen minutes between 11.00 and 11.15am on Thursday, September 1st 1966, when the whole Matthewman clan was gathered around the parental wireless set in respectful silence and rapt attention tuned into the BBC Light Programme to hear Charles Hodgson read 'TO FITTINGS AND LABOUR'.

Many millions across the nation listened to the work of Mr Frank Matthewman that morning. A similar broadcast today on any one spot of the dial could not possibly guarantee the attention of such a generous chunk of the working and leisured population. Today's airwaves give the casual listener a confusing galaxy of choice from local and commercial stations in addition to the five main BBC Radio stations. Add to this, competition from modern viewing habits of daytime television with it's own multiplicity of channels. Thirty-five years ago the daytime Light Programme, which eventually became Radio 2, had a huge, loyal, daily audience for the ever popular 'Morning Story'.

Apart from giving us a valuable social history, Frank Matthewman wrote well because he wisely wrote of his own time, his personal experience and all these stories give us a comfortable feel for that period.

Chapter 7
The Marton Road Gang

In the September of 1941, Keith and Bill Shaw began their formal education at Meadow Lane Infants School which was a healthy and perfectly safe walk of three quarters of a mile across the fields from Marton Road. In contrast to modern habits, not one single child was chauffeured to the school-gates in those days when Chilwell was still quite rural.

Keith has happy memories of Meadow Lane school and told me of the momentous and dramatic event of the 'big bad dog'. Recollections are sketchy, but apparently during one break-time this large uninvited hound invaded the playground causing a general panic - or more probably great pleasure in livening up an otherwise predictable daily routine. The fearsome intruder singled out his victim, very likely a girl who was pungent with the alluring scent of her own much cuddled pet doggy back home.

   The agonising screams of this little distressed damsel on the run awakened in the young Keith Matthewman, an incipient chivalry. With a few equally brave fellow knights, they raced to the rescue and drove the terrible beast out of the school grounds and up into open fields. These heroics were the talk of the school. Eventually the exciting news reached the ears of the headmistress herself who, in Churchillian terms, decided to honour the gallantry of the fearless few during the following morning assembly.

   ".... and now little Wendy [An indulgent nod and gracious smile towards to the now dried eyed and fully composed injured party] *has been delivered back to us from her dreadful ordeal, we must, one and all, give a rousing round of applause to our splendid bold boys who set such a good example and put others before self, making Meadow Lane School, once again, a safe place for us all."*

With an uplifted chin, her curious and expectant gaze cast down over the small sea of little faces -
   "Those boys who chased off the dog yesterday - will now take their rightful place and come up to the platform, proudly, to stand with me."

All eyes turned on the one boy who obediently moved out of line and made his way up to the front of the hall. This single pupil fully expected to be followed by his compatriots, but alas, rather embarrassed, Keith stood with his headmistress alone! The other lads were too shy, or too modest, or just too scared. An indication for the future?

During 'Depot Corner Days', the 'Marton Road Gang', were always ready to stand with Keith Matthewman. Both terms were coined by one of their number, Bill Shaw, who tells us that they were a jolly 'community of kids' -

"Apart from myself, Keith, and his younger brother Ray; our gang included Bob Hales and his younger sister Brenda. Colin Hallam is now a university professor in Tasmania, and there was also his kid brother Paul. Les Hooley and his sister Marina, Geoffrey Huffer, Ray Sewel, Terry Oliver, Pat Cook, Brenda Ashton, Margaret Niland and Louise Hunt. At the bottom of the road lived Bill and Jim Leafe, and Pete and Terry Turner who had a successful career as an RAF officer. Also we had the remarkable Brian Longbottom ..."

"Why remarkable?" I asked.

"To some of his peers he was something of a leader enjoying a certain authority. Brian had leg irons. A metal brace was fitted up to the knee of his left leg and highly visible in short trousers which in those days we all wore up to about the age of fourteen."

Keith tells me that Brian once had a crush on an unresponsive girl call Rita Tew -

"He thought the best way to win her affection would be for her to come across Bill and myself beating him up! He reasoned that she'd stop us, take pity and become his girlfriend. So, one day, when she was walking behind us with some of her school-friends, we pretended to attack poor crippled Brian and cruelly knocked him to the ground. Nonchalantly she came by, looked down with little interest and said - 'Serve him right!' Brian took it in good part - he was a good sport."

The deprivations of war affected these early schooldays. Bill recalls the time when he and Keith, en route to Meadow Lane, saw ahead of them a classmate called Maurice McCourt. He was carrying a strange, intriguing object. Running to catch up, they discovered Maurice holding what looked rather like the severed hand of a jaundiced giant in

74

that it had big fat yellow fingers! This exotic gift, from some remote corner of the earth, had been presented to him by his dad, a naval officer just back home on leave.

"In school I remember watching with amazement as our teacher pulled apart this thing into its separate 'fingers'. She then started to peel away the thick yellow skin which revealed white cylindrical flesh beneath. Thick sticky coin shapes were neatly cut off and equally distributed around all the pupils - who were invited to touch, smell and eat this unusual but delicious tropical fruit. We could all remember having eaten apples, pears and plums, but this was our very first experience of - a banana."

The Second World War also provided an interesting variety of childhood adventures and experiences in Chilwell. Keith, Bill and the gang enjoyed playing in the bomb shelters at the foot of Marton Road. On one occasion, about five or six of them were having such a great time with shrieks of delight and were making so much noise for such a prolonged period, that they enraged a neighbour who had, in her view, suffered long enough! Keith recalls this as if it were yesterday.

"She'd warned us to pipe down or clear off, but totally absorbed in our make-believe play world, over-excited and wound-up to the hilt, we soon forgot. Forgot, that is, until she suddenly appeared and chucked a bucket full of water all over us! It didn't stop us playing in those shelters but we were much quieter about it in future."

The Marton Road Gang made new friends with strange accents when they met up with an influx of London evacuees. This was a mutual education, a cultural exchange of attitudes, different street games and competitions. One competition was rather rude - who could stand on the edge of the pavement and pee the furthermost into the road!

"Repeated contests made the result become more and more predictable. Les Smith was always the winner .... and her brother Charlie always came second."

The London evacuees were not entirely out of danger because Nottingham was a key industrial area and the REME workshops at the Central Ordnance Depot could be a military target. Indeed Keith and Bill found tangible and fascinating proof that the ever threatening German fighter and bomber planes had been frequently menacing the skies of Chilwell. They were intrigued by small pieces of metal which regularly littered the streets. The boys took them to be steel, but they were more likely thin strips of aluminium foil [duepple], ejected from German aircraft in clouds, as a countermeasure by the enemy to confuse, block, or give our radar false echoes. This phenomenon stirred the early entrepreneurial instincts of the young couple. They conceived a plan to make money out of the military by collecting up these foreign fragments, melting the metal over a gas ring and casting bullets in moulds in the ground. The Army, being desperate for ammunition, would pay good prices!

Listening to this extraordinarily optimistic venture, I began to realise why Keith Matthewman is a judge and I am not. Such forward looking initiative 57 years ago! He was prepared to think the unthinkable and give it a go: but alas, it did **not** go. Pieces of the metal, put into a tin jar top, were furiously heated, only to burn a hole through the tin lid which made a mess of Mrs Matthewman's gas stove. A later experiment was more successful in melting lead, but dramatically failed in the casting process. Bullet holes dug in the earth were damp and angrily spat back the dangerous hot molten lead like a volcano! After this Bill Shaw and Keith Matthewman retired from the ammunition industry.

Perhaps their energy and talents were better employed when, at the age of eight in 1944, they joined the First Chilwell and Attenborough Cubs who met at the Chilwell Methodist Chapel which is still there on Clark's Lane. Sadly I was never a scout which soon became clear when Bill said -

"We were thrilled with our new uniform which had patriotic red, white and blue neckerchiefs we still wear to this day. The Akela was to become a second mother to many of us ..."

"The Akela? What's that?"

"Narvel! And you a man of letters! Akela was the wolf-pack leader in Rudyard Kipling's 'Jungle Book' and is the name given to all cub pack leaders. Few folks in Chilwell had heard of Mrs Jane Pembleton, but most knew of Akela because all their sons had passed through the ranks."

Hearing about a childhood more than half a century back, I began to realise the crucial importance of the Boy Scout Movement to the social development these two young boys. This was the time before the cosy indoor distractions of multi-channel television, computer games,

76

mobile phones and other sophisticated toys. This was a time of making one's own fun, a time of being at one with the elements, walking, running, interacting with an extended network of friends. This was the day of the cinema, the comic or the wireless - or perhaps even reading 'Jungle Book'.

Kindly loaned by Bill Shaw, this photograph shows the First Chilwell and Attenborough Scouts and Cubs at their 1946 annual camp in Scarborough. Many thanks to Bob Pembleton, front row, the cub without a neckerchief, who has put a name to most of the 64 faces in this picture. Some of the un-named scouts were from the Trowell group. Jean Hodgkinson remembers that moment during one of the few fine days out of a particularly wet week under canvas.

Front row, left to right - Ray Matthewman, Frank Swain, Neil Walker, Colin Hallam, unknown, David Walker, Terry Turner, unknown, Bob Pembleton, Bob Hales and David Friend.

Second row, the adults - Bernard Clapham, Jean Hodgkinson nee Merricks, Jane Pembleton [Bob's mother, the Akela] George Pembleton [Bob's father 'Skip'] Alf Pearce and the last adult on that row is unknown.

Third row - Derrick Midgeley, 'Tubby' Hudson, Bill Shaw, Tony Gregory, Keith Matthewman, Noel Sisson, unknown and Peter (Spanner) Spence.

Fourth row - the first boy framed by distant trees is unknown. Ken Radford, Pete Turner just above Bill. The next three boys are unknown. The boy with

77

his hand on Keith's shoulder is David Clarke. Derek Bird is left of the unknown in the lemon squeezer hat. The last two boys on that row are Ray Hawkins in the cub cap and the beaming capless Michael Skidmore.

Fifth row, extreme left is fair haired Johnny Rippon. Fourth along is the very fair headed Derek Knight.

<u>Sixth row</u> - *extreme left [and left of the sailor in a white cap] with his head framed by masonry is Patrick Philip Prothero. Fourth along and the first sailor in a dark cap is Jeff Seamer. The very top sailor in a white cap is Dave Rippon and the dark lad to his left is Ray Hollingsworth. The dark capless adult to his right is his brother Derek Hollingsworth. Top row on the extreme right with no cap - Gordon Lucas. To his left is an unknown with white cap and spectacles. Left again is Dave Mellors in a white cap who has his hand on the broad shoulder of the capless Derek Hollingsworth.*

To all the unknowns, my sincere apologies, but please write to me and identify yourselves in the event of a second edition.

"A true Scout," wrote Lord Baden-Powell in a new foreword to 'Scouting for Boys' in 1932, " *... is looked up to by other boys and by grown-ups as a fellow who can be trusted, a fellow who will not fail to do his duty however risky and dangerous it may be."*

From the age of eight to eighteen both lads were enriched by a certain wholesome quality of life directly from Baden-Powell's philosophy of innocence and 'bare-kneed ethos'. We can easily see Bill and Keith, under their broad-brimmed 'lemon-squeezer' hats, marching through the unspoiled beautiful English countryside. In an evening of happy camaraderie they sang hearty songs whilst cooking corned beef over open fires, which would be followed by a deep sleep, the silent sleep of the gods, save the creaking of canvas under a clear black starry sky.

And in the morning a reference to the handbook - *"On breaking up camp, leave only two things behind you - (1) Nothing; (2) Your thanks to the owner of the ground."*

Bill Shaw has remained in the Scout Movement all his life -

"I retired from the post of Group Scout Leader at the end of August 2000. Along with many local lads, we revelled in being in the Cubs and later the Scouts, eventually becoming Patrol Leaders: Keith of the Kestrel Patrol and me of the Owl Patrol. Memories are gilded by nostalgia when I think of the numerous weekend camps over the years in deep woods near Little Eaton and by the Trent at Shardlow. Adventurous hikes followed by rests stretching out in sunny meadows.

Lolling around camp fires waiting for grub to cook, and all the time the jokes and laughing - even when listening to the rain on the tent roof.

Whatever happened to good mates like Derek Midgely, Frank Swain, Derek Knight, Gordon Lucas and Ray Hawkins? Well for starters we grew up - boys became men. It is surprising that many of them still live within twenty miles!"

Or is it? Keith Matthewman, Bill Shaw and a number of their life-long friends have made deliberate career choices which have kept them in their South Nottinghamshire area. A beautiful part of England they know and love, having the advantage of easy near-access to a lovely ancient city of culture with its castle and caves, its music, arts, sport and medieval fair - an endearing environment brought vividly to life in Alan Sillitoe's novel 'Saturday Night and Sunday Morning'.

Not far away the leafy glades of the legendary Sherwood Forest redolent with the old ballads of Robin Hood and his outlaws. A little further west still, the deep green Derbyshire Dales, limestone cliffs under high rough stone crags surmounted by a landscape of wild moorland which all go to make up the Peak District.

It is no accident that Keith Matthewman has always worked, and to this day, still lives near to where the meandering River Trent has created its pleasant, lush, broad, low-lying valley.

The relatively quiet war-time open fields at the top of Marton Road provided young Bill and Keith with their first boyish opportunity to experiment with smoking. In the first instance it was a crude form of home-made pipe, consisting of a straw pushed through an acorn cup stuffed with tea leaves as a substitute for tobacco! A little later, at the age of ten, they graduated to packets of five Woodbines which cost them ten pence ha'penny [4p]. Would-be smokers beware! These small beginnings cost Keith Matthewman a great deal of money over the following 23 years.

"By the time I started in practice at the Bar in 1962, I was already smoking 60 cigarettes a day. Most people smoked in those days. It was seen on the big cinema screens as trendy and glamorous, an acceptable and desirable social activity. At that time, for me, they were totally free of charge from our shop at Aldercar. When visiting clients in the cells at the Shire Hall or the Guildhall, the first thing you would do was to offer them a cigarette - which soothed and smoothed the professional chat to follow. During a meal I recall lighting up

between courses in addition to a cigar after the meal. I was puffing
away, on and on for years and years - until one morning in 1969 ....

   Lying in bed, suddenly I felt as though I had red hot bricks in
my chest. Jane and I stopped smoking that morning - and we've never
had another one since."

In 1947, the paths in life of the Marton Road Gang started to diverge
when they took the eleven plus examination which had been introduced
in the Butler Education Act of 1944. Had they been born four years
earlier, Keith and Bill would not have been entitled to free secondary
education at all. The two friends were separated: Keith to the Long
Eaton Grammar School and Bill to a technical school in Nottingham.

"Keith's appearance at informal social gatherings on the street, or
down the fields, grew noticeably less and less as he started the many
years of study which eventually led him into the legal profession. We
naturally went our own ways. In due course I gained an engineering
apprenticeship with REME where both my dad and Keith's dad
worked."

After studying at Peoples College, Bill Shaw went on to what was then
the Nottingham and District Technical College which later became
Trent Polytechnic. He became a draughtsman and a designer first with
Rolls Royce and then back with the Ministry of Defence. Eventually
he studied for a teaching qualification at Leeds University and lectured
at Broxtowe College and Peoples College.

"Keith Matthewman and I have always kept sight of each other over
the years. In our twenties we were at each others weddings and as
married couples we have continued to occasionally socialise. As
mates, and now both of us retired, I still have the same feelings of
friendship for Keith as when we were boys, and we still live just a few
minutes drive away from where we both grew up.

   When I was the Mayor of Broxtowe in 1990-91, Jane and Keith
were of course among my special guests in the Civic Procession and
Service. As we processed through the streets where years before we
had strolled as lads - we did exchange a few asides here and there."

Apart from his duties as the Chairman of The Friends of the Galleries of Justice, Bill Shaw, a regular speaker on BBC Radio Nottingham, has a keen interest in local history and heritage. Today he runs guided tours, giving lectures and local history courses as 'Shaw's Heritage Services'.

Group Scout Leader Bill Shaw on the occasion of his retirement from scouting after 57 years of membership. Courtesy of The Nottingham Evening Post, September 2000.

Chapter 8
Running Away From Home

In the late 1800's, a young Welsh coal-miner called Albert Lang was making something of a name for himself. With some other colliers, he had helped to found a new union to fight for a decent standard of living and safe working practices in an industry which was notorious for hazards of cave-ins and flooding; not to mention explosive gases and poisonous air due to poor ventilation. Albert was spared the extreme, cruel horrors which his mining grandfather would have witnessed earlier in that Victorian century. Exploitation would have included the cheap labour of naked dust-blackened little children, on all fours, hauling heavy trucks of coal for long hours over even longer years; exploitation which enabled an opulent upper class to live on the surface in cleanliness, comfort, luxury and security. It was this gross unfairness which put fire into the belly of Mr Lang who would, himself, have originally 'gone down the pit' at the age of ten with his pick and shovel. As late as 1900 less than five per cent of British coal was cut by machinery.

Albert Lang was one of the co-founders of the National Union of Mineworkers in Wales before he moved to Birdwell near Barnsley. His daughter, Elizabeth, would eventually marry Frank Matthewman. Little did the militant Mr Lang know that, one day, his grandson would be asked to represent a coal mining community in Parliament. Little did he know that his grandson would eventually become the first ever television judge!

Albert Lang never saw a television set. He died long before the outbreak of the Second World War, but as a senior figure in the NUM, he was able to leave his widow comfortable in a rather large house in Birdwell. For two little boys visiting granny, a spooky rambling old house is a wonderful place for exploration and play. One war time afternoon, Keith and Ray were seriously engaged in an important secret reconnaissance mission to gather up much needed intelligence. Room after room was investigated, drawers and cupboards had to be searched, until - for the first time in many years, an intriguing pile of bright red leaflets came to light. The game came to an abrupt halt as the curious lads (both being good readers for their tender years) each took a garish sheet and pored over the threatening message it delivered.

Nearly sixty years later, that ominous warning from the early days of the NUM was so menacing that the reader, now a retired Circuit Judge, can clearly recall its sinister implications for the colliers and their families to whom it was originally distributed.

"I can't tell you the exact rather grim wording on those leaflets, but it certainly made an impression on us both. Something like -
'Join the National Union of Mineworkers - Or Else!!'
and also -
'If you resist joining the NUM, your life won't be worth living! We'll make sure of that!' *- words to that effect.*

We enjoyed our visits to grandmother's house. During the German air-raids, we found it exciting running down the garden to the Anderson type air-raid shelter."

This was made from the bent-over, corrugated-iron sheeting, strong inverted 'U' shape, partly sunk and covered with a layer of soil.

"In this snug and safe haven, we sat there with grandmother and listened to the bombs falling on Sheffield."

Moving southwards, home again down in Nottinghamshire, the mature man looks back to those dark war days with some embarrassment on the occasions of his rather bad boyish behaviour. A number of German prisoners of war were incarcerated in the Chilwell Barracks. The local boys, intrigued and excited to look into the eyes of the enemy, ran out to see them being marched in long lines along the Chetwynd Road.

"I'm saddened and ashamed to recall that I contributed to the chorus of swearing and abuse directed to those soldiers whose only crime was to follow orders. At least I didn't spit at them like some of the lads."

I asked Keith about the reaction to this ordeal and the expression on the faces of young marchers -

"A far as I can remember, they wore a countenance which was somewhere between uncomfortable and a disciplined indifference which, I suppose, is what you would expect. They knew they'd been demonised through our propaganda and we knew they were killing our chaps and trying to destroy our country. That's the tragedy of war."

84

There was a certain blood-lust and ghoulish enthusiasm when the pupils of Meadow Lane School sat before the wireless set and listened to the broadcast of the Nuremberg War trials.

"In 1946 I was only ten, but clearly understood the proceedings. To us, these leading Nazis were monsters. Each time one was found guilty and sentenced to hang, we all jumped up in jubilation and let out a loud and triumphant cheer!"

Readers will be pleased to know that sentences in a Judge Matthewman court were always given out with careful and sombre consideration, totally without relish and no audible rejoicing was ever tolerated!

But great rejoicing there was at the street parties on Marton Road during the 1945 Victory in Europe [VE] and Victory in Japan [VJ] celebrations -

"Nobody got drunk. It was all good natured and well behaved. However, I do recall a sudden stampede of kids over to one particular neighbour when a rumour reached us that chocolate biscuits were being given out. We'd almost forgotten what they were - but not quite!"

Like all young lads, Keith and his younger brother Ray occasionally fell foul of the parental rules. This following incident would have occurred shortly after the war and the original offence now long lost in the mists of time, but the actual punishment is still clearly recalled.

No argument! Judgement had been pronounced by Lt. Frank Matthewman and the naughty couple had been banished to their bedroom for an indefinite period without food or drink. 'Indefinite' to a child is an eternity - they might starve! In the valuable few seconds between the passing of sentence and the actual incarceration, the senior prisoner quickly conceived a resourceful plan to provide for future nourishment -

"Secretly, I strategically placed a box of apples just under our bedroom window which was on the back, safely out of sight of Mum and Dad's bedroom on the front of Marton Road. We smuggled a length of string to which was attached some metal pointed object, possibly a compass, to use as a spearing device to dig into each apple so it could be hauled up for our mutual enjoyment!"

Around about 1948 the twelve year old Keith Matthewman was working hard and learning the value of money. Near the Chilwell

To celebrate VE Day on Tuesday, May 8th 1945, a street party on Marton Road. The first boy seated on the left hand row is Bill Shaw with his mother standing behind. The second boy is Keith Matthewman.

Bypass there stands a house which, 53 years ago, was a paper shop giving Keith his first ever job as a delivery boy earning four shillings [20p] per week. The Chilwell Co-op butchers was a five shilling Saturday job which added up to a total of a handsome 9/- per week income. The Matthewman household was relatively prosperous with both parents conscientiously working for the well being of their boys. As the Supervisor at the REME workshops, Frank Matthewman was able to purchase and run a second hand Austin 10 at a time when it was very rare for ordinary working people to own a motorcar. Mr Matthewman did not wish to own that other rare, expensive and prestigious item of advanced technology - the television set. However -

"It was a fascinating experience to visit Uncle Allott [At 48 Marton Road, brother of Frank Matthewman] *who owned one of the first televisions in Chilwell. I sat down to view with my cousin Nita. Uncle Allott would first plug in, and then turn on this prized possession. Expectantly, we then sat in front of a blank, silent, nine inch screen. We sat and waited - and waited - and waited. Eventually it warmed up. First there was sound, the sound of the panic stricken squeaky voice of Billy Bunter* [courtesy of Gerald Campion] *and then, emerging from an unfocused blob, we could actually see the stern face of his long suffering teacher, Mr Quelch."*

Nita Higham (nee Matthewman) who still lives in the Nottingham area, told me that she is delighted with Keith's success in life and very proud to have a judge in the family.

Keith was fully aware of the family income which consisted of father's annual £750 and the extra £250 contribution from his mother who worked at a local knitting factory. They had bought him a bicycle for which he was grateful, but, (ever kind and considerate) the elder brother felt that Raymond, only a year and a half behind, should, (in the interests of fairness and equality) **also** be given a bicycle. And why not - one thousand pounds a year coming into one home as opposed to the trifling cost of a new bicycle manufactured just up the road in Nottingham. Twenty pounds a week; more than enough to buy two bicycles! Dad had a duty to support local industry and revive the war torn economy!

With these well crafted arguments honed from the embryonic legal mind, it is easy to imagine the enthusiastic young advocate, with both hands clutching his lapels, hitching an invisible gown, striding up and down the living room (Tony Hancock style) with a measured dignity in front of a jury of un-moved and indifferent parents.

The younger brother looked on with hope, but the father could see a wider picture and his budget had already been carefully planned. The answer was a simple and firm 'no'. Later, we will hear from others that Keith Matthewman, the barrister, was 'not a good loser' and this was an early example of such, when he and Raymond held a council of war. The vocabulary may not quite have been as sophisticated, but the following gives an essence of the youthful outrage -

"This is intolerable! They've gone too far this time. We must make a stand, Ray. We'll teach them a lesson. We'll show them. We'll run away!"

Obediently and ever trusting, the younger helped the elder to gather all the necessary equipment for a long journey to an unknown destination for the purpose of a prolonged absence - compass, spoon and fork, penknife and pocket money. These items were sombrely packed into a rucksack.

"Right. That's it. We're off! We're leaving home and it will serve them right!"

Looking back over more than a half century, Keith Matthewman recalls those two sad boys, silently sitting on that bed separated by that ready prepared rucksack and looking out of the window to darkening skies and ominous weather. It became colder. It started to rain. Their joint resolve started to weaken. At the end of that day, Keith and Raymond chose to remain in the comfort and security of 17 Marton Road.

Perhaps they should run away tomorrow, when it might be a bit dryer and a little warmer .....

Readers may be interested to know that Raymond Matthewman and his wife Marion are now running a successful restaurant in the Northumbrian village of Warenford, see cutting on next page.

Warenford pub is tops – so says Floyd . . !

Regulars of Ray and Marion Matthewman's Warenford Lodge have always known it . . . Marion's cooking is delicious, writes **LIZ MAXWELL.**

Now they have the agreement of flamboyant television chef Keith Floyd whose final judgement last week confirmed her as Britain's Pub Cook of the Year.

Her melt-in-the-mouth civets of venison saw off competitors from all over the country, and the couple were treated to a weekend in London for the grand "cook-off" at Olympia.

The couple have run the pub in the tiny Northumbrian village for the past 12 years, and are the only pub in the north to gain a coveted star in the Egon Ronay Guide for Good Food in Pubs and Bars.

"That was quite an accolade, but we were really thrilled to win this title," said Marion this week.

Her culinary delights – she has been cooking since she was eight – already have a huge following among regulars, both

"The final day was exhausting, and everything went well, except that I discovered I hadn't brought a spoon, and I panicked slightly when the Olympia cooker was in Fahrenheit not Centrigrade.

locals and holidaymakers. The pub and dining room can cater for a total of 92 people, and it's often full.

Marion has had no formal training as a chef, but gives credit for her skills to her mother – "a smashing cook" – and her school, Haydon Bridge, Northumberland, where she got an excellent basic training.

STEW

Marion's winning dish, she explained, is a rich stew of venison, flavoured with pork and fresh herbs from the garden, and cooked with red wine and brandy. She serves it with fragrant herb-flavoured rice and fresh green vegetables.

"Keith Floyd was very pleasant. He runs a country pub himself and he knows all the problems," added Ray.

Venison is very fashionable just now because it is fat-free and very healthy, and it's always a great favourite with regulars.

"We have the best of fresh ingredients in this area. We get fresh salmon from Berwick, fresh white fish from Seahouses, the meat from a butcher in Bamburgh, and locally produced vegetables."

Marion prefers to cook savoury dishes – her grilled mussels, Northumbrian fish soups and casseroles are in great demand – although her naughty but nice steamed chocolate pudding and homemade ginger ice-cream would distract even the most dedicated dieter.

ORGANISED

The competition was organised by the drinks and catering industry's newspaper, the Morning Advertiser, in conjunction with Southbend catering equipment, and the prize was £400 in vouchers for kitchen utensils and £200 in cash.

ACCIDENT

He revealed that they had bought Warenford Lodge purely by accident, after running a pub for five years in Cambridgeshire.

Ray and Keith, members of the 1st Chilwell and Attenborough Cubs

THE GRAMMAR SCHOOL, LONG EATON.

Coronation Year 1953.

Staff and pupils of Long Eaton Grammar School in 1953. The Headmaster Mr F.E. Roberts is the first seated man wearing his academic gown directly above the word 'school'. Directly above his head and slightly to the right in a light jacket is Keith Matthewman. In the same row, fifth up from the bottom, ten places to the left, short black hair, white shirt and wearing a tie - is Jane Maxwell.

Chapter 9
Long Eaton Grammar School

Lawyers have always enjoyed greater esteem and considerably greater financial reward than teachers. Is this because they are more intelligent, I ask myself? In 1969, Keith Matthewman the successful barrister was earning £80 per week as opposed to £12 per week for a starting teacher. When I discovered that Keith had never failed an exam in his life I was very impressed and described him as a brilliant student. He disagreed -

"Not me! I'm not an academic and never was. My interest in studying was only to achieve certain ambitions. I worked hard and did what I did just to get where I wanted to go. English and history were the subjects I enjoyed most."

In an attempt to uncover the 'Real Keith Matthewman' from those distant days of the Long Eaton Grammar School, in January 2000 I put out a general appeal in all the local newspapers. The following response was intriguingly signed - Carol Harper (legs)

"I remember Keith and his brother Ray, then there was Bob Hales, David and Pete Spence. We all went to the Chilwell village hall dances together - what a laugh! Keith was tall, quiet and serious; a very kind caring person. It's no surprise that he's turned out to be a good, fair and honest judge."

Later it dawned on me that 'legs' was a reference to the school; nothing at all to do with Carol's anatomy.

In 1951 the old School Certificate was abolished and replaced with the General Certificate of Education which, with great public confidence, high value, prestige and respect, would reign supreme until it's replacement in 1984 with the new exam, the General Certificate of Secondary Education.

At the Long Eaton Grammar School, it was just one year into the life of the young GCE when Keith Matthewman passed his Ordinary Level in Maths and English Language. In the September of that year, 1952, he entered the Lower Sixth Form and, as a necessity for any student planning the future study of law, he followed a course in Latin and passed the Ordinary Level in 1953. The following year in the Upper

93

Sixth he passed his Advanced Level in English Literature, History and French; results which were necessary for entry into a university. Some of his less ambitious fellow pupils were leaving simply to get a job. In their case it was necessary that they acquired as many 'O' levels as they could possibly get.

For 33 years the GCE had an unrivalled international reputation for being rigorous and sound: a gold standard which was well acclaimed before the arrival of the progressive innovations of 'interpretation' and 'empathy': a gold standard well before Melanie Phillips was moved to write 'All Must have Prizes'. In short, the reader can be assured that to pass such exams in the early 1950's - Keith Matthewman had to know his stuff!

Nick Seaton (the chairman of the Campaign for Real Education) said in the 14.8.01 edition of the Daily Express -

"The introduction of the universal GCSE exam, in the vain hope that one exam would cater for all abilities, was bound to lead to a lowering of standards in secondary schools.

So what has gone wrong and why? The reasons are partly political, partly cultural and, most of all, the product of confused egalitarian ideology that has infected our education system from top to bottom."

Armed with an impressive array of excellent results in subjects of such high prestige, a present day thinker would suppose that all doors would be open to the bright young student - alas, not everybody took that view.

During the high summer of 1953 when the air was thick with floating fine pollen grains, a miserable seventeen year old, suffering from a bad bout of hay fever, went to seek relief from his family doctor in Beeston, a Dr Thompson. After the consultation, the rather frumpish physician said -

"What are you going to read at university?"

"Law. I want to be a barrister."

"A barrister! People like you don't become barristers! Why don't you become a teacher?

This unwelcome advice made Keith determined to succeed all the more, and looking back over his 38 years in the legal profession, he tackles a commonly held misconception, a myth soundly slain by the sword of his own personal example -

> *"Nobody has ever asked me where I went to school. The public and the press think that where you've been to school and college matters greatly for you to get to, and get on at, the Bar - it does not. It's a load of rubbish! At the Bar, all that really matters is if you can do the job and do it well."*

Keith Matthewman aged about 16

At Long Eaton Grammar School Keith showed very little interest in sport or athletics and had very little talent in any of the usual competitive school games - with the one possible exception of hockey. A girl in his year called Jane Maxwell, one of the First Eleven Hockey Team, shared with me a particularly amusing memory at the end of games afternoon when she and a few of her team-mates were leaving the playing fields on West Park.

"After a good game we were on our way back to school, no doubt in a cheery and giggly mood. At the library grounds we found ourselves just a little behind two good looking lads who always stirred up (in us girls) a small ripple of excitement. Geoff Kingscott and Keith Matthewman were walking slowly, languidly trailing their hockey sticks, deep in serious political conversation. They presented a hilarious sight! Frumpish baggy shorts worn well below the knees caused us to fall about in hysterics! None of the other boys with their snappy closer fitting gear would ever be seen dead like that!"

Please note that today, Jane Maxwell is Mrs Jane Matthewman.

On the same theme of the unwilling sportsman, an interesting observation is made by the French Master, Mr Geoffrey Prime -

"It was unusual for a boy without sporting talent or sporting aspirations to be so well liked. The male contemporaries of Keith Matthewman regarded prowess on the soccer or cricket field as the chief reason for approbation, yet he was very popular indeed with both boys and girls."

Mr Prime took up his appointment at Long Eaton Grammar School in the September of 1949. It was his first teaching job and Keith was in the third year -

"I realise now, though I did not appreciate at the time because of my lack of experience, that Keith was in an exceptional group of pupils, one of the best I have had in a full career of teaching. As well as being bright in the academic sense, the form was full of 'characters', young people of charm, wit and quiet determination. Even in the presence of so much talent, Keith stood out. The first thing I remember about him was his cool, frank, appraising gaze. I can imagine many people being apprehensive or uneasy when facing this unwavering look in subsequent years. Even at the age of 13 he had a unique way of being able to express approval or disapproval in a

glance. I don't think I have before or since come across a person with this quality so marked as it is in Keith Matthewman."

Perhaps we should not be too surprised that this young student was able to use his natural charm and be well thought of even in the teeth of a cultural tendency to esteem a flair for football, athletics and other games. In the early 1900's, Lowell Thomas wrote a perceptive article about one of the most successful authors of the twentieth century -

"He was very poor. He milked the cows, cut the wood and fed the hogs, but he still went to college. He soon saw that there were certain groups in college that enjoyed influence and prestige - the football and baseball players and the chaps who won the debating and public-speaking contests. He learned that leadership went to the man who can talk."

Mr Thomas was writing about a man who wrote and self-published a book in 1937 which has now sold fifteen million copies all over the world - 'How to Win Friends and Influence People' by Dale Carnegie.

Keith Matthewman was a leading force in the Long Eaton Grammar School Literary and Debating Society. It is here that he honed and developed his considerable skills of articulate persuasion which, a decade later, would coax juries to weigh up the arguments in his favour. As a fledgling sixth-former he was beginning to follow and understand the process of the Criminal Justice System and noted with some interest the main event of December 11th 1952, when Lord Goddard sentenced the 19 year old Derek Bentley to death by hanging.

The extracts from the school magazine 'THE GOSSAMER': 1953 to 1955 gives a flavour of the issues covered in the debates.

On page 624 the magazine reports that -
"Matthewman showed himself aware of the paradox of Marlow's shyness and sophistication, and he had some good moments in his scenes with Kate Hardcastle who was played by Glenys Radford."

In Oliver Goldsmith's play 'She Stoops to Conquer', Keith was Young Marlow, the proud, impetuous snob who was shy with his equals but amorous with women whom he regarded as social inferiors. In a play control Geary as the Queen's drunken son. Pat Dennis and Dawson were messenger and gentleman respectively, and Pat Malcolm took the part of a " Dresden " shepherdess.

After the interval " The Dark Lady of the Sonnets " was presented This was of a more serious nature. It consisted mainly of Quotations from Shakespeare ; the plot tells of a chance meeting between Shakespeare and Queen Elizabeth when he should have met his own love, the Dark Lady. The latter arrives as Shakespeare is making love to the Queen who eventually forgives the Dark Lady her liason with Shakespeare.

Matthewman seemed to be ideal as Shakespeare, easily swayed but keeping himself safe by his eloquence. Pauline Greensmith as the Queen was a real tyrant (I was particularly impressed by this part). Jillian Colclough was a charming Dark Lady and Pettefar a most intimidating sentry, guarding the palace walls where the action takes place.

M.J.M., UPPER VI.

LITERARY AND DEBATING SOCIETY PAGE 641

The Society's 1953-54 programme, tabulated below, gives some indication of what an extremely successful season this has been :

Debates :

1.10.53   That commercial television would be a menace to the community.

28. 1.54   That the emancipation of woman has led to the enslavement of man.

4. 3.53   That the British monarchy serves no useful purpose.

1. 4.54   Inter-schools debate with Ilkeston G.S. : That modern entertainment has an adverse effect on the youth of today.

9. 4.54   Old Scholars' debate : This house believes in fairies.

Feb.   4.   Visit of Mr. Ernest Ashley, the author, who writes ' detective fiction ' under the name of Francis Vivian.

PAGE 679   Mr. Ashley addressed the Society on the subject of the short story explaining its structure and his own method of presentation.

Mar.   3.   Visit of Air-Commodore W. Cooper of the Telephone

1955   Works, Beeston. Air-Commodore Cooper spoke on the subject of ' Communications,' showing the changes they have effected in contemporary life.

April   5.   Old Scholars' Renunion Debate : " That the decline and eventual fall of the ' Derbyshire Nationalist Party ' is viewed with PLEASURE."
Proposed by Mr. K. Matthewman, of University College, London, and Mr. B. R. Hunt, Treasurer of the Society. Opposed by Mr. A. G. Kingscott, President of the Derbyshire Nationalist Party, Undergraduate of University College, London, and Mr. T. J. Syson, Chairman of the Society.

about the rigid eighteenth century class system this is an interesting role for a budding socialist.

On the evening of March 19th, 1953, the Long Eaton Grammar School Drama Group staged a play by Bernard Shaw called 'The Dark Lady of the Sonnets'. A photograph in 'The Gossamer' shows a young man in Elizabethan garb on one knee entreating an indifferent and haughty young woman. The man is Keith Matthewman playing the part of William Shakespeare pleading with Pauline Greensmith who takes the part of Queen Elizabeth.

Mr Prime gave me his unofficial review and commendation of that performance -

"I love the somewhat equivocal use of the word 'seemed' in describing his performance of Shakespeare. My memory of the play is that he was very impressive in the part, quite an eye-opener to me in fact. I hadn't realised his hidden depths."

Jillian Colclough as the Dark Lady standing over a kneeling Keith Matthewman as Shakespeare in 'Dark Lady of the Sonnets', 1953.

Keith Matthewman -

"I worked hard at school, but not too hard since I had a brain and was always in the top form. I enjoyed my life at school tremendously, particularly debating ... and best of all ... acting on the stage."

These last few words were said with a profound deep and genuine wistfulness. His tone, melancholic and meditative, struck a chord with my own personal misgivings looking back over early career choices. Like me, Keith was a working class boy who had to obtain a 'no-nonsense' position which would give secure regular wages. Like me, he did not have the luxury of a private income or wealthy parents for a financial safety net. Like me, Keith Matthewman was in no position to take risks, to explore and develop the artistic side of his abilities which means that some talents have gone untried and untested.

But acting is not always done on the stage. Bill Shaw remembers a certain cold wet autumn night in 'down town' Long Eaton when he and his friend Keith, both aged sixteen, found it desirable to turn themselves into black and white, movie type gangsters.

"We left the cinema, (no doubt having just seen a James Cagney film) and, for reasons which I can't remember, decided to track down a mutual friend who lived across the road from Keith. Ray Sewell was in the habit of frequenting snooker halls. In those days of the early 50's, particularly in Long Eaton, they were invariably tatty places and regarded by some as where low-life and criminals hung around. By unspoken agreement we adopted what we imagined to be a 'tough guy' image - with rain coat collars turned up, shoulders haunched, fists thrust deep into our pockets and facial expressions to suit. We swaggered into a couple of 'joints' and in a tough voice asked the (somewhat alarmed) receptionist if Ray Sewell was in the place. We didn't find him on that bleak night and had to catch the bus home."

Keith Matthewman was not acting when he had first expressed his admiration and affection for the 'Dark Lady of the Sonnets'. The eponymous lady was played by Jillian Colclough who lived in Spondon. Just after that performance Keith recalls an evening which involved four time-consuming bus trips, just to take Jillian out to the pictures.

"I caught the bus from Depot Corner in Chilwell for the journey out to pick up Jillian at her house in Spondon. We then waited at the stop for the Nottingham bus and eventually arrived at the old

Gaumont Cinema. After the film, another wait for the bus back to Spondon to see Jillian safely back to her front door. Now alone, yet another wait at the bus stop to catch the ride back to Chilwell and home. Out of the total cost of six sets of bus fares and two cinema tickets, I still had change out of 10/-." [50p]

The academic and athletic distinctions of Jane Maxwell are well documented in 'The Gossamer'. In the June of 1952 she took and passed 'O' Level Domestic Science. Those early skills, now improved by the years of experience, are still enjoyed and greatly appreciated today by guests to the Matthewman home and also by the 'Friends of the Galleries of Justice'. In June of the following year she added English Language, English Literature, Biology and Art. In December 1953 she also passed Geography and French making a total of seven subjects.

Long Eaton Grammar School was divided up into three houses named after local rivers - Trent, Derwent and Soar. Living in Belper I was gratified to discover that Jane Maxwell was honourably associated with Derwent House. In 1954 Jane and Geoff Kingscott co-wrote the house notes in which she characteristically concerns herself with the well-being of a long serving member of staff -
"We are pleased to hear that Miss Silk is out of hospital and well on the road to recovery."
In the Derwent house notes of 1955 -
"We would like to mention the fine performance of our two athletic captains - Jane Maxwell and John Panton. Jane won the 100 and 150 yards races."
From 1956 to 1960, Jane Maxwell also played for the Attenborough Tennis Club.

I asked Keith if Long Eaton Grammar School had it's equivalent of William Howitt Secondary Modern School's formidable Mrs Buxcey described in my second book 'Heanor Schooldays' -
"All the staff were good. I don't remember any teachers who were actually disliked ... but we did have a first year maths master called 'Cheesy' Allen! If homework was done incorrectly, he'd throw your exercise book right out of the hopper window: he never missed! Rain, hail, shine or snow, you had to go out into the playground to bring your work back into the classroom."

Many thanks to former pupil Michael Trotman for sending me the following photographs of charming caricatures of the staff and pupils of Long Eaton Grammar School. This is the work of Mr Sanders the

art master who is first on the left. Mr Greenhalgh the geography master is next to the sitting physics master, Mr Robinson, nicknamed, 'Nosnibor'. The very tall Mr Saville, nicknamed 'Tom', taught English and Latin. In front of Mr Saville, Mr Atkinson ('Fras'), taught maths as did the sitting Mr Dillingham ('Dilly'). The two women between Mr Atkinson and Mr Dillingham are Miss Balantyne [sports] and Mrs Wright neé Deacon, wearing glasses, who taught biology. The striding Mr Crompton, ('Crumps') taught Latin and Mr Morton taught sport. With spectacles and smoking is Mr Allton the music master. Also with specs, is maths master Mr Calton ('Felix'), speaking to the pipe smoking French master, Mr Wright, 'Pip', at the extreme right.

The second photograph is overleaf. Michael Trotman was not able to identify the boy on the roof or the boy speaking to Jane Maxwell who in on the extreme left. The boy apparently smoking is David Pettefar in conversation with Peter Harrison. The dancing girl with a pony-tail is Cynthia Clements, just in front of an unknown boy holding a paper. Behind this boy is the white-coated chemistry master, Mr Pritchard speaking to a fellow chemist, the smoking, dark suited Mr Cocking, nickname unsuitable for publication. The English and divinity master

Mr Hunter, apparently sporting sausages and holding a box, is next. The last two men are English masters, the smoking Mr Townshend and the bespectacled Mr Johnson. The history mistress, Miss Cockerell, is on the extreme right. James Williamson is the boy sitting on the roller.

Nita Higham told me that -

"The history mistress, Miss Brooks, was a driving force. It was an excellent school with thriving musical and theatrical opportunities."

It would seem Nita took full advantage of such opportunities. In May 1953, ambitiously the school staged the 17th century opera by Henry Purcell called 'Dido and Aeneas'. A reviewer signed LN wrote -

"Nita Matthewman, I think, deserves a special mention, for she sang with a beauty, strength and clarity which it was a joy to hear."
The Gossamer page 625.

Miss Brooks, a very popular teacher, also ran the Literary and Debating Society. Keith was full of praise recalling the tremendous amount of extra work she did for the school -

"She was a great help and we got on very well together. Hundreds of former pupils will remember Miss Brooks with gratitude and affection."

Keith told me he was very sad to leave Long Eaton Grammar School - *"It was a good school, a great school. Everybody had a lot of fun."*

But life goes on and Keith Matthewman was destined for higher office.

Chapter 10
University College London

The study of law was never a great love in the life of Keith Matthewman. One evening in confidential mood, relaxing after a few drinks, he once responded to me, sotto voce, shaking his head rather regretfully -

"The law? God, Narvel! If only you knew ... it's as dull as ditch-water! Really!

This was a reference to the law, as a subject, as opposed to its human and dramatic practical applications in the courts of law. Perhaps we must look to the creative, artistic and materialistic side of the man to understand Keith's paradoxical statement. As previous pages have testified, there was never any doubt about his consistent ambition to become a barrister (initially and valiantly) for the defence. Looking back on a career as a history teacher, I have to admit that 'history' had precious little to do with it. Furthermore we must recall the words of Mark Patterson when he spoke of Keith, with his embryonic skills of articulation and acting, being impressed with the 'showmanship' in court and the 'dramatis personae in the theatre of justice'.

As I write [October 2000], Judge Matthewman is counting down the last days to his final court appearance which will be in late December. He is overworked, very tired and cannot wait to hang up his wig. Reluctantly, each morning he drags himself out of bed to do a job which is generally seen as powerful, prestigious and glamorous, but in this last year - it is a job he has come to despair of. This feeling has (for the most part) its roots in recent changes which have come down from top officials in the Lord Chancellor's Department. More about this later. Also we will hear more about the sheer hard work, long hours of study and preparation which stretch into personal time, into the evening and swallow up weekends which are no part of the popular public perception of 'His Honour's' rather short day, when he casually utters the familiar -

"I think we will rise now ..."

As a teacher, for similar reasons of pernicious influence causing damaging changes, percolating down from high, beyond my control, I too, at the end, like Shakespeare's 'whining school boy' crept like a snail, unwillingly to school. During his last months on the Bench, I empathised with my friend about my own last few rough years in the comprehensive school. A draining, debilitating and exhausting experience, staggering like a zombie from day to day, weekend to weekend, holiday to holiday - with a diminishing quality of life - up to the point that my health was on the line. I said -

"Is it like that for you now?"

With some feeling he replied -

*"It's **exactly** like that."*

The same as Keith, I began my profession with great enthusiasm inspired by the splendid example of traditional teachers which included a certain young master called Mr Matthewman. When that same young master decided to leave William Howitt Secondary Modern School in the July of 1961, he announced to his colleagues in the staff-room -

"I'm sorry ladies and gentlemen, but I fear that I can no longer afford to stay with you!"

It is a well known fact that the best talent and quality in the classroom very soon moves **out** of the classroom for more money. Keith has never been shy to admit that he has sought to achieve and enjoy all the fruits of a high salary which the law provided. He and Jane have always lived at a high material standard. As you will see, they have resided in large beautiful homes with large beautiful gardens and have stayed at the best hotels and eaten the best food. The law may be dull, but the Matthewmans never were.

So it was that in the July of 1954 a well qualified 18 year old left the Long Eaton Grammar School with the firm intention to read law at the very best university for that purpose. He applied for, and obtained an October place at his first choice, the elite and famed University College London. October! But this was July and it would be many years under canvas before Keith would be able to savour the comforts of the Dorchester Hotel. He wanted money and he wanted it now. Thanks to the influence of father, who was the supervisor at the REME workshops in Chilwell Depot, Keith Matthewman managed to secure his first job.

In the hallowed curriculum of the Long Eaton Grammar School, the repairing, maintaining and testing of tanks did not appear. Therefore it followed that our Keith did not know the first thing about tanks, but, notwithstanding, he was not discouraged to take on this new job! South of the Central Ordnance Depot at the south-western corner of the Attenborough Nature Reserve was situated with suitable challenging obstacles - the Tank Testing Track. Here he was introduced to 'Nodder' the bloke who actually drove the metal beast which was probably a 'Centurion' type, the new post-war British tank. It was a rough old ride but the new boy had a great time -

"Day after day, Nodder and I trundled around the track in this noisy cramped compartment. One day he said (no doubt against the rules) - 'Do you want to drive it?' I certainly did! What a thrilling experience! And what a sense of power driving that 50 ton metal monster!"

Minutes before leaving home for college, with his suit case all packed and ready, Keith was saying his final 'goodbyes' at the front door before undertaking his journey to London. In these final moments, Frank Matthewman was moved to discharge a belated fatherly responsibility, which to him was not easy - not easy at all! His eldest son was about to be swallowed up into the wicked Capital City. Something had not been said - and now **had** to be said. In some embarrassment, he blurted out -

"You know all about sex then do you, Keith?"
"Yes I do, Dad."
With visible relief -
"Fine, all right, on your way ..."

The new student took the train, which in those days, went to London from Attenborough Station. His suitcase was so over-packed and heavy, the porter at St Pancras remarked in unfamiliar Cockney tones -
"Cor mate! Wot ya got in 'ere? Tommy guns?"

Keith Matthewman made to me a revealing and significant statement about this period and himself. The following supports previous comments in which I suggest that his career decisions were made to keep him near to the place of his birth where the quality of life was always good.

"I enjoyed college life; there were lots of pleasant people, but I have to say that I didn't really enjoy living in London all that much."

Perhaps to keep up with some of the more wholesome aspects of his home life, he continued with scouting activities living in a scout residence called Roland House in Stepney, not all that far from the location of the present day Dome. Starting as an assistant Scout Master, he was soon promoted to full Scout Master over a troop at Bethnal Green, just two miles north. In this (still raw) war damaged area, it was the appalling poverty endured by some these East End lads which awakened the social conscience of the young student and pushed him along to the left side of the political continuum.

But Stepney was more than a repository of slums. Keith found it an interesting district with a rich and colourful history. In the Limehouse area he dined in the famous Chinese restaurants, walked 'The Highway', once notorious for its seamen's drinking dens, visited the 16th-century Prospect of Whitby, an old smugglers haunt, and another picturesque inn called The Town of Ramsgate, standing on the very spot where the infamous 'Hanging Judge', Judge Jeffreys, disguised as a sailor, was arrested in 1688 - not an omen we hope!

It was Mark Patterson who suggested that Judge Matthewman had 'something of a hanging judge reputation' in The Nottingham Evening Post 11.3.2000. Lord Chief Justice Jeffreys presided over the infamous 'Bloody Assize' after the Battle of Sedgemoor in 1685, which, on the orders of the victorious King James II, punished the remaining soldiers of the defeated James, Duke of Monmouth. Judge Jeffreys sentenced 200 to be 'hung, drawn and quartered' and sent 800 more to the West Indies as slaves. Biased accounts painted Jeffreys a monster, the Devil in human shape, who joked as he passed sentence. He was probably no worse than other judges at that time and, for the record, we should point out that Judge Matthewman never did wear the 'black cap' and does not approve of capital punishment.

Bethnal Green was a good centre to run a boy-scout troop with its distinctive 1872 iron and glass roofed museum and the vast expanse of Victoria Park known as 'the playground of the East End'.

Scouting in the Capital caused some problems -

"Studying law is very demanding and I found my scouting responsibilities increasingly time consuming and distracting, not to mention - embarrassing! Travelling on the crowded rush-hour tube at 6.00pm from Stepney to Bethnal Green in full uniform, complete with shorts, was no joke!"

It is not difficult to imagine Keith, at 18, rather put out about showing his bare knees, staring hard at the advertisements on the inside wall of the carriage, swaying in motion, feeling out of place, desperately trying to avoid the curious and condescending eyes of urbane be-suited business office workers.

During the following term a fellow law student called Tony Scrivener suggested sharing accommodation in South Kensington which was so different from Stepney, Keith described it as - *'The other side of the world!'* It was certainly on the posh west side of the centrally located University College in Bloomsbury, a district noted for handsome squares, learning, scholarship, the intellectual and the artistic. Together with 'Scriv' and a lad called John Rhind, Keith paid a third of the rent on a ground floor flat in a quiet, refined, Georgian road south of Kensington Gardens. Here the studious trio dwelt in a conservative world of squares, mews and narrow streets lined with smart and luxurious white-fronted residences, antique shops, old inns and intimate cafes.

On one memorable evening, Scriv noticed two intruders climbing over the back garden wall. With some degree of outrage and bravery he marched out to defend his territory - *'GET OUT!'*
　　　　One of the trespassers ignored him completely, continuing his athletic progress, scaling the next wall. The other, with some impatience, responded -
　　　　"Damn it, man! We're Police Officers ... a burglar's getting away!"
With the authority and style of the seminal advocate, Anthony Scrivener said -
　　　　"I don't believe you! Show me your identification."
Reluctantly in bad temper, the chaser answered the challenge of this fresh faced 19 year old and quickly produced the official document (which was carefully inspected) before hastily continuing his pursuit.

To this day it is still not known if that running criminal was ever caught.

In 'Who's Who', Anthony Frank Bertram Scrivener QC., ex-Chairman of the General Council of the Bar - lists car racing as one of his recreations. So it was nearly a half century back when he bundled Keith into his very old, tiny, open-top sports car and raced around the (then) quieter streets of London. He was once stopped by the police for a minor fault and told it was a simple matter to write to the court, plead guilty and accept a fine. But the said Anthony Scrivener, somewhat miffed, had no wish to throw himself upon the mercy of the court and no inclination to pay a routine fine. He would fight! He went to court to make his very first appearance before the poe faced magistrates and eloquently argued against the unjust charge. He lost. But Scriv had gained the admiration of his flat mates. He had actually got to a court, been on his feet, and contested a case before the other students.

Keith found college life a wonderful experience. The lecturers and tutors were all very helpful and pleasant. There was a good Law Society. Law lectures often required students to go out of the large campus of University College London and into King's College for certain lectures, and sometimes into the London School of Economics.

Keith Matthewman took a growing interest in the fast moving political scene. His grammar school days had seen the defeat of the Labour Government in the General Election of October of 1951, when, for the second time Winston Churchill became the Prime Minister at the age of 77. Keith's college days had seen the old man reluctantly resign at the age of 80 on April 5th, 1955 to give way for the aristocratic and refined Sir Anthony Eden who won the General Election on May 27th. The following year, Colonel Nasser, the President of Egypt, seized the all-important oil carrying Suez Canal. In August 1956 Sir Anthony Eden went on television and told the nation that -

"It is a matter of life and death! A man with his record cannot be allowed to have his thumb on our windpipe."

Keith Matthewman and some of the undergraduates of UCL did not agree with this interpretation of the events. Together with the Americans, the Soviet Union and a majority of the United Nations, they condemned the infamous 'twelve hour ultimatum' and our subsequent

110

bombing raids on Cairo and the Canal Zone. They agreed with Nasser that it was - *'an attack on the rights and dignity of Egypt'* and supported the Daily Herald's opinion that - *'the handling of the crisis was a national disgrace'*. On November 19th, Keith was just one of 10,000 people, many with banners, who gathered in Trafalgar Square to chant and demand 'LAW NOT WAR!' Keith recalls that day -

"I was nearly knocked down by mounted police and survived a baton charge! I have no regrets for my actions but have no condemnation for the police tactics. They were simply obeying orders and doing their duty."

It was all too much for the Prime Minister who had cracked up through overwork and was suffering from 'severe overstrain'. His doctors had ordered an immediate rest which took the form of three weeks convalescence in Jamaica. In the January of 1957 he resigned and the Queen asked Harold Macmillan (not Rab Butler as expected) to be the new PM.

As post war austerity receded further into the background and the working classes (with the help of the 'never never') were enjoying a higher living standard, on July 20th Mr Macmillan (now dubbed 'Super Mac') told the nation - *'You've never had it so good!'*

Keith Matthewman was no Conservative but in that same month it could be said that he himself had it pretty good, having just graduated with a Bachelor of Laws degree from one of the best universities in Britain.

He was bright, young, fit, energetic, and raring to go ....

Keith Matthewman the sandwich-board man.

Chapter 11
The Sandwich-Board Man

Ever keeping busy, Keith Matthewman enjoyed working during part of his holidays and the extra money came in very handy. In the summer of 1955 he arrived at a top quality well known store in Kensington to report for duty. His new boss was an aptly named, dark haired, suave and pretty girl who made quite an impression.

"Rhona Angel! I wonder where she is now?"
The new assistant was keen to get started -
"What do I do first?"
"Well ... let me see ... the sale starts tomorrow. You can change the tickets on all the clothes. Here's the box with all the new red sale tickets. Quite simple, just remove all the existing old tickets and attach the new red sale tickets.
"Yes?"
"Well! Get on with it. What are you waiting for?"
"Yes but ... Look, I'm sorry but ... What do I put for the new sale price? How much do I discount?"
"Oh that! No problem. Just write down the same price."

In the following summer of 1956, Keith decided to give the 'are you being served set' a miss. Staying with a few other law students at the Grimsby YMCA, they worked nights cleaning pea boiling machines at Frigid Foods and Frigid Fruits in Cleethorpes. An appalling prospect after Bloomsbury, but he assured me that he enjoyed the experience -

"Quite fun! We went to the pub before the shift started at 10.00pm and sometimes worked right through to 10.00am the next day to get a couple of extra hours overtime. The boss spent all night sleeping whilst we were working, but I suppose that's the bosses privilege. Scriv joined us a few days later, summed up the situation and objected to the appalling low pay and exploitation of students by the management. He called a strike! I don't recall the outcome."

During the last weeks of term, before the nocturnal machine cleaning, Keith went into advertising. He became a sandwich-board man!

With a board each side of his body and one over his head, the Middle Temple student (without permission from Middle Temple) tramped his beat up and down The Strand, advertising Watney's Brown Ale.

"What if somebody recognised me! I tried to grow a beard to disguise myself."

As you see from the photograph on page 110, the top board was part blackboard to display the latest Australia v England test match results. It was part of Keith's job to telephone Watney's each hour to get the latest score and write it up for the benefit of the public. At the end of a fortnight he was paid the princely sum of a crate of Watney's Brown Ale or Pale Ale - he had the choice.

Back at college he joined the Debating Society but was more interested in the Film Society in which he became the treasurer and at one point filmed the Queen Mother who was on a visit to the university. A student called Margaret Booth who was president of the College Law Society shared one recollection -

"I vividly remember watching the long Russian epics such as 'Battleship Potemkin' in (I think) the Chemistry lecture hall which was not very comfortable."

Miss Booth went on to become a High Court Judge and is today Dame Margaret Booth DBE. Small wonder Sergei Eisenstein's work made a memorable impression on young minds having been described by a Radio Times 7.4.01 critic as -

"A key cinematic turning point; a heady combination of montaged imagery, incendiary subject matter and social message."

A wide range of films were made and shown by the students themselves. Some reels were quite experimental such as the time consuming 'stop-go' animations using small plastic figures, after the style of Morph from 'Take Hart'. Keith worked with Joanna Dunham who later became an actress and also he filmed a play in which another young student, Tom Courtenay was acting. Keith remembers Mr Courtenay -

*"A quiet, courteous man, but we didn't have a great deal to do with each other - as is shown by the fact that he can't remember me at all! Unbelievable, but there you are! Anyway it wasn't all **our** work,*

we were a jolly crowd and occasionally trooped out to see the efforts of other film makers: 'Seven Brides for Seven Brothers' was great fun."

They were once visited by the Film Censor! Fear not; it was nothing to do with any questionable production. He was one of the regular guest speakers at society meetings. Afterwards they took him round to the local pub and generously, he asked each member of the committee what they would like to drink. A variety of shorts were requested such as gin and tonic, whiskey etc., until the guest reached the treasurer -

"Thank you, I'll have a brown ale please."

This small faux pas caused a very minor moment of unease among the gathering, but the censor, a gracious fellow, took it in good part and merely said -

"A brown ale! Are you quite sure?"

As a teetotaller and also one who has not moved in the circles of barristers, judges and the titled (in a similar occasion I once asked for a pot of tea) - Keith had to explain to me this social howler -

"We all have to learn the social graces. My choice of drink in that particular situation was unfortunate! It was the same as asking for 'mild' or a Watney's which have working class connotations. An uncomfortable but interesting memory because my uniformed and uneducated request illustrated the gulf between the working and middle classes, especially in the 1950's."

Keith did his last vacation job when he 'went down from college' (graduated) in the June of 1957. Living at the time in Ilford, north-east of Greater London, he spent the summer going all over the Capital on the underground, visiting a multitude of shops, big and small, selling - 'Jubbly'. This was a popular orange drink of the day, sold in tetrahedral cartons made by the Idris Company and referred to as 'Lubbly Jubbly'. The young salesman worked very hard and earned good money on a commission only basis.

Keith's real home was still with Mum, Dad and Ray back in south Nottinghamshire, but in 1957 Frank Matthewman had retired early and they had moved nine miles north-west into Derbyshire, just over the border created by the River Erewash. Mr Matthewman decided to start a new life as a shopkeeper in a small industrial (yet still quite rural) community called Aldercar, just a mile down from the westerly hill top mining town of Heanor.

"Occasionally I helped by serving behind the counter in our family grocers shop at 215 Cromford Road, which in fact sold everything from paraffin to panties!"

Having been served by academia, Keith was now eligible to serve his country. Since the end of the war, two years of National Service had been the norm for all young men who attained the age of 18. With great jubilation, this author recalls the announcement made in 1956 that the 'call-up' was to be abolished in 1960. I was not looking forward to a disfiguring 'short back and sides', marching in time, and being screamed at by the likes of Sergeant-Major Bullimore [William Hartnell] -

'You're an 'orrible little man - wot are you?'

'The Army Game' was a popular Friday night comedy on the new Commercial Television channel which started broadcasting to the nation in September 1955. Keith Matthewman saw the same programme, but his attitude to conscription surprised me -

*"I was looking forward to the experience! I wanted to join the RAF. At the medical my 'flat feet' might have been a concern but the doctor said - 'No problem at all. I'm not bothered about your feet - but, I'm afraid that you **do** have varicose veins! Sorry, but you are rejected.' I was quite put out, especially as up to then, I didn't know I was inflicted in that way."*

Put out and out of work, the former scout, scholar, debater, actor, tank tester, salesman, sandwich-board man, machine cleaner and shop assistant - had now to consider his position. Having a degree in law from however prestigious an institution did not mean he could simply buy a wig and apply to the nearest Assize Court. Further steps were necessary. First he would have to take, and pass the Bar Exam before he could become a barrister. To get into a set of chambers required money and also an introduction / recommendation from a barrister on the inside of chambers. On top of that he needed to be accepted by a senior barrister who was prepared take him on as a new pupil and would also charge a 'pupillage fee' of 100 guinea's.

Until these things were accomplished, as ever, he had to earn his living - and **not** by walking up and down The Strand as a sandwich-board man!

Having an impressive career as a pupil and student, Keith had a healthy respect for the teaching profession. Just as he is remembered today as a first rate barrister and more recently a superb judge; many former pupils recall, with affection, Mr Matthewman as an effective teacher of English.

Ilford, Keith's last London home, was one of three industrial towns close together in the East End, north of the River Thames, which were joined up by continuous housing to make up a large conurbation. The other two towns were Dagenham and the ancient market town of Barking - which at that time had a rough and tough secondary modern all boy's school. Such a school often had vacancies for much needed staff.

In the summer of 1957 they were looking to appoint a new English master ...

Chapter 12
The Soho Strip Club

Teaching has never been well paid, but this was Keith's first real professional position, rewarded at the rate of £620 per year. This modest figure would have been even less if he had no degree and taught outside of London. In 1958, £12 a week was probably an average wage in the Midlands but certainly below average in the area around London. Keith Matthewman would earn every single penny at Barking Secondary Modern School.

It was a deliberate choice! He could have had his pick! Why did the brilliant English master not apply to a nice, middle class, well disciplined grammar school in a civilised leafy suburb: a school where he would be received in silence by upstanding, smartly uniformed, clean, respectful, quiet boys? With his excellent qualifications plus three years at University College London, he could easily have secured a post in a prestigious public school, yet he chose to face 40, and often more, boisterous, unpolished, working class, East End lads who were determined to give the newcomer the works!

The answer is simple. It was a political decision based upon his left wing views and disapproval of selection, by which means the eleven plus examination separated the academic from the non-academic. The eleven plus examination was first proposed in the 1926 Hadow Report but was not actually implemented until the 1944 Butler Education Act. It was to decide if a pupil should go on to a grammar school or to a 'secondary modern' school where the emphasis was on more practical subjects.

At that time, Keith Matthewman agreed with critics of the divisive system who doubted the wisdom of deciding a child's future at the early age of eleven, especially as the exam itself was not always reliable and admission to a local grammar school depended upon the places available. Although a beneficiary of the system himself, Keith might have concurred with the views of the author Barry Hines, as expressed in the BBC Timewatch Programme called 'Grammar School Boys' 14.4.98. -

"Going to the secondary modern meant you'd get a labouring job such as a brickie, or a joiner, or go down the pit. Grammar school meant an office job with collar and tie - to sign on, rather than clock on."

On the other hand, in the same programme, Keith's near contemporary and near neighbour who one time lived in Aldercar, said -

"The eleven plus suited me down to the ground. It was designed for the likes of me, the son of a coal miner, to have the chance to compete with the privileged."

My subject and this particular contributor have much in common. He is Kenneth Clarke the former Chancellor of the Exchequer.

In 1956, Keith the socialist did not agree with the following warning from the headmaster of Eton School -

"The growing number of comprehensive schools were a threat to the quality of British education."

See newspaper cuttings on page 121.

Keith Matthewman believed in the new concept of the comprehensive school, a school which accepted pupils from the whole community regardless of academic ability. But that was the young, idealistic, liberal Keith Matthewman of the late 1950's and early 1960's. After a short teaching career and a lifetime of observations and experience, retired Judge Matthewman of the year 2001 has an entirely different viewpoint.

"I regret the destruction of so many of our excellent grammar schools during these last 40 years. Long Eaton Grammar School served me very well and gave other working class boys a very good start in life. It has been crazy, absolutely crazy, to close grammar schools! It creates a situation whereby academically gifted pupils are not able to use their gifts well.

My own son Adrian went to our local comprehensive which was the George Spencer School in Toton and later to Bilborough Sixth Form College. Fortunately they were very good ones, but in many cases the comprehensive ideal seems to have been high-jacked by left wing trendy teachers who are determined to reduce academic standards to the lowest common denominator, and standards of dress appear to have gone the same way. I'm saddened to hear of 'mixed ability' and the end of whole class teaching, streaming and setting; astounded to find that some departments have abolished marking the work of pupils. I'm appalled to learn that some teachers are addressed by their first names.

HEANOR LABOUR PARTY

A well-attended meeting of the Heanor Ward Labour Party was held in the Labour Club, Heanor, on Tuesday last, when at the close of routine business those present were addressed by Coun. K. Matthewman on the subject, "Education."

The speaker, in his opening remarks, said 80 per cent. of the children in this country were not getting a square deal because of present educational policy, and six out of ten children in Secondary schools were suffering from the acute shortage of teachers.

Coun. Matthewman attacked the systems leading up to the 11-plus grammar school entrance examination, pointing out that only 10 per cent. of children in Rutland could gain grammar school places, whilst nearly 60 per cent. had this opportunity in Merioneth, and these inequalities operated throughout the whole of the counties and county boroughs in the country.

Academic education was not feasible or necessary for all children, but a radical reorganisation was needed, and this could be met by the system of comprehensive education, which was the cornerstone of Labour's Education Policy.

The comprehensive system could either be operated in a large school of around 1,000 pupils, or as in the method now being tried out in Leicestershire, of two junior high schools feeding to one senior high school.

The public schools should be integrated into the State system, and the universities, where a "new look" was needed, required a drastic change in the system of entry, as ex-grammar school boys were now achieving better results than ex-public school boys from university education. It was essential that a higher proportion of the cost of education should be borne by the national Exchequer, instead of becoming an ever increasing burden on local rates.

HEANOR LABOUR PARTY

Monthly Meeting

The main item was a debate on "Peace—at any price," in which Coun. S. Mellors, in proposing, said that the example of America, with its fear and hysteria over nuclear fallout shelters was a frightening prospect, and a revolutionary approach to the problem of nuclear warfare was required from one of the world's key statesmen. Every leading statesman was desperately anxious to avert a third world war, which, Mr. Mellors said, would be more disastrous than any alternative which could possibly arise, and his policy was peace at any price. Coun. K. Matthewman, in supporting, said we must not endanger generations as yet unborn with nuclear explosions, and the danger of a number of small countries possessing nuclear weapons was very real. He thought we were caught up with systems, and not with people, as if we had the opportunity to meet ordinary people from other countries there would be a greater chance of mutual understanding.

LOSCOE WARD LABOUR PARTY

A talk was given by Coun. K. Matthewman, of Langley Mill, on "The Labour Party's Education Policy." Coun. Matthewman spoke about the weaknesses and failures of the present-day educational policy, and emphasised the advantages of an all out comprehensive education policy, as advocated by the Labour Party. He deplored the fact that most men in the street did not know just what comprehensive education meant, and thought that the Labour Party should put out more publicity explaining how it would work, and how it would benefit all classes of children.

At the Bar and on the Bench, I've seen the destructive results of the gradual break-down of discipline in our more progressive schools. At least, in recent years, we are seeing indications of a return to traditional teaching methods and, of late, I've noticed schoolchildren looking smarter."

As I write (September 2001) the current statistics for my former profession look bleak indeed. Writing in the Daily Express 4.9.01, Dr Andrew Cunningham of Cranleigh School in Surrey, paints a depressing picture -

"A survey of 827 comprehensives reveals that up to 6,000 teachers appointed over the holidays could be 'sub-standard', with heads so desperate to fill shortages they have taken on second-rate staff. That same survey suggests there could still be 5,000 teacher vacancies: resulting in the prospect of big classes and four-day weeks.

Meanwhile, 40 per cent of new recruits become so disillusioned they quit within three years. One graduate gives her reasons; 'Children are getting more and more out of control, there is not enough support and the pay is terrible.'"

The extract from the Ripley and Heanor News was printed sometime in 1960. Note the absence of first names and use of formal titles when referring to individuals: Mr or Coun. K. Matthewman. When I researched 'Heanor Schooldays', Keith and other members of the staff of William Howitt Secondary Modern School were unable to give me the 'Christian names' of older colleagues. All masters and mistresses addressed each other as Mr, Mrs or Miss. Jane Matthewman was once asked by one of her pupils (who was puzzled by 'Coun.') if her husband was a Count, like Count Dracula!

Traditional teaching methods reigned supreme at Barking. The uncouth and loutish may have been regarded as, in progressive parlance, 'challenging behaviour', but, as Judge Matthewman said to Jeremy Evans on Radio Nottingham [October 1999] the Barking masters were always in complete control.

"Transgressions were never ignored and justice was never delayed by bureaucracy. In morning assembly we had hymns followed by public canings on the stage delivered by the headmaster. Occasionally a boy would remove his hand at the last split-second causing the cane to swish down and miss. They were ready for that.

That was a signal for the history master and the gym master to leap onto the stage, grab the lad, one each side, holding each arm over the table, face down. The headmaster would then administer double strokes on his bottom.

I hear your listeners crying - **'Dreadful! Cruelty! Brutality!'** *But, I'll tell you this - they never came back for more!"*

William Howitt Secondary Modern School at Heanor two years later, just as 'working class', notwithstanding was an entirely different, kinder and more civilised regime where the cane was always available - but very rarely used. Keith Matthewman attributes this welcome improvement to the mixture of boys and girls -

"Co-education has a softening effect on 'loutish, ladish culture'. With more mature girls looking on, boys tend to be embarrassed by their own boisterous bad behaviour. Result - less need for the stick!"

One particularly difficult Barking boy decided to test his new teacher. He was amusing himself by pinning a steel ruler to the edge of his desk with one hand and causing it to loudly reverberate with the other. The English master told him to stop. The order was ignored -

"Give me that ruler!"

"Yes, Sir."

Promptly the lad hit Mr Matthewman with the ruler on the hand - BANG! These were the days when a schoolteacher could use his initiative, respond appropriately and quickly without fear of reprimand or worse. And he did. He hit the culprit twice.

"Sir!! Bloody 'ell! That's not fair. You 'it me twice an I only 'it you once!

Discipline would have been firm and efficient from a particular master called Mr Ossuski who had received effective training having been a member of Hitler's SS! He was a Pole who was drafted into the German SS during the war and now, nicely solvent, because in addition to his teacher's salary, he was also in receipt of a pension from the British Government, unlike another master on the staff, a 'Cape Coloured' [as they were known at the time] South African called Mr Hendrix. He had no such pension, yet was keen to fight **for** us, only to have had his offer refused. Slightly short of money, like many London teachers, Hendrix worked a second job. He was a doorman for a strip

123

club at the Irving Theatre in Piccadilly. His young colleague, Matthewman, was most intrigued by this very interesting and unusual theatre in the Soho area. To comply with the law, the naughty naked girls on stage had to be completely still. To move would have been **too** naughty! Would Matthewman care to view this spectacle? Yes, he would! In fact he went on a couple of occasions.

Keith was not present on the one celebrated occasion at the Windmill Theatre when a girl known as 'Peaches', in mid tableau, to her horror, saw a mouse! The audience were delighted to see her make a frantic illegal dash from the stage.

One lunch time, in the staff-room, after a typical hectic morning, two drained and drooping masters were relaxing and sinking ever deeper into the beaten-up old sofas. Hendrix asked his colleague if he would like a job -

"I have a job! I'm a teacher."

*"No no. I mean an extra job. A good job. An **interesting** job!"*

"What sort of a job?

"There's a job going at the strip club. The man who shaves the girls is retiring at the end of this month. They're making him some sort of presentation. Long service and all that ... a clock I think. Anyway, I've pulled a few strings and If you want it, the job's yours. How about it?"

Initially, Keith's face lit up like a Christmas tree. He was a red blooded 22 year old, but the way ahead had been carefully planned and mapped out. School teaching was a temporary expedient. Keith Matthewman intended to become a respectable barrister. Given that the sandwich-board situation was classified as 'advertising', he already had an interesting variety of reputable past work experience behind him.

An unwelcome scenario presents itself. Keith standing in a grubby, stuffy little room, pungent with strewn female underwear and shaving lather. Razor in hand, he is about to operate on a prostrate girl when a group of uninvited beefy police officers suddenly burst in -

"'Allo 'allo 'allo! Wot do we 'ave 'ere then?"

These warning thoughts concluded, Keith politely thanked his colleague and regretfully declined his offer. The peace shattering bell urgently rings through the building and 4B, already restive and raucous, can he heard way down the hall. Mr Matthewman slowly rises and reluctantly returns to duty.

Chapter 13
Called to the Bar

Keith Matthewman made his way to the Bar in a different way from most other barristers. The Bar Exam has two parts. Having a law degree meant that he was excused the first part, but law students usually attended special classes to get through the second part. These classes cost time and money. Keith, in a full-time modestly-rewarded teaching post could afford neither. In the January of 1959 he decided to 'grasp the nettle', resigned from his permanent appointment and applied to be a supply teacher (available just three days per week) back in the same school.

The young teacher regretted having to make this necessary career move. Painstakingly, he had built up trust and a good relationship between himself and the boys, particularly the boys in his own form. As an occasional supply teacher for absent staff, he would be known to the pupils, but the valuable pastoral continuity would now be lost and he felt sorry for the lads who would have to get used to a new member of staff.

Again he moved to yet another small flat. This time he located at Crouch End and made the trip to Barking on a slow train.

With the remaining free two days, several evenings and a good chunk of the weekends, Keith Matthewman launched into an imaginative 'do it yourself' path of private study to becoming a barrister.

"I bought five copies of what was then called the 'Bar Calendar' which is a booklet about the Bar and the Inns of Court. Each one contained the past three years Bar Exam papers. Alone, studying from law books, I worked carefully through each of the previous fifteen exams and marked myself using the answers afterwards, learning from my mistakes and getting better each time. No lectures or tutorials, but within the year I passed the real Bar Exam."

In this method of private study we see a preview of Keith Matthewman the individualist who, in later years, will resist the inefficiencies and dictatorship of 'the group' or 'the collective'. Here is Keith Matthewman the maverick, the unconventional and the loner, which is not to say that he is incapable of team work, amply demonstrated later by Keith the socialist councillor.

To qualify as a British barrister, requires even more than a degree in law and the successful completion of the Bar Examination.

This ancient and honourable profession is steeped in mystique, tradition and custom. Just north of the River Thames, between Chancery Lane and Kingsway is situated that small area known as 'Legal London'; an area where 'narrow streets lead to smaller alleys, hidden taverns and minute churchyards.' Here, near the bustle and roar of Fleet Street, we can find peace in the quiet leafy square of Lincoln's Inn Fields or in the lawns and gardens of Inner and Middle Temple. All around are mellowed barristers' chambers and various bygone-century gate-houses. In the Strand we see the impressive gothic Royal Courts of Justice where a slow dignified procession of robed and bewigged Judges can be viewed once a year. Outside, stands a bronze statue of a heraldic griffin, (a winged dragon) which marks the boundary between the City of London and the City of Westminster.

In this area there are the Four Inns of Court: Gray's Inn, Lincoln's Inn, Inner and Middle Temple. These are the original English law schools (which have long since ceased to teach law) dating from the 14th-century. They are ancient corporate legal societies which alone have the power to 'call a person to the Bar' enabling him or her to practice law in the courts. The 'bar' was originally just that - a part of the court-room which separated the public from the proceedings. The word 'barrister' derives from 'the bar'. For the best view, student barristers were once called to the bar to hear cases as part of their training. To be 'called to the Bar' today, signifies the end of their training and receiving a formal qualification. When a barrister takes Silk, he is called 'within the Bar' - more of that when we get up to 1979.

In 1955 Keith Matthewman had to become a member of one of these venerable societies to eventually fully qualify as a barrister. He chose the Middle Temple, (the one nearest the Embankment) and had to fulfil the requirement of eating at least four dinners a term in the medieval and magnificent Great Hall, 'a cradle of English common law'. At a long table they sat in messes of four eating together, efficiently being waited on by smart gentlemen in pristine white coats. There was a choice of beer or wine. On Grand Nights, such as the Queen's Birthday, all the drink was completely free!

Under complex, arched, elaborately carved, black stained oaken beams, Keith and his friends were overlooked by a large portrait of Charles I and other English kings, together with the Armorial bearings of Sir Walter Raleigh. Mediaeval suits of armour establish the connection with the original Knights Templars and wall plaques honour past instructors and readers. Images of prominent Middle Templars decorate the high stained glass windows. 'All eating together' is a remnant of the original purpose of the building, not only a school, but also an inn.

As a first time student, Keith was filled with curiosity -
*"When I first became a member of the Middle Temple, I really had no idea what to expect, but was very impressed with it all. In these first-time situations, you're a stranger and you tend to think - Oh dear! What's it going to be like? Who **are** these people who are going to be barristers? I presumed that most of them had been educated at a public school and then went to Oxford or Cambridge. That may have been so, but as it turned out it didn't matter.*

They were all completely friendly and I was made to feel quite at home on those long tables. After all, some of the others were also there for the first time and consequently in the same boat as me. As I have said before, nobody ever asked me about my background.

There is an enduring public perception that all barristers come from a high social set and look down their noses at the lower orders. They don't. There is an assumption that strong, deeply ingrained prejudices work against minorities at the Bar. It is simply untrue. I don't know where it comes from! In all my experience of 21 years as a barrister and nearly 18 years as a judge, I have yet to see a single example of racism, sexism or any similar intolerance within my profession. If you can do the job, that's all that matters."

Even with the extra two free days off school in early 1959, it became clear that the prospective barrister was going to need more time to study for the Bar Exam. As a beautiful spring gave way to the well remembered glorious summer, he resigned his supply post and returned home to Aldercar with the understanding that he would mind the family shop for just two hours a day. This would give him a full time shot at working towards the Bar Exam which was successfully achieved in the November of 1959.

During the following January the final and hallowed ceremony took place in the Middle Temple Great Hall under the large painting of Charles I. Always having been impressed with the mystique of the judiciary, I imagined a cultured, sonorous voice of authority, echoing through the ancient hall, hazy with burning incense -

'Keith Matthewman! Come forth ... come ye ... COME TO THE BAR!' This followed by a bewigged and elaborately robed young man solemnly walking up to, and kneeling before, an imperious figure who would touch him with some sort of scroll. 'Arise Keith Matthewman! Now get thee hence from this BAR. Go out ... Go. Denounce the wicked and defend the innocent!'

So much for my erroneous perceptions. Each Inn may have a slightly different procedure, but Keith recalls no particular elaborate pomp -

"Sorry to disappoint you, Narvel! On hearing your name you came to the front and bow. Standing before the treasurer, he gives his little speech which is simple and to the point - 'I call you to the utter (outer) Bar'. He'd give you the certificate, you would bow and walk away."

Chapter 14
A Shop in Aldercar

In 1957, the name 'Aldercar' filled me with fear and horror. It was the new local secondary modern school, completed in 1955, which accepted all the Mundy Street Boys School leavers who had failed the eleven plus examination. Some of those same boys, who had made my life a hell at that grim and cruel Dickensian junior school, frequently threatened that 'Aldercar' - would be even worse! As explained in 'Heanor Schooldays', my Red Lion Square address at the foot of 'Tag Hill' (Derby Road) put me (only just) in the catchment area of William Howitt Secondary Modern School which, in complete contrast, turned out to be a culture of kindness which transformed my life for the better.

But unbeknownst to me at that time, 'Aldercar', was also the location of the Matthewman shop. Less than a half mile east of the aforementioned dreaded contemporary academy, Keith's family business was snugly situated between a chip-shop and the local Co-op on the south side of Cromford Road, number 215, opposite the Aldercar Infants School. The same school which was attended by the Rt. Hon. Kenneth Clarke QC. MP between 1945 and 1950. Now demolished, the school was built in 1875 and stood for one hundred years.

On a cold, damp but sunny day in late November 2000, I decided to explore and cycle deep into 'Keith Matthewman Country'. Leaving Belper, climbing up the steep 'Bedlam Hill', over the top and down to Kilburn Toll Bar, I pedalled up Bywell Lane, further up still and then through Horsley Woodhouse and Smalley, down the delightful quiet unmettled Bell Lane, through Manchester Wood and eventually into Shipley Park.

With Osbourne's Pond on the left, I cycled under the old (long disused and dismantled) 1891 Great Northern Railway line, up Buxton Avenue, right at Sunningdale Avenue and up into Marlpool, over the busy Ilkeston to Heanor main road, into the huddled atmospheric Victorian area of Breach, Mill and Prospect Road, down an interesting narrow jitty which emerges at the site of the long gone (and as I recall ice cold) open-air Langley Swimming Baths.

Proceeding northwards down along Aldreds Lane, I crossed the Bailey Brook and emerged into Langley Mill, across Mansfield Road, still due north along the long straight Lower Dunstead Road which eventually ends at the start of the 12th century Aldercar Lane, a direct route to Codnor Castle which is a mile and a half further north.

A right turn into Cromford Road and finally I am in Aldercar. This pleasant name should have held no terrors. Even now in the 21st century, the views to the east and north are open, green and lush. Water loving alder trees once grew here along the 'carr' - low marshy common ground which spreads around the wide River Erewash flood plain. Alder + carr.

The eye travels over the meandering river and distant meadows up to Brinsley in Nottinghamshire. A slight turn of the head to the south east reveals the Great Northern Basin, a symbol of the early Industrial Revolution, where the Cromford, Nottingham and Erewash Canals meet. Little wonder that Keith said -

"After council meetings, I'd walk home down the hill into Langley Mill and then into Aldercar. Cutting the corner by going down Ormonde Street and Ormonde Terrace, [The land was owned by the Marquis of Ormonde in 1792] *a right turn brought me out on Cromford Road very near to home ...*

It was like travelling to the ends of the earth! - especially when it was foggy. You approached that sharp bend to the left and it seemed that everything was swallowed up in mist and darkness!"

Perhaps it was civilisation which had been swallowed up! During the previous five years, Keith had spent almost a quarter of his short life living at various addresses in London, mixing with savoir-faire, cosmopolitan people and moving in a complex sophisticated and smart environment. This relatively rural corner in south east Derbyshire is historically interesting and rich with industrial archaeology: a stark contrast with the refined Capital City to which Keith had now become accustomed.

This is not to say that Councillor Keith Matthewman ever looked down on his constituents. The young socialist of 1960 who turned into the independent judge of the 21st century, has no time for pretentious snobbery. Anyone who gives voice to such class-conscious sentiments is in danger of getting the sharp edge of his tongue.

Cromford Road was part of the Nottingham - Cromford turnpike which was opened in 1776 and the abrupt turn to the south was necessary to avoid the soft marshy area of the Erewash valley. The 200 meter drop from Wood Linkin, a mile up the hill, increased the danger to some drivers who descended and approached the sharp bend much too fast. Keith remembers many accidents -

"Frequently we heard a crash and had to dash out and rescue people from their mangled motorcars. Fortunately nobody was ever killed or seriously injured but it was necessary to call an ambulance and the police."

Duly warned and slowly cycling down Cromford Road, after crossing over the Victorian bolted cast iron railway bridge, I noticed an interesting and romantic old derelict house on the right, surrounded by an overgrown wilderness, un-tended for years. Perhaps forty years back, Keith would have recalled a one-time neatly maintained garden. Next came what appeared to be ancient dilapidated cow sheds and after that - the corner of three shops.

I looked for the Matthewman shop - and found nothing but the faint remnants, fragments of rubble of a long since demolished building hiding underneath a strong, thick stand of healthy weeds towering over me. The chip-shop was also gone, but as for the one-time Co-op: it was still standing! In the Heanor and District Local History Society book 'Heanor - Then and Now', on page 57 you can see a photograph of the building with the modern flats in the background on the site of the old school. I asked a passer-by if he could remember the Matthewman shop. Fortunately he turned out to be a local builder who had lived in Langley Mill and Aldercar all his life - another Keith, Keith Beresford.

"Yes! I do recall the family and even now we still miss the shop. They sold everything. It was very handy."

Albeit his competitor, Lieutenant Frank Matthewman was very friendly with the manager of the Co-op next door. If one shop ran out of a particular product, then the other shop would supply the short-fall. They helped each other in that way, and the Co-op manager was co-operative in alerting Mr Matthewman to a well dressed shoplifter!

"Well what do we do? Do we call the police - or what?"

"Oh no! Certainly not. She'd be offended! She might take her custom elsewhere. We don't want that. No. Just keep an eye on her.

You'll find that she'll steal something and put it in her bag. All you do is to discover the price of the stolen item and add it to her bill."

"And when she checks the bill!!"

*"She'll hardly complain will she? She knows full well that **we** know that she's a thief."*

Frank Matthewman took that advice and everybody was happy. The well turned-out shoplifter continued to steal once a week, but nobody was inconvenienced. Sheila Birch the Matthewman's trusty and efficient assistant also knew her and coped very well with the situation.

In the space where the Matthewman family once walked the shop floor and served the people of Aldercar, there is now nothing but a narrow footpath created by the tramping of many feet over many years, treading down the determined weeds and cutting the corner. This is all there is left of the shop which stayed open many hours and served 'everything from paraffin to panties'.

Chapter 15
The Youngest Heanor Councillor

Perhaps it should not be surprising that Keith Matthewman became interested in politics in the spring of 1960. The keen intellect and social conscience, with studies now complete, had time to reflect and seek out a practical way to make a positive difference to the lives of working people. Keith was all energy and activity! Enthusiastically, he became a governor of the new Aldercar Secondary Modern School which had opened only just five years before. He read a left wing Sunday newspaper of the day called the 'Reynolds News', joined the Labour Party and soon became a very keen and conscientious member, eventually joining a militant sub-group of socialists called the 'New Left'. In meetings at Nottingham and Chesterfield, he rubbed shoulders with Stanley Mellors, Kenneth Coates [the former MEP], Eric Varley [Baron Varley today], and a fiery 29 year old Dennis Skinner who has been the MP for Bolsover since 1970 and in the tabloid press often dubbed - 'The Beast of Bolsover'.

For nearly 20 years I was one of his constituents and, from personal experience, can warmly commend him for his conscientious, unstinting efforts to deal with problems.

Keith's political views were noticed two years later by his pupil-master in chambers, now the retired Judge Thomas R. Heald -

"His politics in the early 1960's were almost Militant Tendency! Interestingly, now that he's ripened, so have his views and today one reads in the press to find him ultra conservative. I have always taken the view that there is little to choose between the very left wing and the very right wing. It's rather like a clock face where the ultra left is at two minutes to twelve and the ultra right at two minutes past twelve. The two positions are really very close together."

Retired Judge Matthewman today gives a more moderate self-assessment -

"Jane and I left the Labour Party even before the 'Winter of Discontent' [Early 1979] when we felt that there was as much hypocrisy as in the Tory Party. My present position is 'independent' and I vote according to the candidate. I believe that the last Conservative Government, under John Major, was the worst of all post

war governments. The appallingly liberal 1991 Criminal Justice Act came from the permissive and misguided doctrines of previous Home Secretaries such as Douglas Hurd [1985-1989] under Mrs Thatcher."

Judge Matthewman's theory gets strong support from the views of Frederick Forsyth which appeared in The Daily Mail 27.4.00 -
"About 20 years ago a new Left-liberal, trendy, progressive ethos began to invade the Law and Order Establishment, moving swiftly from the civil servants, who dominate whoever is in charge of the Home Office, through the Lord Chancellor's department which nominates the judges, down to the magistrates and on to the police leadership."

On a Trent FM / GEM AM Radio interview, Judge Matthewman criticised the 1991 Criminal Justice Act -
"Say a 17 year old gets high on drugs or drink, drives dangerously, loses control of his vehicle, mounts the pavement killing a young mother and her two children. The maximum punishment I can now give for causing those three deaths is twelve months! Twelve months!! It seems to me that most decent law abiding people will regard that as a scandal!"

On the same programme the Chief Constable of Nottinghamshire, Dan Crompton had concerns about the new requirement that -
" ... the courts should not reflect upon the previous criminal history of the accused. Surely past conduct must have an impact on what the court decides to do? I feel that this measure has been included in the Act as a subtle way to try and persuade magistrates to impose more non-custodial sentences because of the cost."

The Home Secretary, Kenneth Clarke was invited to respond, but in the event a junior minister called Michael Jack, rejected these criticisms as -
" ... inventing selective examples'.

Ten years on, and now into retirement, Judge Matthewman is pleased to see the back of the 1991 Criminal Justice Act -
"Thanks to numerous amendments and Michael Howard, the Home Secretary [1993-1997] who said that 'Prison works', there is very little left of that damaging Act. He was a good Home Secretary, and helped us to come out of that dark period of soft laws. I'm pleased

134

to say that Jack Straw [The Labour Home Secretary from 1997 to 2001] *is carrying on the improvements by being tough and effective.*

This is part of a letter from the Rt. Hon. Michael Howard QC MP to Judge Matthewman, received January 25th 1994.
  "I share your concern that the interests of the victims of crime should be taken seriously and that criminals should be appropriately punished."

HEANOR URBAN DISTRICT COUNCIL ELECTION
Saturday, 14th May, 1960

Polling Hours: 8 a.m. till 9 p.m.

VOTE FOR

KEITH

MATTHEWMAN

The LABOUR Candidate

Local Politics DO matter — and your VOTE counts

VOTE FOR

KEITH

MATTHEWMAN

The LABOUR Candidate

HEANOR URBAN DISTRICT COUNCIL ELECTION, 1960

To the Electors of the East Ward.

LADIES AND GENTLEMEN,

I have the honour of being selected by the Heanor and District Local Labour Party and Trades Council as the candidate for the East Ward at the forthcoming election.

While living in Aldercar I have acquired a considerable knowledge of the community and the difficulties which confront its inhabitants today, particularly in regard to the future closing of local mines, the provision of housing and education, and the need to attract more light industry into the district.

Allow me to assure you that I shall, if elected, work throughout my term of office for the welfare of you and your children, and, with my Labour colleagues, would always be available to give help and advice.

Finally, may I appeal to you to use your vote and help to bring about a Labour victory.

Yours sincerely,

KEITH MATTHEWMAN.

215 CROMFORD ROAD,
LANGLEY MILL.

KEITH MATTHEWMAN, your LABOUR Candidate . . .

Was born in a Yorkshire mining village and educated at Long Eaton Grammar School and the University of London, where he took a degree in Law.

Spent just over a year teaching English and History in a Secondary School in Essex and is at present engaged in private studies.

A member of the National Union of Teachers and the Labour Party; Delegate to the Heanor and District Local Labour Party and Trades Council; Auditor, East and South Wards Committee of the Labour Party.

136

Vote Communist

VOTE FOR TED MOORE

END THE SILENCE OVER LANGLEY MILL AFFAIRS

Printed and published by G. C. Brittain & Sons Ltd., for E. F. Moore, 25, North Street, Langley Mill, Notts.

To the Electors of the East Ward of Langley Mill

MOORE, E. F. ☒

THE CANDIDATE WHO FIGHTS FOR MORE HOUSES AT RENTS THE PEOPLE CAN AFFORD

Dear Friends,

Never before has there been such need for Communists on local councils. The Tory Government's attack on municipal housing and social services, their treacherous sellout on German rearmament, their refusal to work for a ban on atomic weapons are questions demanding the maximum opposition of working people. In this locality never was Tory policy seen so bankrupt as on coal. Mass closures of pits causing misery to thousands are eminent because the Tories are furthering the interests of the oil monopolists at the expense of coal. The Tories must go! There is a policy that can make a start.

Council House Rents. As I warned in my last contest, council house rents would continue to be increased unless local councils fought back against the policy of the Tory Government. Councils should **refuse** to raise rents, demand the restoration of the housing subsidy and drop in bank rate to two per cent. Communist councillors will organise local tenants associations to fight back as tenants are doing in other parts of the country.

Private landlord owned houses. The 1954 " Operation Rescue " allowed rent increases on the basis of repairs. The 1956 Rent Acts allowed further rent increases without having to carry out repairs. Is it not time the labour movement fought back against such blatant robbery. Communists are needed on the councils to fight rent increases whether by local councils or private landlords.

Keith Matthewman was selected by the Heanor and District Local Labour Party to stand as the official candidate in May 1960 for the Langley Mill East Ward. He won the seat with the largest majority of all seven wards. For a very young first timer he did extremely well, polling 593 votes, compared to his Communist opponent, Ted Moore who polled just 74 votes on this, his 15th attempt.

The press extracts do not tell you about all the time consuming hard work which can go into winning an election. Weeks before polling day, posters had to be put up on display, leaflets had to be distributed door to door and people had to be spoken to and persuaded. On the Saturday (not Thursday) of May 14th, Keith and his fiancé Jane Maxwell were busy driving around the Langley Mill and Heanor area picking up people from their homes and taking them to the polling station at Aldercar Infants School, just over the road from home. All this activity, not to mention expense, was in the expectation that the grateful voter would favour the hopeful driver.

One particular old woman was picked up from a Langley Mill address on that Saturday and carefully chauffeured to the Aldercar School. After voting, the usual procedure would be to chauffeur her right back to her own front door, but she took it into her head to make a special request -

"Nay lad, am not often in a motorcar! E it's rate grand it is, an av not seen arr Nelly, fa ... oow ... many a while! Tek me ta Nelly oop t' 'ill. A wont ta see arr Nelly."

This turned out to be the daughter who lived in Eastwood. Many potential Labour voters were still waiting for their expected free ride. Keith and Jane were pressed for time but they were amused by the cheek, and perhaps a little touched by this sudden onset of motherly affection. After a two mile drive they eventually arrived at the front door of a neat little terraced house. Ever solicitous, Jane helped the lady out of the car and gallantly Keith went forward to knock at the front door. All three waited with anticipation. Seconds later the door opened to reveal a somewhat hard faced woman of indeterminate age and what appeared to be a truculent disposition. In a moment, her frosty features and cool un-welcoming stare quizzically swept over the busy hopeful candidate and his patient fiancé - finally coming to rest on the sad little figure between them, the dear old mother.

*"Wot **you** doin' 'ere! Wot ya brought 'er for?"*

"I gather this is your mother?"

"Ya can joost 'gather' 'er back in that damn car! A don't wont 'er. Bloody nuisance! Ya 'n all clear off - lot on ya!"

"E ar Nelly! Where's ya manners!"

Keith's patience with this minor drama was now wearing thin, time was short and a quick decision was made. As they drove away down the little back street, Jane turned her head and retains an enduring last memory of the unfortunate mother, who was still standing on that doorstep remonstrating with her hard hearted daughter, now in a state of frustrated and cantankerous indecision.

Heanor Gossip
BY BAILEY BROOK

DERBY EVENING TELEGRAPH, Wednesday, April 27, 1960.

the competition, which is an annual affair between the three referees' organisations.

Another newcomer to the election tussle this year is 24-year-old law student Mr. Keith Matthewman, of 215 Cromford Road, Aldercar A member of Langley Mill Ward of the Heanor Labour Party, Mr. Matthewman is contesting a seat in East Ward.

Mr. Matthewman, born in a small mining village in Yorkshire, where his grandfather was a trade union leader and a Labour councillor, was educated at Long Eaton Grammar School after moving to Chilwell. He then studied for a degree in law at London University on a Nottingham County Major Scholarship and is at present studying at home for professional exams.

SCOUTMASTER

He was a scoutmaster for several years in a tough district of the East End and also taught at a secondary modern school in London.

Local press extracts give samples of a range of the subjects discussed by the Heanor Council in 1960. The debate 'Peace at any Price', page 121 [Chapter 12 The Soho Strip Club] is an interesting example of contemporary socialist thought on the chronic and pervading fear of a nuclear holocaust. I expressed the teenage anxiety about the atom bomb in 'Heanor Schooldays'. With regard to 'Bring Back the Stocks', the comments of the tough Judge Matthewman in 2000 on the liberal views expressed by the young idealistic Councillor K. Matthewman in 1960 - were most interesting -

"I hadn't seen as many criminals at that time as I've seen today, and yet ... there is still a small part of me which wants to agree with the remarks of that naive and distant young man. There is some truth in those ideas, but sadly I'd never say that today. No. We've been too soft. I now believe that many youths are born vandals and hooligans."

139

'BRING BACK THE STOCKS'

Sit vandals in them—Councillor

THE stocks should be brought back and people convicted of vandalism should be made to sit in them in the open market place, Councillor W. T. Slack told Heanor Urban Council last night.

Councillor A. Lee said the council would press for the heaviest possible penalty against vandals who were prosecuted.

Councillor K. Matthewman said he would not like the public to think that everybody on the council favoured bringing back the stocks.

"This sadistic instinct so many people seem to have about such things as flogging and beating should not go unanswered," he said. "Young hooligans and vandals are not born, they are made—by us."

If they constantly saw acts of violence on TV they would grow up with the feeling that violence was the natural order of things.

"I am not against punishing vandals, but we cannot abrogate our responsibility in regard to them," he added.

Councillor Mrs. P. Hart asked: "Will Mr. Matthewman tell us how they should be punished?"

But the chairman, Councillor W. Belfield, intervened and stopped the discussion.

The council had before it reports of damage to trees at Langley Mill, to plants at Broadway Garden, to a wall at Loscoe and to the door of public conveniences at Mayfield Avenue, Heanor.

The council adopted a suggestion by the chief Public Health Inspector, Mr. H. W. Jefford, that the door shall be replaced by a screen.

"The door has been damaged and repaired so many times that I have come to the conclusion that it is a waste of money to continue this losing battle," Mr. Jefford reported.

Councillors clash over a rubbish tip

RATS, smell, litter, dust, crickets and bat-flies were said to be some of the things with which tenants near Heanor's Commonside refuse tip had to contend. And at last night's meeting of the Urban Council, Coun. K. Matthewman said that any member of the council who said he would live near the tip was "either a fool or a liar."

In 1962 Keith Matthewman was still a councillor, still enjoying working with his team on the council and had started work in Nottingham as a barrister which gave his political career further status. He became the Secretary of the Langley Mill Labour Party and the Political Education Officer of the Parliamentary Constituency which in 1962 was called Ilkeston. Frequently he was

140

asked to speak at a multitude of political meetings and he spoke well. Keith Matthewman was making a name for himself. Keith Matthewman was beginning to be noticed.

In the local book, 'Life in Old Heanor', on page 9, there is a 1947 photograph of the Langley Mill Girls School standing in front of the soot-blackened, gothic Houses of Parliament. In this nearly all female picture stands just one man, an old man, but then Keith once told me - *"He always looked old"*.

George Oliver was born on November 24th in 1888, and died in November 1984 at the age of 97. Nearly all Heanorians past their half century will remember George Oliver, but few will know that he was not originally a local man. He was educated at Holy Trinity School in Bolton, Lancashire and then came to Derby to become an engineer at Rolls Royce. On November 16th, 1922 he was elected as the Labour Member for Ilkeston and Heanor when Andrew Bonar Law became the first Conservative PM since 1906 and, for the first time ever, the Liberals were replaced by Labour as the main Opposition. Oliver won the 1924 and 1929 elections, but lost the seat in October 1931 to A.J.[Bob] Flint by just two votes! Bob Flint was the local County Court judge in Nottingham when Keith first began to appear. Keith recalls him as a pleasant, sharp-witted man who had an impressive law practice at the Birmingham Bar before he became a judge.

After the elections of November 16th 1935, the Conservatives had a huge majority in the country under Stanley Baldwin's National Government, but, once again, George Oliver was back in the House representing Heanor and Ilkeston.

And there he stayed, a popular and hard working politician, solid Labour, for the next 29 years until he retired at the age of 76 just before the 1964 General Election. At that time there were very few people who could remember when George Oliver was not looking after Ilkeston and Heanor. *"He was there for donkey's years."* said local historian Frank Bacon.

When George Oliver announced that he would not be fighting another election after the General Election of October 1959, a vacancy for the constituency of Ilkeston arose for the first time in 42 years. The local Labour Party had the difficult job of searching for a suitable candidate to fill the shoes of the venerable Old Man who had been there for so long.

Councillor Keith Matthewman, with the added status of being a barrister, had an ideal background and the qualifications which attracted the attention of party officials and Bert Wynn the leader of the Derbyshire branch of the National Union of Mineworkers. Keith's maternal grandfather, Albert Lang was a founder member of that union and his father was a coal-miner. His views were in accord with those of the far left and certainly would be expressed effectively with skilful articulation. Accordingly, Keith Matthewman, an energetic bright young man in his early twenties with many years ahead of him was first choice and was asked to stand for Parliament in the next election. Mr Oliver was 35 when he first took his seat.

For Keith and Jane Matthewman this was an important offer to be considered very carefully indeed. In this rock solid Labour area, effectively it was a guaranteed pathway to the House of Commons. There could be no possibility of failure. As one of my former school-friends once said -

"A monkey with 'Labour' around its neck would get elected in Heanor!"

But Keith had more intelligence than a monkey and also the talents of public speaking to boot. Once in the House, Keith Matthewman MP would soon make his mark and there was the probability of promotion to a junior minister in Harold Wilson's new Government to consider - **if** Labour won the election.

At the time of these difficult deliberations, the date and result of the next general election was simply not known. It **was** certain that Keith and Jane were very happy together, contented and enjoying living in the Nottingham area. Having to live in London most of the time would be somewhat disruptive. After a great deal of hard work, his fledgling barrister's practice needed building up and was already starting to grow and thrive. He could not do **both** jobs well, the needs of his constituents would have to come first - at the expense of his legal work.

"I was interested in politics and my heart said 'grab the opportunity - be an MP!', but my head listened to my clerk, Michael Churm, who didn't approve of a 'political barrister'."

At long last and after much heart-searching with Jane, he decided to turn down the offer to step into the shoes of George Oliver.

The offer then went to L. Raymond Fletcher, a writer for a well known left wing paper 'The Tribune', who was elected in the General Election of October 16th 1964 when the Labour party was back in power after thirteen years of Tory rule.

Keith told me it was the one career move in his whole life which he most regretted -

"Biggest mistake I've ever made! But there you are. Being an Member of Parliament would have been a valuable experience, and as I always say, no experience is ever wasted."

Warm supportive remarks came from friend and colleague, Judge Richard Benson, who told me that Keith's desire for political office came from his personal generosity, that altruistic part of his personality which wanted to influence events -

"He wanted to make a contribution and it was certainly nothing to do with self aggrandisement. I think he made the right decision because running a barrister's practice and being an MP is one hell of a commitment - riding two horses! What happens when you ride two horses? You're likely to fall off them both - or just go mad! After having the trappings of power very briefly, Keith may have descended into obscurity - we'll never know. We can all say 'what if ...' We'd all like the benefit of 20/20 hindsight. Keith came to a cross-roads and made his decision: he doesn't look backwards - it's not part of his nature."

The subject of this book, generally admired and held to be a very good judge, is big enough to admit to occasional bad judgement. On the political scene there are two famous examples, Willy Bach, now Baron Bach of Lutterworth and Geoffrey Hoon, now The Rt. Hon. Geoffrey Hoon MP, the Secretary of State for Defence.

Keith first met Willy Bach in the mid 1970's when he came from Leicester and carved out a good practice at 24 The Ropewalk. Like the other barristers, Mr Bach enjoyed the same social scene, dinner parties, cocktail parties and the occasional Bar Mess at the George Hotel in Nottingham. It was on such an occasion when Keith was dismayed to hear that his colleague was planning to go into politics in a serious professional way. Willy Bach was an excellent barrister and Keith took the view that his friend should not exchange the security of a promising legal career for the uncertainty and turmoil of public office. During one dinner party, amidst the fun and light hearted banter, perhaps somewhat inappropriately, Keith became serious minded and remonstrated with Willy Bach -

*"Politics!! What on **earth** do you want to do that for?"*

"I'm going to enjoy politics! You ought to know the feeling of it. You've been there yourself. You know all of that. Why not?

"Why not? You're doing so well at the Bar. Why do you want to give it all up? You'll never get anywhere in politics. Stick to the Bar - much better."

In the few years just after he had taken Silk and before he ascended the Bench in 1983, Keith Matthewman and his clerk Michael Churm were charged with the responsibility of interviewing new barristers who applied to practice at 24 The Ropewalk. One such applicant was Geoffrey Hoon, a personable young man who made a very good

144

impression. Unfortunately, he had hardly shaken hands and sat down when he said -

"I'm interested in politics!"

Out of courtesy, the interview continued but as far as Michael and Keith were concerned - that was the end! With references to Judge Benson's 'two horses', Michael Churm did not want to clerk a barrister who would occasionally have to sit in the House of Commons and not always be available to look after his clients. Having made a difficult decision on the same issue some 18 years before, Keith also took the same view. He told Mr Hoon -

*"We'd be delighted to take you as a new pupil and think you'll make a good barrister if you concentrate on the Bar, give it your **full** attention and give up any Parliamentary ambitions. It's a highly demanding job and most likely you'll get nowhere. In politics, like acting, many are called and few are chosen! **If** selected and **if** you win the seat you'll be paid until the next election when you **might** lose the seat. A lot of ifs and mights - stick to the Bar!"*

Geoffrey Hoon thanked his interviewers, said he'd consider their experienced and professional advice, but he was really looking for chambers which would accommodate a political barrister. Eventually he declined the offer at 24 The Ropewalk and went to another set of chambers in Nottingham.

Keith Matthewman looks back on these two massive miscalculations with some embarrassment and regret. Possibly giving a thought to his annoyance with the discouraging and pessimistic Dr Thompson back in 1954, (Chapter 9 The Long Eaton Grammar School) he deserves full credit for this honest admission -

*"My God! How wrong can you be! What a complete lack of judgement I showed with those two! I feel guilty about it. Thank goodness they ignored my advice! Look at them now - one elevated to the Peerage and is Baron Bach of Lutterworth; sits in the House of Lords and is the Minister for Defence Procurement. Geoffrey Hoon sits near the Prime Minister in the Cabinet Room as the Secretary of State for Defence! And **still** they write a foreword in my biography!!"*

Chapter 16
Chastity Belts and Firm Discipline

Geoff Kingscott, a fellow pupil of Long Eaton Grammar School and friend to both Jane Maxwell and Keith Matthewman, had been giving regular record parties at his house since their schooldays together. Jane knew Keith and Keith had known Jane for some years, but only on the level of an acquaintance, a familiar face which had often been seen, noted and admired. They enjoyed the social scene at Geoff's parties and in early 1960 started to get to know each other better. At that time the new compact seven inch 45 rpm record was beginning to out-number the older 12" 78 rpm record. Both were played at the Kingscott record sessions which today we would call a 'disco'. Keith and Jane's favourite song, (which recalls their nostalgic meeting and was often played) would have been one of the older '78's, originally dating from 1952. It was Johnnie Ray's first big hit - 'Walking My Baby Back Home'.

In my book 'Heanor Schooldays' I described the deputy headmaster of William Howitt Secondary Modern School, who had taught there for 31 years as -

'... a smooth sophisticated gentleman with a relaxed and supremely confident class control ... greatly respected, fondly remembered and much loved by thousands of Heanorians'. This was a reference to Maurice Brentnall - 1910 to 1998.

It is interesting to note that this same Mr Brentnall used a similar level of high praise to honour a headmaster who, at approximately the same time, taught at Wilsthorpe Secondary Modern School in Long Eaton -

"Tommy Maxwell! You know him? A first class professional! A superb headmaster! Let me tell you all about Tommy Maxwell ..."

Mr Brentnall was speaking in May 1960 to a new young member of staff, a Mr Matthewman. The latter was particularly interested because the headmaster in question was the father of his new girl-friend, Jane Maxwell.

Mr Thomas Maxwell (1905 to 1957) was also very well regarded by one of his former young masters who became a High Court

Judge, Mr Justice Smedley. Jane herself has affectionate memories of her father taking morning assembly -

> *"On walking into the hall, he never had to say 'rise' - just a silent gesture of the head, an 'eyes up', brought all the children to their feet. He was adored and the pupils would have done anything for him."*

Jane Matthewman.

To get into chambers and start his career as a barrister, Keith Matthewman needed money. He applied for, and was appointed as an English and History teacher at the William Howitt Secondary Modern

School, Loscoe Road, in May 1960. This is an unusual time to join a staff, but it is possible that he was an early replacement for the formidable, Victorian Mrs Maud Buxcey who was retiring in July after 44 years of faithful service.

It was very a fortunate career move for hundreds of Heanorians and this author. Many commentators have described Keith Matthewman as an excellent judge, but, if it is at all possible, he is a better teacher. I say 'is' because all the instincts and skills which go to make up a good teacher are still an integral part and parcel of the person we refer to as Keith Matthewman.

I have come to the writing of this life with no legal or judicial background and no specialised knowledge of the law, but notwithstanding - I write on! However, in this section of the life, the area of education, I claim some small qualification having been (albeit briefly) a pupil of the master and having experienced a teaching career which followed. It was the teacher part of Keith and Jane Matthewman (another good teacher) which encouraged me to write "Death on the Derwent". In this they both displayed a fundamental quality of an effective educator - to inspire and buttress confidence whilst still being realistic about what can be achieved.

A number of former Howittians have shared with me complimentary recollections of their studies under the Matthewman regime of instruction and classroom management. I found the most revealing from Dorothy Wincott nee Frost -

*"Mr Matthewman! Oh yes. Definitely the best of the lot of them - and certainly the most yummy! He had a way of making you work and learn ... almost in spite of your self. He made you **want** to learn and did it with a gentleman-like, moderate approach, never raising his voice."*

Ann Roberts, nee Thorpe, recalls a kindness during a school trip to Austria and Italy in the spring of 1961 -

"Just 13 years old, very nervous and a long way from home for the first time ever. To top it all I broke my wrist and had it in plaster! Mr Matthewman was so very considerate, organising a group of boys to carry my luggage. I liked him ... well, we all liked him."

From the letter below it will be seen that Mr Matthewman was (in effect) still teaching twenty years later when he made a strong impression on a group of fourth years visiting Lincoln Crown Court.

K Matthewman Esq QC
Barrister-at-Law
24 The Ropewalk
NOTTINGHAM

THE CROWN COURT
Holborn House Newport Lincoln LN1 3DG

Telephone (0522) 31421

12 March 1980

In our social education course this term we have been studying Crime and Law. It is all very well just sitting down and learning what the teacher is telling us, but when our teacher said that we would be able to visit and see a Court Case, we were all very pleased. We were actually going to Lincoln to watch a court case at the County Sessions.

A lot of us did not realize that the court was actually situated in the castle grounds and that the setting was very beautiful. This contrasted to the interior of the court itself, which had a serious atmosphere which was emphasised by the dark and stately victorian trappings of the court and the mainly black clothing of the officials. We didn't need to be told or warned to be quiet. We sensed that appearing in court was a serious matter.

Finally the Judge entered and we all stood up. The case which had been started the day before continued. It was a rape case. Many people might think it wasn't suitable for us to watch but we learnt something very important. A topic which we might laugh and joke about amongst friends became very serious in reality. We were sorry when it was adjourned and we had to leave, to get back to school.

As we came out into the sunlight and discussed what had happened we felt that if more teenagers went to see a court case, there would be a drastic reduction in crime rate. Even the toughest of us admitted we found it frightening.

Thank you Mrs Coupland and Mrs Tnought for taking us.

Howard Lyon
Fourth Year Social Education Group

Colin Morley is a barrister who has known Keith both at the Bar and on the Bench. He reflected on the similarities between Keith the judge and Keith the schoolmaster -

"Certainly he was always master in his own court and quite rightly because the judge is the only person who controls the proceedings in court. The teacher has the same responsibilities. If a teacher can't maintain order in his class he'll never get his message across and won't be able to do his job. There's no harm in Keith Matthewman running a 'tight ship' in court, but I feel the reputation of a hard disciplinarian is not justified. [See following letter]

I'm concerned to see that over the years he has acquired the reputation of a heavy sentencer. This surprises me because in private life I've always found him to be not only a charming and delightful man, but also very compassionate. When I appeared before Judge Matthewman, I always found that he was by no means a heavy sentencer, except where the crime warranted it. In a judge's life there are cases that demand a severe punishment. Keith has never shirked his duty in such cases."

150

```
His Honour Judge Matthewman Q.C.
Nottingham Crown Court
60 Canal Street
Nottingham
NG1 7EL

16/02/99


Your Honour

I realise that it is not usual – but I hope not inappropriate – for an
offender to write and thank you.

However, just because I walked from your court a free man does not
mean that I have put the events leading up to and following my trial
altogether out of my mind.

I am conscious that it would have been quite expected for you to
impose a custodial sentence on me for causing death through
dangerous driving.

The mercy that you have extended towards me, my wife (who was
present throughout the trial) and our children by imposing a suspended
prison sentence is much appreciated. On reflection I am left with the
distinct impression that I would rather have my fate determined by the
judicial professionals than the laity, however honest and well
meaning.

With my best wishes

Yours sincerely
```

In the Radio Nottingham interview of October 1999, Jeremy Evans was left in no doubt about Judge Matthewman's view of the modern teacher -

"This year I've had three cases involving schoolmasters giving evidence before me. Not a single one was wearing a jacket and tie! When I was in the profession we would not have dreamed of coming to a Court of Law dressed in an old sweater! Looking like that - how can they expect their pupils to respect them? Their appalling attitude is subtly communicated to our young - 'It doesn't matter; relax; be selfish; do what you want regardless of how your conduct impinges on other people.' It all comes down to the fact that children, no longer taught good manners or respect for institutions, grow into parents with similar deplorable attitudes."

As an impressionable adolescent, the first meeting with Mr Matthewman was indeed memorable. A short history lesson vividly recalled 40 years later! I wonder how many of **my** pupils will speak about the history lessons of Mr Annable in the year 2035? When he walked into Mrs Cook's class on that day in 1960, he brought with him an unaccustomed charisma of personality and a level of energy which was well ahead of the norm. There was more going on in that room besides the subject. I was admiring the hold, the skills of delivery, the professionalism, the voice and the command. He had an ability to pass on something of his own success, indeed, even at that tender age, I distinctly recall being excited by the scent of success.

Looking back at those school years, the retired judge of today also feels something of the thrill of success and satisfaction -

"In my whole career, either at the Bar or on the Bench, I have never had any moments happier than in teaching young people. At the end of a school day there is no more satisfying experience than to find that the kids have learned something. Winning an un-winable case in court does not come any higher on the scale of satisfaction."

The title heading of this chapter is best explained by reading 'Heanor Schooldays' or the Introduction in this book. Keith does not actually challenge the distant subject matter of that memorable lesson of 41 years ago, but has expressed doubts about the accuracy of my imaginative and enthusiastic interpretation!

When he left William Howitt Secondary Modern School in the summer of 1961, it may have been a good day for Rolls Royce and ultimately the legal profession - but it was a bad day for education.

Keith described his 15 months at William Howitt Secondary Modern School as -

"Marvellous, I had a great time but was still mindful of the final goal, the ultimate prize - practising at the Bar. I needed to be saving more money to have the necessary money behind me which was simply not happening on £600 per year as much as I enjoyed teaching."

He cast around for better pay and wrote to Raleigh Cycles in Nottingham: no reply, the same with Ericksons, but Boots invited him for an interview. An interview for a job is a two way process and in this instance it was the candidate who refused the position offered.

Rolls Royce also gave Keith an interview which (thanks to his impressive presentation, legal training and current passport) resulted in the offer of a position as Commercial Assistant to the Group Licensing Officer [Frank Pickles] in the International Division. He was given his own secretary and a princely starting salary of £950 rising over five years to £1350 by his 30th birthday. His task was to draft licenses and negotiate fees with other firms. It sounded complicated so I asked Keith to explain -

"Companies need to do research and development in order to produce their product. Very often they hit on an idea which would be very useful to another business. Supposing a firm made steel girders and during the course of manufacture they came across something which would help make excellent propellers. As an negotiator, I would be sent to the HQ of that concern to offer X number of pounds to have their design, exclusively, to make better propellers. I'd then return to Rolls Royce and write out a contract including provisional figures for the approval of my superiors. If we had something another company wanted I would be dispatched to negotiate in the same way."

It was a great job. In the short nine months of employment, Keith never went abroad but he always went first class on the train to different cities in the UK. His secretary would ring for a car to take him to Nottingham Station and a car would be waiting for him at his destination. Glasgow was his favourite venue where he was always politely greeted and transported by the chauffeur in a Rolls Royce motorcar!

"It seems silly to say it now, but one of the reasons why I hesitated to leave Rolls Royce was because I was about to get my own office with my name on the door!"

Why did Keith Matthewman give up such a well paid and prestigious situation? Answer - because he still had his eye on the ball and also because he and Jane paid a chance visit to a public house called the Bulls Head in Breaston sometime in the early spring of 1962.

They were enjoying a drink when his college friend, Brian Smedley just happened to walk in with Dilys Waldren who was the secretary at Wilsthorpe School and had been secretary to the late headmaster, Thomas Maxwell, Jane's father, who had died in 1957. There followed one of those rare and decisive conversations which have a dramatic effect on the direction we take in life. After five years there was a great deal of news upon which to catch up. Sir Brian recalls that meeting -

"I have no objection to being credited with the introduction of Keith Matthewman to the Nottingham Bar, but I should make it clear that I accept no responsibility for what happened thereafter!

When I joined the Chambers in Castlegate in September 1960 I was the junior member of a set consisting of six barristers. It was the largest in Nottingham! Now when I look at the Law List and see over 100 names I'm amazed at the expansion and frankly wonder where all the work comes from to keep them all in business. I do remember that the pressure of work was so great in those days that frequently in the afternoons we (certainly John Hopkin and myself - but I am not sure about Keith) would go to Woodthorpe Park to play 'pitch and putt' with our clerk!"

Brian, aware of Keith's legal qualifications and ambitions, heard about the Rolls Royce position -

"Why don't you come to the Bar at Nottingham? Well at least consider giving it a try. Come and see us anyway."

In those days Keith did not even know there was a Bar in Nottingham and expressed concerns about procedure and cost. But here was a persuasive invitation from an old friend on the inside who was kind enough to encourage and arrange a smoothing of the way.

"So there it is, Brian Smedley gave me the start I needed; he gave me everything; I'll always be grateful."

The second big event of 1962 was his marriage to Jane Maxwell on the Saturday of October 20th as can be seen in photograph and press-cuttings at the end of the chapter. In his private life Keith Matthewman is essentially a very private man. Accordingly, in very personal questions, I always proceed with diplomacy and great caution. However, he did respond in full with commendable honesty, and no small amount of generosity, when I asked him to appraise the importance and impact of his 39 year marriage to Jane Maxwell -

*"Over a large number of years my career has been what many people regard as 'a success'. That, of course, is a matter for their judgement, not mine. What I **can** say is that what ever success I have achieved would not have been possible without the patience, support and love I have been blessed with from Jane and, as he has grown up,*

Adrian. Only I know the hard times they have sometimes had to endure resulting from the pressure of my daily life. Only I know what rare qualities they possess, not merely to take it all in their stride, but to do so uncomplaining. Without them, this book could not have been written. I owe them more than I can say."

BARRISTER AND TEACHER

They met at school... wed

A NOTTINGHAM barrister and the youngest member of Heanor UDC, Mr. Keith Matthewman, of 215, Cromford-road, Aldercar, was married at Breaston Parish Church today. He met his bride, Miss Jane Maxwell, a teacher at Longmoor County Junior School, Breaston, and the daughter of Mrs. and the late Mr. T. Maxwell, headmaster of Wilsthorpe Secondary School, Long Eaton, when they were fellow pupils at Long Eaton Grammar School.

Mr. Matthewman is now in his last year as a councillor representing Langley Mill.

After leaving London University, he was called to the Bar of the Middle Temple in 1960. He taught history and English to secondary school pupils in London and the Howitt School, Heanor, and before practising as a barrister in Nottingham earlier this year, worked with the International Division of Rolls-Royce for several months.

He is the eldest son of Mr. and Mrs. F. Matthewman. of 59. Maylands-avenue, Breaston.

The bride, who was given away by her brother. Mr. Richard Maxwell, wore a full-length dress of white organza and satin. with a rose and tulle bouffant headdress.

She carried white freesias. stephanotis and lilies of the valley. Her sister, Mrs. Anne Gilbert, attended her in a lemon nylon dress, and holding lilies of the valley. Mr. Raymond Matthewman was the best man.

TAUGHT IN HEANOR

Mr. Matthewman was born near Barnsley. He moved with his family to Chilwell, and after leaving school went to London University to read law. In 1960 he was called to the Bar of the Middle Temple.

He taught secondary school pupils in London and at the Howitt School, Heanor.

From last September until March he worked in the international division of Rolls-Royce Ltd., Derby, as commercial assistant to the group licence officer. He then left to practise as a barrister, and is in chambers at Nottingham. His family moved to Aldercar 4½ years ago.

PRESENTATION

Yesterday afternoon Miss Maxwell was presented with a crystal water set from the staff and pupils of the school, and last week the couple received a clock and tray from Langley Mill Ward Labour Party.

HE'S STILL WITH US

Mr. Keith Matthewman, the Heanor councillor who married and left the district last month, will not resign from the council, though he will not seek re-election next May. He announced his decision in a letter to the council which met on Tuesday night.

The couple were both pupils of Long Eaton Grammar School. Several years after leaving school they met at a New Year's Eve party.

Chapter 17
Chambers in Nottingham

To me, the term 'chambers' still conjures up an image of dark, medieval rooms with thick stone walls housing ancient, bewigged, musty and dusty gentlemen scratching away on parchment with quills. In reality they are simply a suite of offices where barristers work.

Retired Judge Thomas R Heald told me that -

"Brian Smedley introduced me to my new pupil Keith Matthewman. He came to us in 1962 at 16 Castlegate when the surrounding buildings were all being pulled down to be replaced by Rodney House. Ours was the last building to be demolished, practically over our heads! Denis Cowley QC, the Head of Chambers at that time, had decided to buy 24 The Ropewalk, but there was not enough space, so Keith and I had to share, and squeeze into, a very cold room at 23 Regent Street which was full of my books. Even after he became fully qualified, we continued to share a room up until the time I became a judge in 1970.

Having the interests of my pupil at heart, I made sure that Keith started on the Easter Tuesday of April 3rd, one day before Ian McLaren (now QC) *who was the new pupil of Brian Appleby.* (now His Honour Judge Brian Appleby QC) *This meant that Keith was always senior to Ian in chambers.* (Wednesday April 4th was also the day that James Hanratty was hanged for the A6 murder.)

Barristers specialised to some extent but in the provinces they turned their hand to anything that was offered. My practice was partly criminal and partly family and 50% civil with some property work. Keith Matthewman, preferring advocacy and being put off by civil work, came into a practice of a type which he would not choose to follow."

Judge Heald gave me some fascinating background information about the chambers at Nottingham at that time. It seems that Denis Cowley, who had been a criminal barrister since the end of the war, was quite a character. He flew in the Battle of Britain, was shot down over the English Channel, stayed in the water for 36 hours before being rescued by the Germans and promptly interned in a prison camp.

He attempted to escape and failed. In his second attempt he succeeded in getting to Switzerland and waited nine months before boarding a flight into Portugal, eventually, after many adventures, ending up in occupied France. Judge Heald has considered writing a history of the Bar in Nottingham.

To jog Keith's memories during those early days, I suggested that we watch an old and witty Boulting Brothers film. 'Brothers-in-Law', which was set only a few years before in 1956 and based on the novel by Henry Cecil. The contrasts and comparisons were interesting -

"It was accurate in that barristers helped each other but Tom Heald, my pupil-master, didn't rush about like the absent minded Miles Malleson! Neither did I endure the appalling adventures and mishaps of his apprentice Ian Carmichael. Tom was very kind, caring and always took time to talk to me and teach me the ropes.

*On the Bench I'd occasionally get a note from an usher to say that Mr X was doing his first case. I well remember my **own** first case so I was always prepared make the necessary allowances for a novice. Even with experienced barristers I never shouted or screamed but, from time to time, needed to make a remedial comment!"*

I asked Keith about his first ever case -

"A peeping tom through a hole into the ladies lavatory! It was heard in the Magistrate's Court and my client 'Tom', pleaded guilty, so I didn't really defend but 'mitigated'. I had to stress to the magistrates Tom's previous good character and as it was his first offence, he was thoroughly ashamed and wouldn't do it again ... etc.

Shortly after that, a distraught Nottingham City bus driver was in deep trouble charged with careless driving having collided with a car. I defended him and I won. Great elation! It was my first ever victory!"

For the first six months of his year long pupillage, Keith could only appear in the Magistrate's Court. He was not allowed in the higher courts known in those days as the Assizes or Quarter Sessions which were closed in 1972 with the passing of the Courts Act 1971. Consequently, these early days were a lean period for the newly married Matthewmans, but there was always work in the Magistrate's Courts of the Guildhall and the Shire Hall -

"It's where we 'cut our teeth' and wasn't too badly paid. Basically we were defending and earned three guineas [three pounds and three shillings] *(legal aid) per case if your client pleaded guilty. It was the experience which really mattered; getting on your feet and mitigating, saying something in your client's favour to persuade the magistrates to pass a low sentence. If you were lucky it was a contested case and then you'd get five guineas.*

Our clerk, Michael Churm, was very helpful persuading solicitors to send us their small criminal cases. Also, I learned the basics of my craft in the Magistrates' Courts of Leicester, Lincoln and Derby. It was very good training."

A recalled insignificant comment, made by an elderly solicitor at that time, makes a very significant point about the huge growth of the Criminal Justice System in the last half of the 20th century -

Elderly solicitor - *"Which chambers are you in then?"*

Keith Matthewman - *"16 Castlegate."*

Elderly solicitor - *"Oh yes. Tell me, how many barristers do you have now?"*

Keith Matthewman - *"There are eight of us."*

Elderly solicitor - *"Good Lord! It must be like a rabbit warren up there!"*

The point being, that here and now in the year 2001, few chambers contain less that 40 barristers and many have up to 100. Sir Brian Smedley referred to a set of six in 1960, the largest chambers in Nottingham at that time, and Michael Holford saw the Ropewalk chambers enlarge to 25 barristers during the period 1968 to 1971.

As a young inexperienced barrister, Keith had to cope with many new expenses, not least the pupillage fee, and his income fell well short of total requirements. The new matrimonial home was built upon the open fields where he had played as a boy 16 years before. It was a semi at 22 Redland Drive, Chilwell, just around the corner from his parents' original house on Marton Road. At this point, Jane's schoolteacher salary was an essential part of the family income, but in the early 1960's when private motoring was very expensive, even the two combined incomes could not possibly support the buying, maintenance and running of a car - and private mobility had been essential when Keith was at Rolls-Royce and even more so now as a barrister.

Father had come to the rescue with the purchase of a used Morris 1000 on the basis that his son would repay a part of the loan, when he was able to, at a later date. These were very favourable terms, but when it came to putting them on their feet, Lieutenant Frank Matthewman was a generous father to both of his boys. In due course Keith repaid the loan in full. During the severe icy winter of 1962, the worst since 1947, that Morris 1000 turned out to be excellent value. Despite no garage, standing out-side, exposed to the cold winter blasts, often covered in inches of snow, it started first time every time and never broke down!

During that first meeting at Breaston, Brian Smedley had suggested to Keith that he could earn extra money on something called the Land Registry Titles. Judge Heald told me that this was a sideline developed by one of his previous pupils, Alan Prichard, who later became Professor of the Law Department at Nottingham University. These titles would normally be checked by the Land Registry personnel but they had become so overloaded by work that they turned to barristers to help them out at a guinea a title. Keith explained -

*"Our task was to make sure that the papers showed valid title (ownership). I would certify it and thereby guarantee the title of that piece of land to the 'prima facia' owner or last purchaser before sending it back to the Land Registry. In other words I was making sure that Mr A really **did** own the land before he sold it to Mr B. It was possible to do two or three titles an hour. In 1962 three guineas an hour wasn't a bad rate but some titles could take up to two hours."*

I have always been most intrigued by the relationship which exists between a barrister and his clerk. The latter could be described as a manager or agent who was employed by the former. This is illustrated by the usual form of address - 'sir', whereas it is common practice for a barrister to address his clerk informally by his first name. With regard to the recent TV series about barristers, 'North Square', Peter Moffat, the writer and former barrister himself, said of the clerk's function -

"He's a pivotal figure and can be ruthless when it comes to touting for work. He can make or break a barrister's career! When a solicitor rings up, the clerk can sell him X or Y and not even mention Z

if he's not in favour. He - and it is almost always he - wields an awful lot of power." Radio Times 25.11.00.

Michael Churm was certainly nothing like the 'hiss-worthy, panto villain, scheming, unscrupulous,' fictional Peter McLeish, but he has clearly been a major player and important influence in the early career of Keith Matthewman -

> *"He was an excellent clerk; briefs used to pour in. Michael was not only good at getting us work, but also good at advising us **how** to work. In our chambers there seemed to be an unspoken pecking order of seniority with regard to the clerk. Most barristers would knock on his office door and wait to be told to enter, but more senior barristers (including myself) just walked in. I remember him with a great deal of respect and affection."*

Michael Churm exerted his authority in October 1962 by cutting short Keith and Jane's honeymoon. They had been to Jersey and were enjoying the last few days at home when Michael phoned to say that a solicitor called Nora Healy needed him in court the next morning. Private time and marital bliss being interrupted, Keith admitted to me that his impulse was to say 'get stuffed', but one did not refuse a brief from a solicitor who used you frequently in court -

> *"I'm still on my honeymoon, Michael!"*

> *"I'm sorry about that, sir! She needs you, she wants you and you'll just have to come, honeymoon or not!*

Thirty nine years later all is forgiven and Jane said -

> *"Michael Churm was a stickler for professional discipline. Not all sets of chambers were so exacting. There was an occasion in the Shire Hall coffee room when a solicitor came over to Keith and said -*

> *'You'll be Mr Matthewman'.*

> *'How did you know?' said Keith.*

> *'Simple! I'm briefing you and you're the only person here wearing a black jacket and striped trousers - therefore I know you're from The Ropewalk.'"*

This is consistent with the recollection of Colin Morley -

> *"Keith Matthewman was very much a Dandy, having a style which is immaculate and always in the best possible taste."*

Ex Chief Superintendent Michael Holford told me -

"It was 1968 and I can clearly remember my very first sight of Keith Matthewman. Fresh faced, bright and bushy tailed, very smartly dressed in formal mourning clothing of striped trousers, black jacket and wearing a bowler hat. What a sight to behold! He cut a dashing figure under the strict influence of his clerk Michael Churm who exercised strict Victorian values. He insisted that all his barristers follow the example of the Head of Chambers who was a QC of great standing. Denis Cowley was an immensely talented and popular gentleman."

No doubt Mr Churm was only too well aware that some judges (such as the future Judge Matthewman) were very particular about correct dress in their court. An incorrectly dressed barrister is likely to receive a strong hint when His Honour remarks - *"I can't hear you Mr X!"*

Under the guidance and stewardship of his clerk, Keith learned an early, valuable lesson. One day he entered chambers to hear -

"Good morning, sir. Here's your brief, you're in the County Court today."

It was the very first time Keith had seen the brief! He was representing a garage owner who had just been made bankrupt. Knowing nothing about bankruptcy, nevertheless, he read the brief quickly and then, post-haste to the court ready to be on his feet in front of the District Registrar, Mr Alan Hibbert. On arrival he had a word with his client only to find that the current stage of bankruptcy was not in fact that part upon which he had been briefed. Perusing the papers -

*"God! There's bugger all about today's hearing in this brief! This appears to be the **second** stage of the proceedings."*
He looked sadly at the forlorn garage owner.

"I can't represent you. I'm sorry!"

There was no more to be done so the young barrister left the court and the man, as they say, had to 'face the music' alone. Returning to chambers, he saw that Michael Churm looked puzzled at this unexpected early appearance. After explanations, to use Keith's own words -

"Michael Churm went spare!!"

*"You **left** him! Alone! You **never**, ever leave a client alone in court. Get back there and defend your client the best way you can. Return right now, sir, and look after your client."*

Keith hurried back to the County Court by which time the whole thing was virtually over. Alan Hibbert, having now heard all the evidence and about to deliver his judgement, looked over his spectacles and noted the silent arrival of the barrister - who of course had been absent throughout the proceedings! Exercising tolerance and courtesy, which is the gentlemanly mark of kind conduct from the experienced in the way that they treat and deal with the inexperienced, the District Registrar said -

"Ah! Mr Matthewman. Is there anything you would like to add?"

Mr Matthewman responded in the negative but the now worldly wise judge looking back at that unfortunate event, told me it was 'a lesson well learned'.

Most contributors describe Michael Churm as a good clerk but not all liked him or could get on with him. He had his quirks, but to some he was a father figure giving wide ranging advice and help, far beyond the usual bounds of his professional responsibilities.

Under his expert stewardship, Keith's practice grew and thrived to the point that in 1967 at the age of 31 he was earning £4,000 per year, nearly £100,000 at today's value. Contrast this with the original £1350 promised by Rolls Royce and the, even smaller amount of income on offer, had he not traded in the 'mortar board' for the 'lawyers wig'! At this stage Mr Churm became the financial advisor.

"You're earning a fair amount of money now, sir. Don't waste it! Get some endowment policies. Might I suggest ... "

"I took his advice and all the insurance policies came up trumps - every single one. An example of his managerial skills and guidance. He got me work when I was unknown and sifted the work when I was known. I owe him a great debt of gratitude."

Keith Matthewman soon became known because, not only did he have ability, he also worked very hard indeed - as we shall see next.

Captain Adrian Matthewman.

Chapter 18
A Riotous Robing Room

Jane Matthewman continued to teach at Longmoor County Junior School in Breaston until July 1966. I had an idea that she probably left her job to allow more time for supporting her husband on the legal social scene, but I was quite wrong. Like her late father, Mrs Matthewman had an excellent professional reputation, was very popular with her pupils, but also strict, and achieved good results with her own individual tried and trusted methods. When these successful methods were called into question by a more 'progressive' management, Jane was beginning to *'swim against the tide'*: a scenario very familiar to this writer. She reflected on her present position -

"I don't like the term 'housewife'. It implies you have little intelligence and can't go to work, don't want to go out to work, preferring to sit in the house listening to 'Mrs Dale's Diary' and doing mundane jobs. I'm not like that and never quite know how to describe myself. I wear so many hats per day - it just isn't true!"

What then of the parties: the duty to be charming and smile sweetly at all the big names? I put this question to Jane a few months before the retirement of Judge Matthewman and the answer came back with some feeling.

"There is little social life attached to the life of a barrister. People think it's one long social round, an endless get together - it isn't! There simply isn't the time. Keith is working all hours and has been working all hours for 38 years! He's working even harder now than in the early days when he worked very hard indeed - sheer hard work!"

From barrister to judge, Keith Matthewman has worked every day with the exception of Saturday, and sometimes even then! He told the Nottingham Business Post, 'My Week' 25.7.00, that on the Monday he arrived home from court at 4.30pm - *'... had a gin and tonic and then disappeared to work in my study ... had a meal at 7.00 and then back to the study to work until about midnight ... it just **had** to be done before the next day."* At the end of Tuesday he finished at 10.30pm *" ... an early evening!"* At the end of Wednesday - *" ... have to read the cases for tomorrow. Quite an early finish - 10.00pm."* Come Friday - *"I left* *the court at 4.00pm and, thank God, it is Friday evening. I always give myself a holiday on Friday evening."*

Looking back over the years, Jane told me that she particularly hated Keith having to work all day on, as she put it, *'Sunday, bloody Sunday'* when the rest of the world was either relaxing or at play.

"Nothing less than the best will ever do for Keith. As a barrister he had to get his case together and it had to be absolutely superbly correct. You can't go into court when you're not properly prepared and he was determined to be well prepared no matter how late the hour.

When our son Adrian, three years old at the time, was asked - 'What are you going to be when you grow up?' he said - 'I'm going to write lines under words like my daddy.' He'd been watching Keith, studying and poring over notes, underlining and highlighting key sections of cases for the next day. Would that it had been so simple as through the eyes of a child!"

Adrian Matthewman eventually decided against writing lines under words, but has undertaken a more demanding profession - an Airline Captain. (See photo on page 164) Keith and Jane are very proud of their only son. His mother told me -

"All through the years he has not caused us one moment's trouble. We've financed his training but he's had to work very hard to get to his present position. He's been a forecourt attendant, worked in a ceramics factory, done kitchen work in a leisure centre, worked on the ramps at the East Midlands Airport ... all good character building experiences!"

I asked Captain Matthewman to make his contribution to this biography and am most grateful to have received the following skilful appraisal which turns out to be amusing, generous, direct, honest and sensitively written.

"One may think that being tasked with writing a piece with the loose title - 'What's It Like Being a Judge's Son', would be simple. Knowing and living with my parents for 21 years is, after all, long enough to ponder such a task. Despite this however, simple it is not. The following ramblings and ad hoc memories will, hopefully, form some sort of comprehensible and reasonably interesting text!

*My early memories of family life are happy ones, Mum and Dad made sure of that. I didn't wake up one morning and think 'My God, my father is a Barrister!' It was natural, it was life. Not up until school-age really, did I notice that my friends' parents' jobs were, lets say, not quite the same as my father's. I am often asked as to whether I was in any way taunted at school for having a father who had a rather different job. I can honestly say that this never happened. I put this down largely to the fact that I have a (fairly) normal personality and had few enemies. There have been a couple of instances, though, where a friend's father or brother has actually been sent to prison by my father. However, these events thankfully took place after school leaving age and so the prospect of having to confront one another in the morning assembly did not arise! It is perfectly possible, indeed probable, that in the course of 17 years of going to 'the local', you will bump into someone, or someone who knows somebody else, who has been locked up by your Dad! Therefore for the man in the pub, a period of assessment is necessary before announcing that your **Father is a Judge**; just a precaution against false teeth! This is by no means to say that I am in any way ashamed of what my father does - quite the reverse, I am very proud.*

*An area of life in which I understand my father has regret was in my younger years. He regrets not having spent more time with me. Certainly, he did work very hard. After having been in Court all day he would arrive home only to start reading a large pile of papers for the next day, often not finishing until the early hours of the morning, not to mention being study-bound at the weekend as well. Despite this I have no recollection of actually thinking I was being neglected. Yes, Mum and I did spend more time together (and she put up with me very well), but isn't this the case with most families? Perhaps I thought it was the norm. Let's face it, for my family it **was** the norm! Holidays, Birthdays, Christmas and New Year were always happy times as a child and after all, I think these are the events one remembers the most from childhood.*

Certainly the standard of living which my parents and I were accustomed to, would not have been possible without the long hours that Dad had to work. My future career would not have happened without those late evenings and weekends. Despite the looks of amazement on the faces of many of my parents' friends when told of my *decision **not** to go to The Bar, I decided I would like a career in Aviation. Why Aviation instead of Law? This question is as old as I am, and I cannot answer why, because I do not know. What is known is that without the large sums of money they have helped me with along the way in order to get me here, now, my flying career would have never occurred.*

*Mum and Dad, thank you for this and for supporting, over the years, what **I** wanted to do.*

It is worth saying here that, as may be ascertained from the above announcement, my parents never once pressured me into considering a career (i.e. Law) which didn't interest me. As a result I find myself doing a job I love with a good view out of the office window!

This then, is what being 'The Son of a Judge', or should I say Retired Judge, is like. Bloody great, actually!

As with the teaching profession, for barristers and judges there is a tendency for the public to measure the length of the judicial day from the comfortable post 10.00am start to the adjournment, typically a little after 4.00pm when, in the public's perception, the judge gets a little bored and says *'We'll rise now'.* Out of those six hours, subtract one for lunch. Anyone who has ever been on jury service will know how intense and concentrated those few hours can be. Keith tells me that thirty years ago the court day was longer -

"We'd come out of court at 5.00pm if we were lucky. Sometimes sittings would last up to 6 or 7.00pm. Then it was back to our busy chambers (civil and criminal) to see what we had to do - there was always something to do; get urgent matters out of the way, get things organised for the next morning, make telephone calls ... "

"What about dinner?" I said.

"Dinner? Dinner was a case of 'as and when'!"

When Keith became a judge in 1983, the job did not get easier -

"The public have no idea how hard it is and the long hours involved in being a judge. If only they thought about it for just one second! When does he read the papers before hand? How can he sum up unless he's read, gone through, crossed bits out and formed a summing up? It all takes time. Last Friday [23.6.00] I had 27 defendants to read about! The amount of paperwork was such that I had to get an usher to take a trolley to move the stuff from my car into

my chambers! Every night there is something to be done. You have a whole day's evidence to go through, sort out, cutting out the irrelevancies - and then you've got to read the whole bloody lot all over again!! I never used to do that, but with so few judges and such a heavy work load, things are getting very tight indeed."

In his early days at the Bar, Keith and his colleagues were earning high salaries for their hard work, more than barristers get today -

"I came into the profession at just the right time and met some super people. We thoroughly enjoyed our work. It was a great life, a bundle of fun in the Shire Hall robing room, a laugh a minute!"

After a little gentle probing, it was surprising to discover that these (generally held to be) dignified and learned colleagues of the robing room were enjoying such merrymaking. I suggested that this atmosphere of high comedy might have stemmed from tension, the seriousness of the job, having to deal with the harsh realities of people in deep trouble, the stress of lives in crisis?

" ... not to mention the pressures of the work load, but the jokes would fly. There was hilarious repartee between the witty Brian Appleby [today Judge Appleby QC] *and Dick Benson* [today Judge Benson] *who can be a very funny man. We were a great team: lots and lots of barristers: Willy Bach, Denis Cowley* [QC and now deceased] *John Deave, Tom Dineen* [now deceased] *Willie Everard, Andrew Hamilton* [Judge Hamilton] *Geoff Hoon, John Hopkin* [Judge Hopkin] *Richard Inglis* [Judge Inglis] *Calder Jose, Bill Joss, Humphry Lewis, Richard Maxwell* [QC] *Ian McLaren* [QC] *John Milmo* [QC] *Richard Payne, Michael Pearce, Christopher Pitchers* [Judge Pitchers] *Brian Smedley* [Mr Justice Smedley] *John Stobart, John Warren* [QC] *and David Wilcox* [Judge Wilcox].

One of the most entertaining barristers was a London practitioner, called James Hunt. [now Mr Justice Hunt] *whose character added greatly to an already great Robing Room. James was just as entertaining in court with a wit which carried juries with him during the course of a trial.*

The witty Graham Richards [now a District Judge in crime at Stoke] *was a broadcasting football commentator at the Derby County Ground as well as being a barrister.*

James Orrell [Judge Orrell] *was a great source of information. If anything happened, such as a barrister going to be promoted, James was always first to know and would tell the rest of us all about it.*

There was a tremendous sense of camaraderie. Every day was a day to remember. Every day in those long-ago, heady exciting days was a day to look forward to.

As space is limited, apologies to all the un-named barristers who played a part in that jolly gathering.

During those early days, Keith and his colleagues found time to enjoy their leisure in style at the Victoria Club in Nottingham, which was owned by friends of the Matthewmans, George and Ellen Akins and has recently been re-opened by their son Sean.

George Akins, the Chairman of Geo. Akins [Holdings] Ltd, is a local entrepreneur who started out with a bookmakers business and later went into property. When the Shire Hall closed in 1988, George Akins bought the freehold from the County Council and then sold the venerable old 1770 building to the Lace Market Trust at a very generous and public spirited low price.

As a barrister in the early days, Keith worked for Mr Akins under the Gaming Acts to apply for the opening of new premises. The years passed and they lost touch until the occurrence of a chance re-union on February 16th 1998. This was at a reception to celebrate the appointment of the then Lord Chief Justice, the Rt. Hon. Lord Bingham of Cornhill, as the Inaugural President of the Museum of Law Trust Company which is housed in the Galleries of Justice. Bill Shaw the Chairman of the Friends of the Galleries of Justice had already asked Keith if he would be the Inaugural President. Since that time, 'The Friends' has been one of Keith's principal pastimes.

George recognised Keith and Keith recognised George after this gap of many years. Learning of the new group (the Friends of the Galleries of Justice) and being interested in the local history of Nottingham, George Akins was keen to join and generously offered to donate £5,000 to launch the venture. George, Ellen and Sean eventually became members and joined the other 'Friends' to help support the Galleries as a major educational resource and tourist attraction. Quarterly meetings are held in one of the historic courtrooms where we are addressed on each occasion by an invited distinguished speaker. This is followed by a very pleasant social gathering in the Grand Jury Room where Jane Matthewman thoroughly spoils us with a bountiful spread of various delicious items in an attractively presented buffet with Carole Brown providing an array of tasty cakes. During the party Keith, (who has considerable social skills which I envy) graciously moves around all the guests spreading joy and happiness!

For all those readers who (quite naturally), might be somewhat nervous about meeting a real live judge you will discover that all your pre-conceived notions of the quintessential, remote, 18th century, stern autocrat - will dissolve into nothingness within the first few seconds of chatting to the amiable host of 'The Friends of the Galleries of Justice'. Apart from the character on the wrong side of the law in the dock, Keith has this magical effect on everybody he meets.

From personal experience over the last few years, I can warmly recommend the Friends of the Galleries of Justice to anyone who seeks the companionship of an assorted cordial collection of interesting people.

More information can be obtained from Carole Brown, Secretary of the Friends of the Galleries of Justice, Shire Hall, High Pavement, Lace Market, Nottingham NG1 1HN, or phone 0115 9520555.

On the same subject of judicial affability, Colin Morley remembers the social scene in the 1960's -

"A few close friends from the Bar and their wives were frequently invited to dinner parties at the Matthewmans. They were both very attentive and a more generous and hospitable host than Keith is impossible to imagine. He was interested in fine wines and always arranged for splendid refreshments. Jane, a very good cook with an expert eye for presentation, went to endless trouble and would lay on a wonderful spread.

For many years, my wife and I were invited to celebrate the arrival of the New Year at Keith and Jane's well known and much loved annual party. Keith would play records of his favourite artists but was never high brow in his taste. The nostalgic voices of Al Martino and the lovely Jo Stafford often sang through the Matthewman speakers. Just thinking about those relaxing times in their comfortable modern home, eating, drinking, listening to music and telling stories - it all brings back many happy memories."

The above modern house referred to was the next move in 1968 from 22 Redland Drive. A time of prosperity and a measure of Keith's success as an 'often asked for' barrister was bringing him £4,000 as opposed to a basic teacher on top salary at £1,500 per annum. Keith paid out £3,500 for a good sized plot of land in Toton and his brother-in-law, architect, Alan Gilbert designed a splendid house which, when complete, totalled £11,500 - all cash paid, no mortgage, no loans. Alan married Jane's sister, Anne, who is now a textile artist and watercolourist and the Vice President of the Living Threads Group.

The faithful old Morris 1000 had long since given way to a flashy white Triumph sports car with bright red seats, and this 'tart trap' (as it was dubbed by a friend) made way for a series of new cars, one for the husband and one for the wife, brand new, every year, paid for in cash. This is indeed impressive affluence to this author who has spent a lifetime of long, penny pinching years struggling to pay off mortgages and car loans!

Keith's main hobby and great love is his garden. Praise comes from several sources, Colin Morley says *'He does it exceedingly well'* and Tom Heald said -

"Jane and Keith's garden puts ours to shame, but they were more sensible than we were in that they always had a garden of manageable size. We still have some plants which come from their garden."

The Matthewman's present home, situated in a very pleasant quiet part of west Nottingham, has (to my eyes) a large impressive garden which is indeed very well managed by Keith, Jane and their part-time gardener.

"We've done it all ourselves." said Jane as we stepped of the generous sized patio. *"When we took it over, the property had stood empty for months and the garden was a wilderness with grass three feet tall!"* At this point we were startled by the sudden leap of a frog. *"There are lots of those. We also have blue-tits, gold-tits, greenfinches, blackbirds, but too many crows and magpies."*

172

Having been a guest on a number of occasions, I have been privileged to see the welcome regular night visitors to the sweeping Matthewman lawn - wild foxes. The long expanse of grass tapering towards the lovely distant rolling parkland / countryside giving the illusion of extra length. The neat lawn is flanked by conifers, cherry trees, herbs, shrubs and a profuse variety of flowers.

Growing success at the Bar in the 1960's brought with it growing social opportunities to meet 'the great and the grand'. I was most intrigued by a casual reference to 'The Judge's Lodgings', an exclusive residence situated quietly somewhere in the leafy, quiet, environs of The Park. This is where visiting High Court Judges stay and occasionally invite their colleagues for dinner or cocktail parties. Not a private hotel, not a private club for the judiciary, but simply 'exclusive' in the literal sense of the word: accommodation for High Court Judges and occasionally Circuit Judges only. As the precise location is kept very confidential for obvious reasons of security, I was privileged to have a brief chat with the butler, Colin Lane, who has, with his wife Myrtle the housekeeper together with a cook and three cleaners, conscientiously and faithfully served their distinguished guests for the last 24 years.

Back in the 1960's I was a regular visitor to an impressive mock gothic house in The Park, complete with ballroom and its own tower! Based on these opulent memories, I conceived an image of an impeccably dressed 'Lane' silently padding over plush carpets and, deferentially with a slight bow, serving a drink on a silver platter to an eminent grey haired gentleman comfortably reposing in a good quality arm chair reading The Times.

These charming images of quiet and gentle 'olde worlde' courtesy, not far from the centre of a bustling modern major city, are consistent with the mystique and charisma which still surrounds the judiciary - even if exaggerated.

Mr Lane spoke affectionately of his long acquaintance with my subject -

"Mr and Mrs Matthewman are extremely nice polite people. Judge Matthewman is discerning and has excellent taste in wines, but he was also a hard working judge who gave offenders exactly what they should get!"

In the early days Keith arrived home one day to find Jane unusually quiet and concerned about her first invitation to a dinner party at The

Judge's Lodgings. Having never met a High Court Judge before she was anxious about what to wear, how to behave, how to address these illustrious lawyers in conversation etc.

"Oh haven't I told you, darling? It's quite simple really. You must wear a long white dress and, as it's your first occasion, you will walk backwards into the room. Under no circumstances must you look directly at a High Court Judge until after a formal presentation and a respectful deep curtsy. Don't worry, darling. You'll find them absolutely charming."

But Jane did worry -

"It was so awful! I was really wound-up about it all. I remember going into Jessops looking and thinking - 'Where the hell am I going to get a long white dress? Would my wedding dress do? No! You'd look a right berk in your wedding dress!' Arriving home, still fretting, I was almost in tears when finally Keith said - 'But surely you didn't believe me!'

Well of course I believed him! And do you know, Narvel, he let me believe that for two days! He actually let me believe that nonsense for two whole days!"

In the intervening years since that mischievous deception, Jane has moved in the circles of various eminent QC's and High Court Judges. She told me her present perception is very far from the exalted, untouchable image which was so intimidating in her younger days.

The prosperity enjoyed by the Matthewmans in the late 1960's was soon to be tempered by the chronic economic crisis and punitive taxation of the following decade. Against all expectations, the Conservatives under Edward Heath swept to power in June 1970 and income tax on all earnings above £15,000 went up to 91.25%! After the paralysing industrial disputes of December 1973, Britain went on a three day week. In March 1974 the Prime Minister called a General Election putting the simple question *'Who rules Britain, the democratically elected government of the people - or the trade unions?'* The result was almost a draw and the headlines screamed out - 'WHO RULES BRITAIN NOW?'. Harold Wilson (Labour) only just managed to form a government with no real power, but after a second election in October 1974 he scraped through with a tiny majority.

Disaster followed disaster. In December wage settlements averaged 26%. Teachers received a pay rise of 32% which helped to push inflation up to 20%. In the following February of 1975 the coal miners accepted a pay hike of 35% and unemployment passed the million mark in April. In May the pound went into free fall losing 25% of its value and inflation reached an all time high of **26%** in July! Mr Wilson announced a maximum £6.00 per week pay rise and a total freeze on all incomes above £8,500.

In the midst of all this economic chaos, Keith Matthewman and his 'learned friends' were now paying 83 out of every 100 new pennies from the top portion of their incomes. To a successful barrister, this made a big difference in living standards.

The Matthewmans had become accustomed to holidays in luxurious hotels: the Dorchester and Hilton in London were frequent favourites but in the summer if 1974 they were reduced to an afternoon at Wollaton Hall, which had free admission!

"An afternoon we thoroughly enjoyed. [said Jane] *Adrian,* [then six years old] *was fascinated by the displayed insects. I recall that we had to drink orange juice when we got back instead of the usual gin and tonic. A barrister's wife was grumbling to me about the hard times.*

'Do you know, Jane, things are getting so bad: my bras are dropping to bits!' - to which I replied -

'My dear! You'll just have to ask your husband for more support ...'"

But orange juice and bras still had to be paid for and Keith Matthewman needed to be 'on his feet' to support his family. On this particular occasion it was his first appearance in the Divisional Court in London when he defended a Mansfield publican who had been accused of selling alcohol to youngsters under age.

To make the most of a day out, Jane decided to accompany her husband and, by coincidence, so did the wife of the publican's solicitor. So it was that four people entered that rather old fashioned court on that day when the case was called on. The two women were especially audible in an old echoing Victorian Court with no carpet or curtains to absorb amplified sounds. Jane was wearing fashionable stiletto heels with steel tips which made an embarrassing sharp sound on the bare floor boards. Worse, much worse, the solicitor's wife had her leg encased in plaster with an iron support under her foot which filled the Court with a disconcerting loud noise as she slowly, and painfully, progressed across the reverberating boards.

The presiding judge, with a somewhat irritated countenance, had cause to scowl all the more when the solicitor, making **his** progress, further disturbed the erstwhile peaceful proceedings with a clattering suitcase full of clanking shandy cans as part of the evidence.

When all these noisy agents finally came to rest, peace reigned briefly as the case took its course.

At the conclusion and dismissal, Keith Matthewman, gave the customary bow to the three judges and began to leave the court accompanied by his small band of involuntary and embarrassed percussion - filling the Court with noise. The next case had started - *'Your Honour, I appear for ....* '. The voice struggled to out-shout the plonking, clattering, clinking, clanking and rattling ensemble which seemed to take an eternity getting over to the exit. To their horror the door was locked! The presiding judge glowered and Keith gave a second bow as the whole disruptive cacophony was repeated in spite of a conscientious effort to be as unobtrusive as possible. Once at the correct door, the now grumpy judges were relieved to accept a final bow from the quartet who then plonked, clattered, clinked and clanked all the way down the echoing corridor ....

One of the delights of visiting the Matthewman home is enjoying the inspiring experience of a warm and charming chemistry between Jane and Keith: a marriage which is one of the principal successes of his life as demonstrated by this thoughtful assessment by Jane -

"Although Keith spent many, many hours away from his family in the infernal study, he has always been a loving father and husband. Adrian, Keith and Jane form a mighty triangle which, as the years sped by, became more and more impervious. We were a team, a loving, caring, fiercely protective team. That is the situation that has endured throughout a very happy life together. It seems one cannot speak about one without referring to the other. Keith Matthewman is a great person, a clever and accomplished man and without the dedication and commitment to his chosen career he would surely have faltered. He therefore had to be allowed free rein to develop and become ever more skilled, ever more assured. Some may ask did this make him selfish?

Did this make him arrogant? To these questions I would reply - only when applied to the job - never to me or to Adrian.

I have a sneaking suspicion that despite the fact that he is now retired, the engine of the power-house is not yet cold, that it may be impatient to jerk into life again. Who knows? He may yet continue to amaze and enthral us, entertain and amuse us, shock and thrill us. All I know is, I hope that he does, for he is unique, a one off and he's the nicest most caring man I have ever known and my life (and I know that of Adrian) has been enriched as a result."

Chapter 19
Silk, Rape and Murder

History was made at the Nottingham Crown Court on December 21st 2000. It was the darkest day of the year but the court staff, in high spirits and jolly mood, seized and arrested Judge Matthewman! He was escorted to the dock of Court 1 to stand trial. Such a brave action had never happened before. The correct and formal proceedings were opened by experienced usher called Mike Walvin -

"All persons having anything to do before Her Majesty's Listing Officer draw nigh and give your attendance."

Maria Lunn the Clerk -

"Are you His Honour Judge Keith Matthewman?"

They all shout -

"Two - tees - Q - C!"

The judge replies and Maria continues -

*"Your Honour Judge Keith Matthewman, QC, you are charged on this indictment with aiding and abetting the Criminal Justice System. The particulars are that you did, on various dates between 1983 and December of the year 2000 continuously, remorselessly and without fear or favour, strike terror in the hearts of innumerable defendants, the public **and** some members of the Bar. How say you? Are you guilty or not guilty?"*

Judge Matthewman replied -

"I'll plead guilty and get it over with. They all do in Court 5."

This delightful surprise for Keith was indeed an unprecedented and massive display of sincere affection from those who held him in high regard. He was deeply moved -

"It was an unforgettable moment! The first time a judge had been honoured in this way in the Crown Court, Quarter Sessions Court, or Assize Court in Nottingham. I'm deeply indebted to the Court Manager, Pat Gamble, and her splendid hard-working staff for looking after me so well over the years and especially during these last few stressful months."

One usher, Trish Briggs, told me -

"This is really a very sad day for us. We're going to miss Judge Matthewman terribly. We're fond of him. He was always the gentleman, so considerate and with such a good sense of fun."

The case continued and each time the judge was named they all shouted - *"Two - tees - Q-C!"* No doubt this reflected an in-joke from the many instances when staff prompted each other to write down His Honour's full and correct details.

Keith appeared before Her Honour 'Judge' Kath Haywood who was told that she came across as more formidable than a real circuit judge. Sharon Thompson enthusiastically prosecuted and the prisoner was stoutly defended by Michael Auty and Sue Davis who, at one point said -

"My client is already the subject of a biography. He is a media star. He will continue with several of his committees and is to begin as a ...

Oh, may I refer to my junior, Your Honour? I think there's an error on my notes .... "

Judge Haywood -
"Certainly."

Mrs Davis -
"Oh yes. A misspelling Your Honour. He is to begin as a 'lecturer' in law at Nottingham Trent University. Actually it is amazing that he has found any time at all in these past years to appear on the Bench! My client has often set the Listing Officer certain challenges over the years. However he has been a most sociable judge, attending staff retirement parties, presenting gifts, drawing raffles and recently firing a starting pistol at this year's Fun Run."

This last caused Miss Thompson to interject quickly with -
"I would like to ask the court to take into consideration one count of discharging a firearm in a public place!"

This additional offence was a reference to the 'Fun Run' of January 2001 when the Nottingham Crown Court legal team raised £3000 to help breast cancer sufferers. In the next photograph [courtesy of The Nottingham Evening Post, January 23rd 2001] one of the entrants [centre left] Sharon Thompson next to Judge Matthewman make the presentation to Maxine McCoy from Breast Cancer Care.

As the Crown Court reporter for The Nottingham Evening Post, Judy Cullimore has, over the years, had more opportunity than most to observe Judge Matthewman's conscientious concern for court staff -

"He fiercely championed the clerks and ushers who respected and liked him very much. He was also protective to the members of his juries and not averse to making a fuss when it came to matters of their comfort and convenience, raising many a smile from the panel by some of his comments. [See 'Not fit for a dog' in 'A Copper's Judge?']

And fans from the public! There was Violet. She was an elderly lady who, despite great disability in mobility, travelled by bus most days from her house in Long Eaton to sit in the public gallery and listen to the cases. She read my articles about Judge Matthewman's trials avidly. Imagine her feelings when he sent her a message, via me, asking if she would like to have lunch with him in the Judge's Dining Room! She was so overwhelmed at the prospect that Keith asked me along to give her support. 'I'll be too nervous to speak, never mind eat anything.' she said. Keith Matthewman went out of his way to put her at her ease and she spent an hour happily chatting to him. Later she confided - 'I'll never forget today as long as I live. What a lovely man!'"

'Taking Silk' is one of those intriguing mysteries hidden in the charm and magic of the judicial world. It has been said of Royalty - 'Do not let light in on magic', but illumination here is part of my job. In the first place to become a 'Silk', obviously, you need to be an exceptionally talented and practised barrister. Space does not allow for all the complimentary comments which poured in praising Keith's competence at his chosen craft. His Honour A.R.M (Bob) Ellis told me -

"He appeared before me many times and always mastered his brief whether prosecuting or defending."

Ex Chief Superintendent Michael Holford QPM, will have plenty to say in the next chapter and Colin Morley, a barrister in the same chambers, had a number of years, close up, to form an opinion stretching from 1967 to 1988, when Mr Morley left the country to take up an appointment as a magistrate in Hong Kong.

"When you join a new set of chambers, you're not always welcomed with open arms! A newcomer provides competition and some existing members are resentful. Not so with Keith Matthewman, who at that time was a well established member of the Junior Bar and had a flourishing criminal practice which took him into court daily. He was always helpful and we soon became good friends."

But 'good friends' often appeared against each other -

"Keith was a feared opponent! He was beautifully prepared, never took any short cuts and knew his brief like the back of his hand. He was extremely competent and extremely successful because he had an easy way with people which gave him the ability to put his point of view over to juries. In no time at all he would have them eating out of his hand. Using his keen intellect he started as a great defender but ended up doing more prosecutions.

I remember one of Keith's remorseless interrogations before Sir Basil Nield. Under clever cross-examination the defendant was getting into deep trouble, telling lies to try to get out of this trouble and getting into greater and greater difficulty! He was driven to take refuge in the frequently heard retort - 'Oh, I didn't understand the question!' There was no possible way the questions could have been misunderstood, and this prompted an intervention from the judge who said -

'Come now, Mr X! Just mind what you are saying. These questions are exceedingly clear.'

They were crystal clear. So there you have it from the mouth of a High Court Judge - Keith, well on top of his job."

In the early days Keith Matthewman was prosecuting a case of affray when Richard Benson (now Judge Benson) was defending two of the several accused. A number of witnesses had not come up to proof, that is, they had not said in open court what they had said in their witness statements. Colin Morley told me the same story and said -
"It's always a blow when your star witness lets you down! This man had said something completely contrary to what he had been expected to say."

In quick response, Mr Benson made a submission to Judge Ellis that there was no case to answer. In dealing with this, Keith Matthewman was moved to say to the judge -
*"May it please Your Honour ... my impression of what the witness **meant** to say was ... "*

Judge Benson recalled this desperate attempt of his struggling opponent with admiration -
"A forlorn case: he'd lost it! It was hopeless but he never gave up. It was so typical of Keith. He'd fight on to the last round of ammunition - to the end!

Chatting over dinner, Keith once made a profound statement which, at first hearing, I found somewhat alarming -
*"In all my years at the Bar and on the Bench, I've only ever come across **one** single person in the dock who I was sure was innocent of the charges. He was an alleged burglar I was defending at Derby Crown Court."*

In 39 years only one innocent person! On reflection this should not be too surprising considering that the police have taken time, trouble and great care in putting together an indictment against an Accused. After such a thorough, searching examination of the facts, I suppose we should not expect to see too many innocent folk in the dock. This comment moved me to ask Keith the hoary old question often asked of barristers - if you really believe your client is guilty, how do you cope?
"You cope by being thoroughly professional. Being human you may well have your own views but this should not affect your duty to

put your client's case. It is a matter for the jury to make the decision as to the guilt or innocence on the evidence presented. Your duty is to win the case fairly within the rules for your client which ever side you represent.

*What you must **not** do, is to act in any way dishonestly. You spell out to your client the strengths and weaknesses of the case, for and against. You do not deceive the court in any way; so, if your client tells you he **is** guilty, you cannot allow him to give evidence that he is not guilty. If he insists on giving evidence of his innocence, having told you that he is guilty, you withdraw from the case as prescribed by the Bar's Code of Conduct.*

If, however, he insists on his innocence, despite your advice that the evidence against him shows clearly that he is guilty, then he is entitled to put forward his case and have you argue in his favour. As I have said, it then becomes a matter for the jury.

As a barrister your job in not to be the final judge of the case, merely to present it to the court. You are not there to indulge in sympathy or antipathy for your client. Emotion does not enter into your considerations. Any barrister who suffers from emotion will soon discover failure at the Bar, and, therefore, unhappiness in the job."

I began to realise that 'innocent' and 'not guilty' were not at all the same thing. No one is ever found 'innocent'. Innocent means you did not commit the crime as a matter of simple fact. 'Not guilty' means there is not sufficient evidence to **prove** you **did** commit the crime and the prosecution has failed to persuade a jury to convict because they are not sure of guilt. This is not the same as saying they are certain of innocence.

There was an occasion when the evidence did collapse in a case of manslaughter before the High Court Judge, Mr Justice Ashworth. This goes back to the days when Keith was a 'Junior' to the late Denis Cowley QC. In certain cases a client can have the benefit of two barristers, the Junior is 'led' by the more experienced 'Silk' who is a Queen's Counsel or QC. Either barrister may question a witness, but the Leader will do most of the questioning.

Mr Cowley for the prosecution had reached the stage where he had decided that 'there was no case to answer'. This meant that the prosecution evidence did not warrant a conviction and therefore the case should stop and a verdict of not guilty entered. Accordingly the judge was asked to instruct the jury to bring in a verdict of 'not guilty'. After reviewing the facts of the case, Mr Justice Ashworth disagreed with the learned counsel and still wanted the prisoner to be brought to the test. He leaned forward -

"Mr Cowley."

"Yes, My Lord?"

"Mr Cowley: I think you have made the wrong decision!"

*"I'm sorry, My Lord, but I have **not** made the wrong decision. It is my decision. I am counsel for the prosecution, and in these circumstances I - make - that - final - decision. With the greatest of respect, My Lord, you - do - not -make - that - decision."*

Keith recalls this gallant exchange with awe -

"This was brave stuff! To challenge a High Court Judge on such a point was courage indeed!"

After a brief argument, His Lordship suggested the appointment of different prosecuting counsel -

"Well," said Denis, *"I'll make enquiries, My Lord."*

Enquiries were made. The police rated Denis Cowley as a senior silk and very popular barrister due to his thoroughness of preparation and high success rate. Naturally, he was much less popular with the police when he was defending! On this occasion, the police and County Prosecution Service said -

"No. You are our counsel and in charge of this case. We will not be briefing another barrister. You have made the decision and we stick by your decision."

Mr Justice Ashworth had no option but to direct the jury to acquit.

Keith spoke warmly of his association with Denis Cowley QC.

"He put his heart and soul into a case! He'd take a great deal of time and interest, making copious notes, going through everything with a fine tooth comb.

Times without number he'd invite me round to his flat in The Park. Sometimes he was still in bed! The prosecution evidence came to us in 'depositions' - i.e. statements from witnesses. Not content with that, he'd write it all out in his own note book and I'd have to go through each page with him, line by line, and work out our case compared with the prosecution case. We'd have to work out where his cross-examination was going to. It used to take hours! If nothing else I saw precisely what thoroughness was.

About lunch time we'd have a sandwich. He'd have a couple of glasses of whisky and water and I'd have two or three gin and tonics. Then we'd spend the rest of the afternoon going on and on, working into the late evening, going through the case - line by line, item by item .... "

I asked Keith about the strengths and weakness of his other 'leaders'. Was this the real basis of his legal education? Did he try to emulate these legal legends?

"You can't do that. You must be your own person, but learn and take on board the way they did things, the way they spoke, their attitudes and try to take in as much as you could to increase, implement and help your own vocabulary, your own presentation and your own persuasiveness. It was a joy to hear some of these people. "

Was he prepared to name names?

"Gladly. Like Denis, I was a big note taker, but listening to Brian Appleby's [Now His Honour Judge Appleby QC] *brilliant cross-examinations, opening and final speeches, you'd think he been up all night making copious notes! In fact he'd probably barely scribbled 25 words on a whole set of depositions. He didn't need to take notes because it was all in his head. Extraordinary!*

At the end of prosecuting one murder trial, Patrick Bennett QC was equally efficient with a similar shorter style. He asked the defendant just five questions. I wouldn't have dared be so brief, but he had such a quick brain and knew that further questions would not have helped his case. "

A Leader generally examines 'in chief' all the important witnesses himself, but Keith recalled occasions when a particular Leader made sure the Junior kept awake. This was when he was Junior to Edwin Jowitt who later became Mr Justice Jowitt.

"To my horror, at the very last minute when it was time for a witness to give his evidence, Edwin turned to me and casually said 'You take this witness, Keith.' This happened upon more than one occasion with no prior warning. Result: you learned to be completely prepared all the time to examine any witness because you never knew

which one it would be! After taking Silk, I copied his example and
sometimes surprised my own Juniors."

At one gathering, in jocular mood, Keith introduced me to his 'boss'.
A puzzle, since I did not think judges had bosses beyond the remote
and grand Lord High Chancellor, but this was not Lord Irvine, this was
His Honour Judge Christopher Pitchers, the 'resident judge' of the
Nottingham Crown Court. In the late 1960's and into the 1970's, Keith
did a great deal of work for Derbyshire Prosecutions Department at
Derby Crown Court. Eventually, Christopher Pitchers came on the
scene and began to replace Keith for prosecutions.

"I didn't mind because I could concentrate on my work in
Nottingham. Christopher was another positive influence. A powerful
speaker and very good prosecutor."

Appropriately, Judge Pitchers spoke the first tribute to Judge
Matthewman on the occasion of his retirement on December 22nd,
2000.

I have always felt that the most disappointing aspect of a
funeral is the sad fact of the principal guest being unable to hear and
appreciate all the kind and generous comments laid at his door. So it
was, with great satisfaction, that I enjoyed the privilege that morning of
seeing Keith, sitting there in the midst of the multitude, alive and well,
with all the modest demeanour he could muster, soaking up the deluge
of affection and praise. A range of entertaining lawyers and non-
lawyers, with a judicial use of humour, stood up, one by one and
skilfully expressed their warm appreciation of his life's work.

I say 'privilege' because Court One, the largest court in the
Nottingham Crown Court, was literally overflowing with some staff
actually crowding outside of an open door. The room was packed full
of judges, Silks, junior barristers, solicitors, clerks, ushers,
representatives of the Probation Service and Crown Prosecution
Service. Judge Pitchers said -

" I first met Keith Matthewman in the robing room at Derby in
1965. I found him friendly, down to earth, full of common-sense, no
side to him at all and those, I have to say - and those of us old enough
to remember those days will confirm it - were qualities which you did
not find in all members of the Bar or, dare I say it, judges, all those
years ago.

Thereafter we were often opponents, always having the right kind of contest in criminal cases, no quarter given in court, but out of court, complete friendliness and co-operation.

On a personal level, those of us that sit here will miss him very much indeed. He is a most enlivening and enjoyable companion. The lunch table will be a great deal less fun in his absence and we will miss his company out of court."

In 'A Judge for the Victim' we have seen Judge Matthewman in disagreement with Mr Justice Rougier, but this same High Court Judge, as a Silk was another respected and esteemed mentor -

"He taught me how to get witnesses to say what you want them to say. Richard never shouted, screamed or bullied, not that silks do, but he had the facility of asking questions in a silken voice; in a charming way, such that he could persuade a witness to go along with him and make them feel that, perhaps, they were being churlish if they didn't agree with him.

I admired the advocacy of a Leicester practitioner, Brian Woods. [Eventually His Honour Judge Woods of the Derby Crown Court] *His mitigations at the Derbyshire Assizes in front of a High Court Judge were a delight to hear. You'd just sit there and be mesmerised by his superb delivery, his vocabulary, his syntax, his approach in that persuasive, smooth, silver tongue. Every sentence was beautifully constructed. Every word was thought about before he said it. I'm not sure if he wrote it all down, but it just flowed.*

Brian Smedley had similar qualities, strong, persuasive and again a joy to hear. John Owen [later Mr Justice Owen] *was another good Silk. Igor Judge was one of the best cross-examiners I've ever come across. Other Silks, especially those who took Silk after me, too numerous to mention, also had an influence on my practice and advocacy.*

*Not for a minute am I suggesting that I'm as good as these stalwarts of the courtroom, but one learns from them, **not all** the tricks of the trade (you have some inherent within yourself) but a lot. I'm deeply grateful for their examples."*

In 1978 Keith Matthewman took soundings from senior colleagues and judges on the subject of his taking Silk. 'Go for it!' was the general response. To become a QC a barrister needed two High Court Judges to act as sponsors. One of them, the Senior Presiding Judge of the Midland and Oxford Circuit, Mr Justice May said -

*"Well, I'll have to tell you that I'm already sponsoring two others and you will make three. It may be that the currency is being devalued and, don't forget, Keith, I **will** have to tell the truth about you!"*

Fortunately the truth was in Keith's favour because only a small proportion of applicants for Silk were successful upon first application.

So what is 'silk' and what does it mean? A Silk is an experienced advocate and a member of a small legal elite, about one tenth of all barristers. In Keith's day a Silk always appeared in serious complex cases leading Junior counsel. Silks obviously commanded higher fees because of the importance of the cases in which they were engaged.

As to the magic and mystery, literally, 'Silk' originally referred to the very expensive black silken gown worn by the prestigious barrister, but in modern times not all the gowns are made of real silk.

Being 'called **within** the Bar', involved for Keith, a visit to the House of Lords in April 1979 to be sworn in by the then Lord Chancellor, Lord Elwyn-Jones. After that he had to go the court of the Lord Chief Justice, Lord Justice Lane and bow four times. One bow to the Bench, one bow each side and one final bow to the people sitting in the public gallery. This ancient ceremony had to be repeated in other High Courts.

Keith took Silk at the same time as another colleague and long standing helpful friend - Igor Judge, now Lord Justice Judge (Senior Presiding Judge for England and Wales) who invited Keith to change into his new silk robes in Mr Judge's chambers in London.

Congratulations came from many other colleagues and friends including Anthony Scrivener QC who had been through the ceremony himself in 1975. He made a well remembered ribald comment to Keith during the tense moments just before he was called, about to move forward and bow - *"Don't your balls look funny in tights!"*

Tense it may have been, but Keith had to smile.

Having just received a warrant from the Lord Chancellor, Keith Matthewman is now a Silk and is pictured with Jane and Adrian standing outside the House of Lords in 1979.

This is a splendid story of great success. Here was Keith now at the pinnacle of his career as a barrister. I suggested that his parents would be bursting with pride. I was in for a surprise.

When Elizabeth Matthewman was told about her son achieving the level of a QC and shortly afterwards being invited to a garden party at Buckingham Palace, her response was rather less than gracious -

*"Why you? What have they invited **you** for?"*

It took Jane and Keith some minutes to explain to me this extraordinary response. He reminded me where he came from -

"I'm proud of being a Yorkshireman, but Yorkshire folk can be very odd. They don't care what people think and can be tactless. They can be both proud and, at the same time, embarrassed by success."
Jane -

"They can be in awe of success and not know how to deal with it. Keith's mother was steeped in honesty but was inward looking and felt inadequate. I'll never forget the retort when we told her I was having a baby - 'About time an all!' A down to earth woman. She didn't know she was being hurtful."
Keith -

"My mother was really a very pleasant person but unfortunately she came across as a somewhat jealous personality about her boys. That sounds awful but it's true. We went through our young lives on the basis that she always thought that we were trying to get above our station. It's all part of life and has made me what I am. At the end of the day it doesn't matter. It just made me push on all the harder."

But success can also bring with it painful decisions. Now a QC, Keith was in greater demand than ever. He was offered the chance to take over the London chambers of a former Solicitor General, a golden opportunity which needed serious consideration. To take full advantage of his new elevated status in the legal profession, to get 'the big London stuff' as Keith put it, he would certainly need chambers in the capital.

"As a Silk, if you are going to the top, the financial top, then you had to have a London practice to make it an utter success."

Some 15 years before he had to make a similar painful decision when a seat in the House of Commons was his for the taking. A similar opportunity which could have led on to great things. Once again Keith and Jane were plunged into deep heart searching discussions. London chambers, the promise of a smart life style were set against their comfortable home in Toton and the familiar quality of life which was to be enjoyed in Nottingham. Daily commuting to London was possible but hardly convenient. As in 1964, once again, after taking everything into careful consideration, the Nottingham practice gained the upper hand. He would stay put. Rather wistfully, Keith told me -

"At the time, I decided it wasn't for me. I was doing well in the provinces making a lot of money. Everybody knew me here ..."

I sensed a 'but' on the way -

"Hindsight is a wonderful thing. Don't get me wrong, I'm not grumbling, it was my decision - but I often wonder whether it was a mistake."

There was plenty of excitement waiting for Keith back in Derbyshire. A man he described as 'pleasant, charming and personable' was out in the countryside shooting rabbits when, suddenly, he accidentally came across two of his neighbours out in the open engaged in sexual activity. An excruciatingly embarrassing experience for all three concerned which resulted in violence, rape and murder. On first hearing this appalling episode, I assumed that the violence erupted from the humiliated man caught in the act. Not so, it was the observer who later became Keith's client, pleading guilty to rape and a double murder.

The deep and mysterious workings of the human mind are difficult to fathom, but in this particular horrific scenario the defendant said he was enraged because the woman, his neighbour, looked up and recognised him! He shot both lovers and then raped the woman who was probably already dead.

The point about this grim story is in the first line - 'Pleasant, charming and personable'. Keith told me that in his experience, murderers were the 'nicest' people to defend!

"True! Just think about it, Narvel, most of them were ordinary, decent, honest people with no previous convictions. I can hardly approve of their conduct! We're not talking about planned contract killings here, these are cases of a sudden flair up.

The rabbit shooter, brooding in his cell, was so mortified by his crime and so ashamed of what he had seen that day up in Derbyshire -

he actually tried to gouge out his own eyes! I had to go and see him ...
give him some comfort, calm him down ... it was a terrible job. "

The compassionate barrister above could be seen at odds with the popular tough perception of this same lawyer who later became Judge Matthewman - all part of the fascinating mix of this intriguing personality. In The Nottingham Evening Post, 11.3.00, Mark Patterson reflected the general view when he made two references to Keith's 'hanging judge' reputation by giving out sentences 'often above tariff'.

However, Keith has made it perfectly clear to me that he is opposed to capital punishment - *'It is too final'* and he once joked - *'I was glad to see the back of those black caps'*.

If a murderer was the best client to defend, who was the worst?

*"A fraudster, no doubt about it. If acquitted, it's to their credit, they answered the questions in court correctly because they were totally innocent all along and it had nothing at all to do with me. If convicted - it was all **my** fault! It had nothing to do with the client: the defence barrister was poor. "*

Keith took Silk in the April of 1979. In the February of that year some public service unions made a decision to cause chaos which would come to be know as 'The Winter of Discontent', remembered by paralysing strikes which, amongst other miseries, caused overflowing dustbins, dangerous, untreated icy roads and unburied dead.

In June the British electorate made a decision. They voted for a change of government which would see Margaret Thatcher as the Prime Minister for the next eleven years and the Conservatives in power for a total of 18 years.

Some years before 1979, Keith had already made a decision, forming an ambition to take Silk and become a judge before he reached the age of 50. The latter he achieved with three years to spare.

To become a judge or not to become a judge? That is the question pondered by a real life barrister, Mark Rodgers of St Mary's Chambers, Nottingham in the Radio Times 21.4.01. He was talking about the fictional barrister Kavanagh QC who, facing this dilemma was concerned that a judge may be speaking at people rather than for them. Mr Rodgers suggested that a barrister's life style may be seen as more glamorous in contrast to a judge's life style which could be seen as more sterile - *'Since a judge cannot really influence events.'* Keith Matthewman expresses a different view on this subject in Chapter 23.

Tom Heald was surprised that Keith (the first of his pupils to become a QC) became a judge so soon after becoming a Silk -
    "Normally you remain a Silk for about ten years before going on to the Bench."
    I presumed that this particular wisdom was connected with the earning power of a Silk, often being greater than that of a judge. It is a frequent refrain, heard said in the life of Keith Matthewman that he only spent so many years doing this, or just a few years doing something else. I put this point to my subject -
    "That's my style. I move on. I don't go for long term. I've always wanted to do as much as I possibly can. Retirement is yet another opportunity and I've a whole lot of interesting experiences to get through!"

Chapter 20
A Copper's Judge?

Down the long, twisting, turning path of research for this biography, occasionally I heard - 'Judge Matthewman? Oh yes, he's the copper's judge.' It did not sound like the judge I knew so I decided to investigate.

I needed to talk to a policeman who had known and observed Keith Matthewman as a barrister and a judge. The ideal candidate was Michael Holford, a policeman who had actually worked with Keith.

Since 1990, Ex Chief Superintendent, Michael F. Holford QPM FBIM has been the Head of Safety and Security at Nottingham Forest Football Club. A position made all the more necessary after the worst ever disaster in British sporting history at Hillsborough in Sheffield, when Liverpool played Nottingham Forest on April 15th 1989, which left 94 dead and 170 injured due to crushing.

Mr Holford, a bouncy and enthusiastic character, cheerfully agreed to give me information about his former colleague of whom he had fond memories. Greatly encouraged and sensing a productive interview, it was early on August 2nd in the year 2000, a pleasant day of sunshine and showers, (more sun than rain) that I set off on the long cycle journey from Belper to the City Ground in the centre of Nottingham.

Following the former route of coal from the collieries of Shipley and West Hallam, I made good use of the nice flat, and historically fascinating, cycling track along side the Nutbrook Canal. It starts in Shipley Park and, south bound, links up with the Erewash Canal which, once again, took me deep into Keith Matthewman country.

I left the canal at the point where it goes through the grounds of the Long Eaton Grammar School which stood, somewhat quiet and deserted in midsummer, but handsome and solid surmounted by its distinctive central cupola. Main roads were avoided as far as possible by cycling north east along Station Road up to Nottingham Road. Time was short, but I decided to take a quick look at some of the places which had been so vividly described to me. Just after crossing the River Erewash and into Chilwell, I turned up Stapleford Lane and right into Chetwynd Road, keeping the Central Ordnance Depot and nearby Tank Testing Track on my right.

Marton Road soon came up on the left and I was able to get a discreet look at Keith's boyhood home. Cycling on through High Road and now, an opportunity to glimpse Meadow Lane School before studying the map and finding the access to the Beeston Canal via Dovecote Lane and Trent Road.

This is a clear, traffic free path which would eventually join the Nottingham Canal and take me directly into the city centre. To my left, beyond Castle Boulevard and up the hill, the desirable area know as The Park which holds pleasant memories in the early days of Keith Matthewman, as indeed it does in the early days of this writer.

A little after Nottingham Castle came the Canal Museum, a great temptation which had to be resisted. Suddenly to my immediate left, aggressively, hard up against the canal side, towering above me, I noticed an uncompromising, stark Derbyshire gritstone, massive, mountainous wall - which somehow looked familiar.

Of course! Canal Street! This was the much abused 'back side' of my subject's place of work, the eight million pound Nottingham Crown Court which was opened by Lord Chief Justice Lane on February 3rd 1988 to replace the 1770 Shire Hall (just up the hill) now the Galleries of Justice Museum.

Architect, Paula Havard's ultra modern building came 'under attack' on Saturday February 17th in 1996 when, next to a large colour photograph of Judge Matthewman, the front page headline of The Nottingham Evening Post screamed out - NOT FIT FOR A DOG, with a sub headline - JUDGE'S VERDICT ON CITY COURT - by Simon Harrison.

During a trial for assault and affray the jury had to be repeatedly sent from the courtroom while points of law were debated. Judge Matthewman apologised to the jurors describing them as *the most important people in the building*' and added that the windowless jury room was *'not fit to keep a dog in.'*

Most of the rooms inside the building are without windows and only one of the nine criminal crown courts has access to natural light. Speaking to Simon Harrison, Judge Matthewman made wider observations that the new Crown Court was too functional and clinical, lacking the gracious charm and authority of the dignified, majestic court of yesteryear -

196

"If you build a court which looks like a coffee bar, then people will treat it as if they are in a coffee bar. When you went into the old Shire Hall you knew you were entering somewhere where something serious and solemn was going on. You don't get that feeling here."

The beautiful oaken panels of the Shire Hall certainly do give a strong atmosphere of judicial antiquity born of long past dramas in the old court room. On one quiet occasion, alone with Keith, I was admiring artistic wooden carvings and the skill of Victorian craftsmen when he casually mentioned that the building had its own ghost!

"I've never seen it myself but gather that she makes an occasional appearance."

No ghosts in the new court, but before pedalling off, I looked up to the windows on the off-chance that I might see a familiar face: there was none.

From the city centre, the east bound canal takes a sharp turn to the south where it will join the River Trent at Trent Bridge, my final destination. It is 15 minutes before my appointment at 2.00pm: just enough time for a quick lunch which reposes in the saddle bag. I leave the cycle track at the Trent Navigation Inn where it is just a short walk to the Nottingham Forest City Ground.

After a friendly welcome, I was invited to address the very senior Ex Chief Superintendent as 'Mike'. He started as a young constable in the inner City of Nottingham in 1957, the beginning of a long and varied career. By way of introduction he gave me a brief outline of this career, skipping along, lightly mentioning, almost apologetically (in typical British style) that he had been awarded the Queen's Police Medal for distinguished police service following the Miners Strike.

This major event in the history of Nottinghamshire (which has the country's second largest coalfield) lasted from March 1984 to March 1985. Mrs Thatcher appointed a new Coal Board Chairman, Ian MacGregor, who proposed to close 20 'uneconomic' pits, an action which would shed 20,000 jobs. Nottinghamshire miners resisted going on strike without a national ballot and the majority worked normally throughout the conflict. Under the leadership of Arthur Scargill, the President of the National Union of Mineworkers, hundreds of militant and illegal secondary flying pickets from Yorkshire, in pitched battles, engaged hundreds of police officers sometimes mounted and sometimes in full riot gear. The daily news showed ugly scenes of brick throwing fury and anguish as raucous, striking miners shouted 'scum' 'scabs' 'traitor' to working miners trying to get to into a colliery.

On several occasions a bitter and ranting Arthur Scargill waved his arms and denounced 'the biased decisions of Tory judges'. Perhaps he would exclude Judge Matthewman, a former left-wing politician and the grandson of a founder member of the NUM. Judge Matthewman presided over several strike related trials including the very last trial of the famous 1984-1985 Miners Strike, reported in the Nottingham Evening Post. See next page.

A policemen working with barristers was unheard of, but the Criminal Justice Act of 1967 paved the way for Detective Sergeant Michael Holford to save time and streamline justice in a cost effective way. Mike told me -

"It had never been done before and it has never been done since, but there was great optimism at the time and a belief that police officers wouldn't have to spend so much time in court giving evidence.

In my new promotion in 1968, representing the Chief Constable, I had the exacting task of preparing the prosecution paperwork for barristers, substituting for a solicitor because at that time they didn't have enough solicitors to go around to do the job.

A unique position for a policeman being accredited to sit in court like a solicitor and instruct a barrister! This was my new job, a novice pseudo-representative of the legal profession, notwithstanding that all my discipline was that of an enforcer of the law, because I had been sworn in as a constable (as all police officers are) to uphold the law and prosecute offenders and defend the peace.

For the next three years I was on the biggest learning curve of my life, improving my knowledge of the criminal law, looking at case papers, preparing statements which would support the charge, nice sheets of paper (the brief) all tied up with lovely red ribbon and handed to a barrister - such as Keith Matthewman."

No evidence offered on assembly charges

A DECISION not to press prosecution of 19 men for unlawful assembly at Babbington Colliery, Nottingham, during the miners' strike was made after day-long discussions at Nottingham Crown Court yesterday.

And the position of 62 other demonstrators due to appear in a series of seven trials as a result of incidents at Mansfield, Babbington, Warsop, Silverhill and Manton is to receive "anxious consideration".

Decisions will be notified to their solicitors in due course, said Mr John Milmo, QC, prosecuting, offering no evidence after an unemployed Bulwell man, a Worksop miner and 17 Yorkshire miners had pleaded Not guilty to unlawfully assembling at Babbington on July 25, 1984, with intent to carry out a common purpose, to endanger the peace.

Entering Not guilty verdicts in the case of David John Deverill, 22, of Leen View Court, Crabtree Farm Estate; Clayton Tindle, 27, of John Street, Worksop, and the 17 Yorkshiremen, Judge Keith Matthewman, QC, said: "I take the view in all the circumstances that that is a just and sensible decision."

With their consent, the 19 defendants were all bound over in the sum of £100 to keep the peace for 12 months.

Mass picket

Mr Milmo said 57 people were arrested on July 27 after a two-hour mass picket at Babbington Colliery. All but two came from Yorkshire.

Attempts were made to cordon the demonstrators, to allow free passage along the A610, access to miners wanting to work and generally to preserve the peace.

NCB lorries were stoned, a number of working miners' cars in the colliery car park were dented by missiles, one working miner was assaulted and others threatened, said Mr Milmo.

It was not possible to identify any of these defendants as taking part in these activities, and it was not suggested they could be regarded as ring leaders or instigators.

●Judge Matthewman ... 'sensible decision'

There were insufficient policemen to cope with the demonstrators.

The alleged involvement of these defendants related to pushing and shoving officers in the cordons, breaking free and encouraging others to do so.

Of the 57 charged, 43 had been committed for trial after a seven-day hearing before a stipendiary magistrate.

At that stage, the prosecution was entitled to conclude there was unlawful assembly and that each defendant was involved,

But although a number of men had been convicted of unlawful assembly in Nottingham on their own confession, Not guilty verdicts had been recorded in a case which finished last week.

Following a 12-week trial, the jury had then returned unanimous verdicts in the case of eight defendants after a retirement of certainly no more than 15 minutes.

Mr Michael Mansfield, defending, said the agreement of the defendants to be bound over was not an admission on their part that there was an unlawful assembly or that they played a part in it.

The waiting for trial had played havoc with their lives for over a year, he said.

Nottingham Evening Post

Yet again I was treated to happy memories of the notorious Robing Room, the fun and the laughter, as Mike, over a cup of coffee, discussed with solicitors and barristers the close detail of cases in preparation for a trial. But not all the work was done in office hours.

It was one Sunday afternoon at about 6.00pm when Mike, after a busy week, was relaxing at home, sinking deeper and deeper into the comfort of his favourite easy chair, half listening to 'Sing Something Simple'. Suddenly, his peace and rest was rudely interrupted by the ominous shrill ring of the telephone! It was Keith Matthewman! He was calling from a luxury flat in The Park, the home of Denis Cowley QC - no less, the barrister who was leading him in an important case.

"Michael! Sorry to ring you at home, but since you're instructing me in this case I need you. Denis is very angry because we haven't got this and we've not got that piece of evidence .... he's going up the wall .... and I've been up all night! I need you here - now! Can you get here in ten minutes?"

"From Mapperley? I think it'll be a bit more than ten minutes, Keith, but I will come straight away."

Michael Holford described Denis Cowley as a 'much respected master of perfection, but also a tough slave-driver' so, without delay, he hot footed over to that posh part of Nottingham, the lush, leafy area known as The Park to be met by -

" .... a bleary eyed Keith, looking worn and tired, being worked like a dog, going through papers over and over again. This was an important and serious case in which a conviction would result in a lengthy prison sentence. They wanted my help to be completely prepared for Court at nine o'clock in the morning - the very next day! We had to do justice to the evidence."

Three hours later Michael did his best to explain to his wife why he had suddenly 'chased off' on a Sunday evening -

"Look, I had no choice, you don't argue with the likes of Denis Cowley QC! We had to get this sorted for the morning."

To cut a long story short, all their work paid off. After a lengthy trial the guilty were convicted and imprisoned for a long time. But it was the sight of Keith Matthewman, the consummate bright professional which stayed in Mike's mind -

"It was a tough case. Denis raised issues, Keith took exception and was slapped down - and came back with further arguments. That's how it went."

Mike amused me with stories from the early days when Keith was 'cutting his teeth' on the minor end of the criminal law in the Magistrates Court defending the worldly wise 'Ladies of the Night' who inhabited Arkwright Street and other areas of the Meadows.

"A very difficult job because Keith, having to meet high standards in chambers, was up against the main prosecution witness, often an experienced detective who was going to say exactly what he saw. Such confident evidence would be hard to refute, but occasionally Keith was able to cast a doubt in the Magistrate's mind and get an acquittal."

I speculated on the chances of an innocent woman being arrested for prostitution? *'Non-existent!'* was Mike's firm reply.

With heart-felt, sincere admiration, Michael Holford recalled his prosecution days instructing Keith Matthewman -

"He gave it his absolute 100% effort and attention! I don't think I've ever seen a better prepared counsel. He had great ability to articulate, speak succinctly and with authority. This was particularly important when some of the judges were not easy to convince and could be quite crushing in their comments to hapless barristers who needed a thick skin to do that job. Sometimes I used to shudder at the sharp riposte from a judge responding to a vexed legal point - 'You don't know what you're talking about' snapped one judge to a man with years of legal training behind him!"

But in order to be an effective prosecutor, I suggested that the barrister needed full support and a lot of hard work from his solicitor -

*"Indeed! I was instructing Keith on one particular day at Lincoln Assizes when, suddenly - 'Michael, on this item we need additional evidence.' That meant 'Get on and do it - **now**, not tomorrow'. It was very much 'time driven' and I had to move quick. It was a lengthy trial, Keith gave it his all, and after weeks of research and hard work we expected a good chance of victory because we don't bring a case lightly. I particularly remember the judge saying in his summing up -*

'I am the judge of the law, you, members of the jury, are the judges of the facts.'"

Alas, in the end, the defendant was acquitted.

"Keith Matthewman was not a good looser! Deeply disappointed because he had been passionate about this case at Lincoln. However we live in the real world and have to accept the occasional perverse verdict of a jury. From a prosecution and police point of view, we wanted a barrister who wanted to win and we certainly had one in Keith Matthewman!"

At this point I sprung my principal question. Was Keith Matthewman a favourite prosecutor for the police? A pro-police, copper's barrister? Was there any truth in this occasionally heard expression - a copper's judge?

Mike answered by recalling his very next case after Lincoln, two days later, when he was instructing a different barrister. Guess who was appearing for the defence?

*"Keith Matthewman!! An incredible situation where 48 hours before I'd been instructing a barrister who was working **with** me, prosecuting, wanting to win the case, fairly within the laws of evidence to send the culprit to jail: now, this same man is going to make my life as difficult as possible, using all his formidable professional skills to work **against** me - if possible putting a criminal back on the streets! Remember: Keith doesn't like to lose - no, not one bit. He was ruthless!*

In years past as a police officer, I've stood in the witness box myself and been cross-examined without mercy by Keith Matthewman the skilled advocate and daunting opponent. Other police officers learned that when Keith was defending, they were in for a hard time in that witness box.

*Those who said that Keith had a pre-disposition to be friendly to the police did so on the basis that he carried out his professional duties as a prosecution counsel with a great deal of sincerity and vigour. What they **didn't** see, as I often saw in my unique position, was when the boot was on the other foot, he could be just as vicious defending. He fought tooth and nail for every one of his clients who pleaded not guilty; yet minutes later in the Robing Room he was chatting, laughing and joking with no hard feelings."*

A copper's judge?

"A copper's judge? Never! It stems from the fact that he is seen as a strong supporter of law and order. Judge Matthewman is held in high esteem, not just by police officers, but by the local press and many others who observe our Criminal Justice System. He's regarded as a 'no nonsense judge' who tells it like it is! As we've all discovered, [See cutting below from Nottingham Evening Post 26.07.00] a tough judge is also tough on the police as well as the wrong-doer. We had to be scrupulously accurate to get all our facts in order and correct."

City judge spares police

NOTTS police have escaped the embarrassment of having one of their own officers jailed by a judge.

Last month Judge Keith Matthewman threatened to jail an unnamed officer after hearing statements he requested from the police had not been obtained.

Last month he adjourned a case against teenage burglar so he could hear the impact of the crimes on their victims. But when no statements were produced on Monday, the Nottingham Crown Court judge was furious.

He said: "The police are not immune from arrest and are not immune from action for contempt of court. I don't expect my instructions to be disobeyed. They will do as I say, otherwise they will take the consequences."

Yesterday, the case was listed again and the statements were duly produced.

Three victims said they might never get over it. A fourth was considering moving after the break-in.

Meden Vale, near Warsop, admitted four charges of burglary and one of attempted burglary. He asked for 28 similar offences to be taken into consideration. Most of the crimes happened in Sutton-in-Ashfield and were to pay for heroin.

Julie Warburton, for said: "He accepts what he has done is disgusting. He is now drug free."

The judge said had HE been older he would have got five years — and deserved every moment.

Judge Matthewman added: "Sentences in this country are generally far too low for dwelling house burglary. Perhaps it's time there was a rethink."

He ordered to serve three years, three months and a further six months from a previous detention order.

The conversation turned to the time when Judge Matthewman threatened to send a police officer to prison in June 2000 for failing to provide requested statements. He told the officer -

"I don't expect my instructions to be disobeyed. They will do as I say, otherwise, they will take the consequences!"

I see nothing has changed much from the days of William Howitt Secondary Modern School! Mike said that the police force have a healthy respect for the power of judges and went on to recall an incident in which he was personally involved.

A High Court Judge, very senior in age and experience was presiding in the Shire Hall, when, suddenly, the whole building started to tremble due to the deafening roar of a low swooping, thundering jet aircraft. For a few seconds it was so loud that His Lordship could not hear himself speak, nor could he hear the speech of counsel. Immediately incensed and convinced that the jet was flying below the legal limit, with temper and great agitation, he screamed to his clerk to have the matter investigated. A Group Captain [the rank above Wing Commander and below Air Commodore] in charge of the guilty base, somewhere in Lincolnshire, was ordered to present himself before Mr Justice X at 9.00am the next day to give an account and explain the 'appalling conduct' of one of his pilots.

This particular senior officer was quite prepared to assume full responsibility for the actions of those under his command, but found the judge's order simply incredible! Regardless of any long standing duties or appointments in his diary for 9.00am the next day, all must be swept aside to make way for an early start; a long journey into the busy and crowded City of Nottingham, to stand before the majesty and power of the law, in the form of a furious judge!

*"Not to mention the time consuming journey back to Lincolnshire. And for what? Some idiot dips a bit low over a court house and rattles a dusty old wig ... Are you **sure** about this? Damn it all - I won't go!! It's dashed inconvenient! **No!** Go back and tell the old fool - NO!"*

"I'm sorry, sir, I'm afraid I must insist."
Replied the Police Officer.

"Insist all you like! I've work to do - a base to run. Good afternoon: the door is over there."

The calm, ponderous officer, slow of speech, still standing his ground, at attention, with hands behind his back, did a very British deep knee bend before significantly clearing his throat -

"Let me try and put it to you this way, Group Captain; either you voluntarily travel to Nottingham tomorrow morning, in time to be in the box at nine o'clock prompt, or, I will be forced to take you there, under arrest, in a police car - possibly hand-cuffed!

Seriously! Failure to obey an express order from one of Her Majesty's judges is seen as a contempt of court which may result in you going to prison. I'll be leaving you now, sir, to reflect upon your position."

Just before the court appearance, counsel advised the Group Captain -

"Please do try to be respectful to His Lordship, who is not, this morning a fan of the RAF, and tender your humble apologies."
This was done together with a regretful and diplomatic explanation of why His Lordship's court was rudely disturbed and shaken the day before. It was a mistake and the pilot would be - *"... given suitable advice!"*

In a measured and formal response, the judge, sounding rather like the angry prince in 'Romeo and Juliet', said -
"If your fighter aircraft ever disturb the peace of my court again - I will have you brought back here, in contempt of court, and your freedom will pay the forfeit of the peace. For this time you may depart away."

To conclude, Mike told me -
"I saw a white faced, contrite Group Captain stepping down and leaving the Shire Hall."

Michael Holford has now been retired from the Police Force for eleven years and has followed the career of Judge Matthewman through occasional appearances on television, listening to him on the radio, reading about him in the local and national press together with hearing first hand accounts from former colleagues who still give evidence in court.
"Personally and professionally, these experiences of preparing cases held me in good stead hereafter in my police career. No other policeman was ever allowed to do the work of a legally qualified solicitor, a unique opportunity and at the end of it I was promoted to Inspector."

I asked Mike to briefly clarify the police ranks. An Inspector looks after a team of police officers including constables and sergeants. After Chief Inspector comes a Superintendent who is in charge of a sub-division of several hundred officers. Michael Holford became a Divisional Police Commander in 1986 with the rank of Chief Superintendent, in charge of a complete division, about 600 officers and 400 civilians.

Escorting me from his office, through the maze of secure corridors and eventually outside to unchain the bicycle, Michael Holford was summing up on the judge who was no 'copper's judge' -

"We could do with more judges like Keith Matthewman. I've never known another one quite like him who was so fearless and could grasp things so quickly. Few judges are prepared to be as outspoken and put their profession on the line about matters which affect the judicial system. His heart-beat was, and still is in tune with that of society."

With that candid and heartfelt commendation still ringing in my ears, I mounted and waved goodbye to my hospitable and helpful former police officer.

Belper! Which way? I decided there was just enough daylight left (it was well past four o'clock) to enjoy a high quality, traffic free route home. Back on to the Nottingham Canal tow path which runs into the Beeston Canal tow path. On this return journey I avoided the busy streets of Chilwell by continuing to follow a well metalled canal route which, alas, eventually deteriorated into a non-cycle-friendly, many stiled, very rough footpath through the, lovely, but seemingly never ending Attenborough Nature Reserve - quite magnificent in the early evening sunshine. Any observing, intelligent crows would be puzzled to see me navigating south-west to get to Belper. It would be about 8.00pm when I reached Trent Lock and rested at the Steamboat Inn for a much needed meal. The final leg took me due north up along the Erewash Canal. Two hours later, in darkness, I was slowly struggling up the steep hill to Openwoodgate and back down into Belper.

A copper too far? Not at all. It was the end of a very enjoyable and successful day.

Ex Chief Superintendent Michael Holford QPM.

Chapter 21
Doddering Old Fools

These words were used by Judge Matthewman in The Nottingham Evening Post 19.7.93 to describe the perception of judges! In the Express and Star 16.4.93 he referred to them as *'A bunch of out of touch old duffers'*, called them *'Fuddy duddies'* in the Guardian in April 1993, *'Pompous, pratty and toffee nosed'* during a Radio Nottingham interview in October 1999.

In these high profile utterances, Keith was **not** abusing his friends and colleagues on the Bench, but, on the contrary, suggesting to Andrew Culf in The Guardian that by appearing on television he would be able to -

"Disabuse the public of these unfortunate ideas they have about the judiciary; ideas of aloofness which are constantly fed to them by the media. Judges live in the modern world and most are modern thinking."

In spite of his strong support of the regalia, dignity and tradition, he told Judy Cullimore in the Nottingham Evening Post that -

"I can see no reason why we should be morose and pompous as portrayed by camera shots of judges processing in ceremony with long wigs which give the impression of antiquity, a feeling that we are not efficient, an image of living in the past. I may wear an 18th century wig but my head is very much in the present!"

In 1992 Mike Morley had executive responsibility for a range of network and regional current affairs and documentary programmes at Central Television. Through various newspaper articles and local radio he gradually became aware of a very unusual phenomena - a controversial and outspoken judge. Unusual, because until recent years, as former barrister Rosalind English put it -

"English judges have cocooned themselves in a web of restrictions known as the Kilmuir Rules which, conveniently, forbade any member of the Bench from speaking to the media. In the days of reverential journalism, that was a perfect formula. The silence of the judges kept them aloof and safe from criticism."
'BBC Worldwide' July 1994.

In the year of Keith's birth, 1936, the general complacent attitude was expressed by the then Lord Chief Justice, Lord Hewart, who defended the immunity of judges from tough questions when he said -

"His Majesty's judges are satisfied with the almost universal admiration in which they are held."

Even after the Lord Chancellor, Lord Mackay of Clashfern, lifted the ban on judges speaking out in public without permission and the scrapping of the Kilmuir Rules, Rosalind English still found that most judges refused to be interviewed -

"Lest their comments be quoted out of context in an unsympathetic piece. The few judges who did condescend to see me fended off mildly critical questions with a salvo of blandishments and platitudes - with the exception of Judge Matthewman - one of the few who is making an effort to rescue the public image of his profession.

Keith Matthewman QC is passionately anxious to demonstrate that judges are human beings after all. This might be due to his daily exposure to the raw end of life, the mad, bad and desperate. His unjudicial humility might also be a result of the fact that as a Crown Court judge he is obliged to leave the final decision to 12 members of the common public - the jury."
BBC Worldwide 1994.

Ms English, who also interviewed Judge Matthewman on the BBC World Service in 1994, goes on to make the point that having been protected for so long, judges are now ill equipped to defend themselves from the growing intolerance and frequent excoriation from a hostile press who paint the judiciary as 'out of touch, doddering old fools' - a description which hardly fits the Judge Matthewman I know, who has the drive and disposition of a man more than 20 years younger.

One interviewer, recalling the judge who once famously said 'Who are the Beatles?' attempted to prove a point by asking Keith on Radio Leeds to name all the Spice Girls. Somewhat disappointed he found that Judge Matthewman had actually heard of the pop group, but was gratified that he could not name the famous singers. Keith said -

*"I expect that many people in my age bracket in an assortment of jobs would fail your test, but, as a matter of interest - can **you** give me the names of the Everly Brothers?"*

The interviewer had heard of the singing duo, but was unable to recall Phil and Don. As a barrister, Keith was once upbraided by the judge when he referred to 'motorcycle gear' -

"Gear! What, exactly do you mean by 'gear', Mr Matthewman?"

In these instances, I suggested that possibly the judge is not so much ignorant as exercising his responsibility to clarify terms for the benefit of the jury. Keith agreed, but pointed out that some judges can be deliberately obtuse and pompous regarding terms of popular culture -

"Also you can get an element of 'showing off', 'one-upmanship' and trying to be smarter than the barrister."

Judge Benson made a point about the past scarcity of judges which may have added to their remote, out-of-touch image -

"With so few judges 50 years ago you hardly ever came across them. You had a vague impression of erudite, aloof old men living in ivory towers on a private income. Only a few years back, when I went on the Bench in 1992 there were 70 High Court Judges and about the same number of Circuit Judges. Now with 104 High Court Judges and 550 Circuit Judges you're much more likely to meet a judge."

In the Express and Star interview of 16.4.93, Peter Rhodes put it to Judge Matthewman that -

"You may not be from the mould of public school and Oxbridge and you are certainly not an 'out of touch old duffer', but you do inhabit a world which has been by-passed by public awareness. When somebody breaks ranks like the outspoken Judge James Pickles he becomes a pariah. Could this happen to you?"

Refusing to make any reference to his fellow Yorkshireman, Judge Pickles, the schoolmaster side of Keith stoutly and effectively defended his growing public reputation to Mr Rhodes -

"I think the public ought to be better informed about the practice of the courts and the judiciary. I do make public pronouncements but don't aim to be controversial or do any show-business which would detract from the dignity of my office."

Such a pronouncement reached Frances Gibb, the legal correspondent of The Times, 12.4.93, when she wrote -

"Judge Matthewman recently protested about inadequate sentences for joy-riders and urged Parliament to consider a change in the law."

Privately, Keith gave me a more hard-hitting response to the issue of his public perception. He said he did not care what people thought about him!

"I know that sounds awful but it's true. I plough my own furrow. I go my own way and if people don't like it they can lump it! If people don't like me, I'm not bothered, they can avoid me. I don't particularly want to be liked - I really mean that. People's opinions of me cut no ice. Perhaps this is a bad thing but it's my quirk. Life is easy if you don't care what people think about you!"

Receiving this startling statement, an unbelievable and untenable position, I looked to Jane in the hope of receiving some mitigating clarification.

*"If Keith has an epitaph on his grave-stone it should read - 'I don't care!' He's a lovely dear man and I love him to death, but it does worry me, always coming back to this theme - 'I don't care' - because he **does** care!"*

When that particular transcript had been checked and returned, Keith had written underneath Jane's last comment in a bold hand -

"No I don't!!"

As a humble schoolmaster I was awe-struck during the few occasions when Keith invited me to lunch with his colleagues in the impressive judge's dining room at the Nottingham Crown Court. Sitting at the massive wooden table which created a vast distance between the judicial diners, a magnificent panoramic view of old Nottingham could be enjoyed through an ultra modern colossal window. The eye was drawn up high to the lofty, 15th century, perpendicular St Mary's Church tower and the Old Shire Hall which both crown the steep rock of the Lace Market area. A forest of roofs indicated the noble houses which were once the pride of great families.

The generous courtesy and consideration from these prestigious 'lords of law' soon put me at my ease and eventually I was able to assess an independent and collegiate view of my subject.

His Honour Judge Richard Benson defended Keith's high profile.

"I've heard it said that Keith is 'a bit of a loose cannon', and no doubt some people resent his publicity - not having had any themselves! We're all different. I try to keep my head below the parapet but Keith is outspoken and never a man not to call a spade a shovel. Keith is something of a non-conformist and what is wrong with individuality? Who is to judge what is the right thing to do? Who indeed is to judge the judges? Are we all to be automatons?"

Retired Judge, His Honour Tom Heald, once the Secretary and later President of the Council of Circuit Judges, took the view that the Lord Chancellor's directions on publicity were out of date. He told me -

"On the subject of broadcasting and press interviews I side with my former pupil, Keith. If judges sensibly give explanations of what they have done, then we would become more user friendly and show ourselves in a more human frame. Keith Matthewman's occasional appearance on radio and TV, expressing his views, is of benefit to the judiciary as a whole and gives the public a better understanding of how the judicial mind works."

On one occasion, going through the numerous newspaper articles in a scrap-book of cuttings which chart Keith's career, we came across a regular column in The Guardian entitled 'Male Chauvinist Pigs'. In this particular week the subject was a rape case -

"She went to investigate and was grabbed, pulled on to the bed, and raped. Her 20 month old son was asleep in the bed at the time. In mitigation, the defending barrister said -

'There was at least no actual physical violence in the second case and no weapon was used.'"

Here comes the big surprise: the barrister was Keith Matthewman! With considerable interest we both digested and pondered these words from the past and I was treated to the small drama of an experienced Judge Matthewman reprimanding a younger Keith Matthewman QC.

*"My God! What on earth was I saying? She was **raped**! The poor woman was raped!"*

This is a good place to introduce you to Julie Dunn. In 1991 Julie was observing a rape trial in Court 5 at Nottingham Crown Court. Julie had a job to do and handed the usher a note explaining that she was a researcher for the Channel 4 'Dispatches' programme which was investigating men accused of several rapes. Each case was tried without any mention of other rape charges. Julie was appalled with the outcome in some of the trials -

"Clever barristers can win an acquittal. In one case, just after the jury had given their 'not guilty' verdict, I was dismayed to hear the prosecution counsel stand up and say -

'Your Honour, may I request that the defendant be remanded in custody pending three further charges of rape.'

I well remember that moment because of the horrific expression on the faces of jurors knowing they had probably released a guilty man onto the streets. Some jurors were in tears."

Judge Matthewman was intrigued to learn of this proposed documentary and the Channel 4 researcher sitting in his court. He wanted to know more. The usher returned and gave Julie a note summoning her into the Judicial Presence -

"Oh no! He wanted to see me! What is a judge going to say to me? I was petrified. Nervous and inexperienced, I wasn't ready for this. As it turned out I needn't have worried because, once in his chambers, he was welcoming and friendly -

'Hello, Julie, come in and sit down. Tell me all about your programme.'

I explained that it was aimed towards victims because we felt that justice was suffering. We hear a lot of fuss about wrongful convictions but nobody seems to make much noise about the guilty getting off.

Judges usually keep their personal views to themselves and we only seem to hear from them when they make a bizarre comment, so I was surprised and delighted that he agreed with me in such an enthusiastic and outspoken way. I said - 'If only we could get a judge to say that on television.' Suddenly he replied with -'I'd say it!' I nearly fell off my chair!"

Lynn Ferguson, Julie's boss in London, could not believe her good luck.

"Are you sure, Julie? You're joking! A serving judge is prepared to make statements like that on national television? This I must see!"

And see she did. A meeting was arranged in which the three had a long chat in which Lynn, who had expected to hear the usual careful, cautious language was impressed with Judge Matthewman's -

" ... bravery, honesty and having the guts to speak up for these women."

After a great deal of research and hard work the programme called 'Getting Away with Rape' was screened. Julie told me -

"Keith was fabulous! He made a profound statement -

'Someone wrongfully acquitted of a crime is equally as bad as someone being wrongfully convicted of a crime.'

We received loads of letters from the public and, in my opinion, largely due to Keith's contribution to the programme, the documentary won the Royal Television Society Award for Best Journalism.

This was the beginning of a friendship and trust which built up over the years between me and Keith. He knew our heart was in the right place, that our work was 'victim orientated', that we didn't stitch people up or trick them into saying anything. So he was very helpful in other programmes regarding legal points."

I enjoyed my bubbly interview with Julie Dunn, a very sincere, down-to-earth, amusing and entertaining character. She was so thrilled to have stumbled upon her 'outspoken, plain-speaking judge' and emphasised his total lack of snobbery -

"There was little me, just a commoner and never once did I feel that he ever looked down on me ... like the time he took me to lunch ..."

The following is much the same adventure which I experienced in the Judge's Dining Room but Julie gave the story a more colourful and candid spin -

"In response to a question, Keith had said something about 'we can deal with that later' and I wasn't even sure that we were actually on our way to lunch. There we were, twisting and turning along this maze of judicial corridors, somewhere deep in the bowls of the Nottingham Crown Court. Suddenly: we were in this big room, great window and ten judges sitting around this massive table all looking at me! It was like the Supreme Court! All males and I barely knew Keith at that time. I was mortified but he said cheerily -

'Hello everybody. This is Julie, a researcher from Channel 4.'
Going scarlet with shaking knees, I forced a smile and struggled out a weak 'Hello' to this eminent judicial assembly.
'Come over here, Julie, and help yourself to a drink.' said Keith and added 'Are you all right?'
In a small voice I said -
'It's just that I'm embarrassed and a bit nervous.'
Keith boomed to his colleagues as much as to me, -
'Don't be embarrassed, Julie, everybody's friendly here!'

Eventually I managed a tomato juice and a little something to eat. I felt like a lost child. They asked me all sorts of questions but Keith was so nice. He guided the conversation to make sure that I was never uncomfortable or out of my depth. After a while we were all laughing and joking."

With the growing public outrage over a minority of juveniles getting away with persistent re-offending and making life increasingly miserable for the suffering majority, (See 'Laughing at the Law') Mike Morley wrote to Keith Matthewman in 1992 to see if the judge would consent to air his strident views about the behaviour of teenagers on camera.

"It was unheard of for a serving judge to comment on anything other than the case they were presiding over - and very often not even then! I fully expected to receive short shrift; to be told about protocol, custom and practice, but as it turned out, I was more than pleasantly surprised!

Instead of Keith launching into a predictable speech on how bad the youth of today were, he unleashed this blistering attack on how poorly the Home Office was coping with the demands of juvenile crime, how he wished to lay out stinging punishments that would halt kids on the road to crime, but how his hands were tied, and instead the best he was allowed to do was to pass unacceptably low sentences dictated by Parliament and the Home Office.

This gave me the backbone of one of the most important documentaries I ever made. We called the programme - 'Caution - Our Hands Are Tied'."

Rapists are walking free, claims judge

A NOTTINGHAM crown court judge has given his backing to a television programme which claims that too many rapists are being freed by the courts.

And Judge Keith Matthewman has called for changes to the way victims are cross-examined, particularly in relation to their previous sexual history.

In Channel 4's *Dispatches* on Wednesday, Judge Matthewman agrees that many defendants in rape cases are being wrongly set free.

"It may very well be that as judges we ought perhaps to tighten up on the sort of cross examination that you appear to say we are allowing of the complainant.

"If we are allowing questions that are unfair, then we are allowing a state of affairs to exist which favours guilty defendants.

"And if that is so, it shouldn't be allowed," said Judge Matthewman.

The programme examines cases of acquaintance or "date" rape heard by courts in London and Nottingham.

In those before the Old Bailey, all those accused of stranger rape were convicted. In cases of acquaintance rape the figure was just 32%.

The programme features three men, each of whom has raped several women, and in almost every case has been acquitted.

Professor David Canter, of the University of Surrey, said: "If somebody who is guilty is let off, then they learn from that process.

"Next time round they are a bit more slick about it, have thought it through a bit more, they know what to expect."

Professor Canter is an expert on the psychological profiling of offenders.

Nottingham Evening Post January 1991

As we have seen in 'Laughing at the Law', Mr Morley exposed how the police and judges had to follow Home Office guidelines and give hard-core juvenile offenders chance after chance after chance ...

"Some kids were committing seven to ten serious crimes before receiving any punishment at all. Keith Matthewman was the first credible figure to expose this scandal - and he pulled no punches! His criticism of the Criminal Justice System touched a public nerve. His

comments received national publicity, the programme secured exceptionally high ratings and ultimately a Royal Television Award, the highest acclaim available. But most important: the long suffering public were rewarded with a U-turn in Home Office policy.

At the end of it all I was mighty pleased with myself and considered it quite a coup to have got a judge to have been so outspoken.

I then realised it was the other way round! Keith Matthewman had simply seized my programme and used it as leverage to get what he wanted, an improvement to the Criminal Justice System. He had no burning desire to bathe himself in TV exposure, but had seen a real chance of using TV to force 'the powers that be' into changing their will to suit his and the public's beliefs."

Judge to deliver his verdict in weekly television slot

Andrew Culf
Media Correspondent

A JUDGE with a reputation for tough sentencing is to become the first serving member of the judiciary to have a regular weekly television slot.

Judge Keith Matthewman, QC, a circuit judge in the Midlands, is to air his views on crime and punishment in a programme to be edited by Mike Morley, the producer of Central Television's Dennis Nilsen documentary, which the Home Office tried to ban.

Judges have previously been discouraged from appearing regularly on television, and few did so, apart from Judge James Pickles, who gave his trenchant views on an ad hoc basis.

Mr Morley says Judge Matthewman's agreement represents a positive approach towards openness, which is being encouraged by the Lord Chief Justice, Lord Taylor, and the Lord Chancellor's Department.

Mr Morley said: "I was very impressed with the judge's comments and openness, and asked how he would feel about the opportunity to comment on a weekly basis. At first he thought it would not be possible, but he talked with his colleagues and found no opposition. It is a very positive development."

Judge Matthewman, aged 57, will appear live in the studio during the new Crime Stalker programme, featuring John Stalker, former deputy chief constable of Greater Manchester, which starts on April 16.

He will have total editorial control, but will not wear his wig or robes for the one or two minute slot.

Judge Matthewman, a circuit judge since 1983, tried the seven-month British Rail Derby fraud case at Leicester crown court in 1991 and the three-month fraud trial of Birmingham solicitor at Nottingham crown court last year. He is president of the mental health review tribunal.

He declined to discuss his involvement in the series, which will be shown in the Central and Westcountry ITV regions. Although he will not receive a fee, Central may make a contribution to charity.

The Guardian

Daily Mail, Friday, April 19, 1996

JUDGE Matthewman is known for his outspoken views and tough sentencing.

Last December, he backed a Nottingham shopkeeper who boiled over and gave a tearaway a clip round the ear after being plagued by a gang of boys.

He quashed a magistrates' order that Geoffrey Thibeault should pay the 11-year-old boy £100 compensation, saying the youngster had been the author of his own misfortune.

Judges are normally discouraged from appearing on television, but three years ago 60-year-old Judge Matthewman aired his views on crime and punishment on Central Television's Crime Stalker programme.

For years he has blamed MPs and reformers for encouraging the kind of leniency which led to young offenders 'leaving the court laughing'.

The judge, who has sat in Midlands courts since 1983, has said that the view that prisons are universities of crime is 'pseudo-sociological claptrap'.

Chapter 22
Crime Stalker

Mike Morley has an impressive CV. Among many other well known programmes, he produced the 'Cook Report' and 'Monarchy: The Nation Decides'. In the 1980's, he presented Central's award winning, live debate show - 'Central Weekend' and helped to monitor and record a major event in Nottinghamshire history when he reported throughout on the 1984-1985 Miners Strike for Central and ITN. He devised and produced Central's first factual network show from Nottingham "Part of the Union?" - a live studio debate between miners' leaders Arthur Scargill and Roy Lynk.

Mr Morley was Head of Regional Programmes at Central Television in 1993 so I asked him about the birth of 'Crime Stalker', presented by former Deputy Chief Constable of Greater Manchester, John Stalker and former ITN newsreader, Sue Carpenter, described as a 'behind-the-scene look at how detectives use advanced forensic science and psychological profiling to solve the most baffling cases'. The first 'Crime Stalker' was horrific! It went out at 10.40 on Friday, April 16th, 1993 after News at Ten. John Stalker described it as -

"One of the most disturbing crime scenes I've ever visited! The musty smell stayed with me longer than the pitiful sight of untouched cups of tea, a completed pools coupon and a pair of spectacles. The victims were made to watch each other die."

Talking to Graham Young of the Birmingham Evening Mail 10.4.93, Mr Stalker was referring to the sadistic murder in Northfield, just south of Birmingham at the home of 71 year old Harry Smith. He was found during November 1992, stabbed more than 100 times together with his stabbed and beaten wife Mary, and their helpless, gagged and bound, 47 year old disabled son Harold who was also found stabbed to death in his wheelchair. Criminal psychologist Paul Britton told Derek Weekes of the Birmingham Evening Mail 17.4.93 -

"These murderers, probably male between the ages of 14 and 25, came to enjoy what they did. It's highly likely they'll do it again."

I do not know if they did it again or not. They were never caught.

Mike Morley was very enthusiastic looking back on his new ground breaking programme -

"Led by experts, people who have built brilliant careers on catching major criminals, Crime Stalker was much more than a regional alternative to Crimewatch. We did make appeals for witnesses to crimes but we also ran a number of original and controversial features. 'Judge for Yourself' was probably the highest profile of these features; basically a short slot in which we encouraged Keith to speak on any issue of law and order that he liked.

Even before he had spoken the first word it was causing trouble! We had all the daily press wanting preview scripts and Keith had the Lord Chancellor's Department peering over his shoulder wondering what on earth he was going to say next. In truth, Keith was very careful about his comments. He was only too aware that there were jealous senior judges who would put both him and the programme to the sword given half a chance!"

Judge Matthewman remembers the original approach from Mike Morley.

*"Since the media was so anti-judiciary, almost without thinking, I said 'yes'. It was important that a judge got his views across. I had a word with the Lord Chancellor's press people who said - 'What a good idea! Go ahead.' I did not ask the Lord Chancellor himself or my Presiding Judges who at that time were Richard Rougier and Igor Judge: I didn't think it was necessary because they were not my bosses in that way. I did send Igor a test tape but that was **after** I said I'd do it and **after** a great deal of publicity about the first ever judge who was going to have his own slot on TV. Obviously Igor wanted to know all about it; he was entitled to know so we had a chat.*

I received the impression that they would have preferred me not to do it, but to be fair to them both, neither tried to dissuade me, for which I'm grateful. They didn't actually say 'no': well ... they couldn't say 'no': they knew I would have still gone on TV! Having made my decision they were both supportive."

The conversation went along the lines of -

"Well, Keith, if that's what you really want to do, as long as you're careful, we won't stand in your way. But remember you're a Circuit Judge and many people will delight in criticising you if you put a foot wrong."

When the series started, Keith featured in a Guardian article headed 'A judge in our sitting room'. He told Andrew Culf -

"I'll have total editorial control of my segment, but will be following guidelines laid down by the Lord Chancellor's Department which means not commenting on individual cases or sentences passed by individual judges."

At the end of the 12 week series, nothing was said on the programme which could possibly be criticised. In the Law Society Gazette 16.6.93, Jonathan McLeod described Judge Matthewman as -

"A fledgling TV personality with a plain-speaking style. At his own initiative to work up a script that will keep people watching when they get back from the pub is very difficult indeed."

Judge Matthewman told Mr McLeod -

"The workings of the law are a mystery to the general public. So many misconceptions; If I can put right even 5% of them, I will be quite happy. Legal history has been made, but my image has not been tarnished, nobody has complained, the viewing figures are increasing and the world has **not** *come to an end!"*

The world did not come to an end, but as somebody else said at that time - 'Fame costs'! Judge Matthewman was told by an interviewer from the Birmingham Post -

"I do hope you realise that your life will never be the same again! Oh no! After the programmes are seen by millions of viewers, you'll be recognised, stared at, and embarrassed by complete strangers addressing you in public places."

Keith was sceptical but contemplated the possible horrors of being a celebrity -

"Oh! Look oo it is! you-a that jooge on't telly arn't ya? That's right, Jooge Math - you - man! That's you in tit? Aye up, look arr Olive, look oo this is - it's that jooge! [crowd gathering] *Nay lass it inna! Ay oop Fred, coom over ere, it's im wit wig ... "*

A much stronger warning about fame came from Peter Rhodes in the Birmingham Express and Star 16.4.93, who interviewed him in the Central Studios just before the show. He pointed out to Judge Matthewman that Crime Stalker would be *'a shade more lively than*

His Honour seems to think.' in its highly popular, Friday evening, prime-time slot, formally occupied by Mike Morley's 'Central Weekend'. As Mr Rhodes put it -

"The live show which did for reasoned debate what the Visigoths did for the Forum. Consequently the world will be watching and you're about to become a television celebrity and public property. From now on the media will pay special attention to the sentences of the 'television judge': Panorama might ring you for a quote: Celebrity Squares might want you. Tomorrow morning your jovial horn-rimmed features will be instantly recognised in the queue at Tesco."

"Ah, If only I could get him into Tesco." chuckled Jane.

When Keith went to do the next programme and stopped at the security barrier to the studios on Lenton lane in Nottingham, the gate keeper did his job -

"Who are you, sir?"

"Judge Matthewman."

"I'm sorry. George ... who?"

So much for fame! In the early weeks, even Keith had some difficulty recognising himself on TV -

"The man up there didn't sound like me! It wasn't me. It wasn't the way I normally speak. It sounded like a man reading things from an idiot board."

Judge Christopher Pitches had a similar view -

"Keith, it's OK but it's just not you. It's not what we expect of you, not how you come across as a real person."

In the Law Society Gazette 16.6.93, Jonathan McLeod said -

"In the first few episodes, Judge Matthewman appeared wooden and reminiscent of the proverbial rabbit caught in the glare of the headlights. Two months into the series he's much better, more used to it and more relaxed."

Mike Morley said Keith was hyper-critical about his performance and annoyed that he was not instantly as good at presenting his piece as a professional presenter who had been on screen for 20 years -

"He'd turn in very presentable stuff, but he would want to do take after take after take. I often had the unenviable job of telling 'His

Honour' we weren't going to do any more takes. You could see him mentally searching for ways to imprison me for impudence!"

But Mike Morley is very grateful to Keith Matthewman for helping to make Crime Stalker a success -

"Every policeman, from chief constable to police constable that I've met knows of Keith Matthewman. Every lawyer that I've ever met knows of Keith Matthewman. Every journalist I've met knows of Keith Matthewman.

"He's left his mark and it's a benchmark of fair play and justice. Quite an achievement in any day and age, let alone the here-today gone-tomorrow sound-bite age in which we live."

Chapter 23
Death Threats and High Drama

Judge Matthewman first became 'Judge' Matthewman in 1977. His new post, the first rung on the judicial ladder, was known as Deputy Circuit Judge. Today such a position is known as an Assistant Recorder. These positions were part time and temporary. Keith told Jeremy Evans on Radio Nottingham about his very first sitting at Leicester Crown Court -

"It was very strange! I was a bit nervous, as anybody would be doing a thing for the first time. I was used to being down on the floor with the other barristers and yet, here I was, up high, being received in a respectful, standing silence. Arriving at my judicial seat, for a tense moment I looked at them and they all looked at me. They stood and I stood. Awkward seconds passed. Why don't they sit down? The tension was broken when it clicked that I had to bow and sit down, before they could bow to me - and sit down!"

Keith enjoyed this experience and eventually the message came down from 'on high'; would he like to become a circuit judge if a position became vacant? As a result he let it be known that such move would be viewed very favourably. Accordingly, Keith was sworn in as a circuit judge on March 28th 1983 on the Midland and Oxford Circuit, mainly sitting in Nottingham. He also sat in Leicester, Derby, Lincoln, Grimsby, Scunthorpe, Boston, Spalding, Buxton and Ilkeston.

Judges are appointed by the Lord Chancellor, but they did not (in those days - it is different today) 'apply' for the job in the usual sense, such as the case of a teacher seeking promotion. There was no interview except for an informal chat with the Lord Chancellor's Permanent Secretary and 'two others'. It all sounds so civilised and intriguing. Until the recent changes, Dominic Egan in his fascinating biography 'IRVINE Politically Correct?' described the old judicial appointments procedure as -

"Little more than the Lord Chancellor having a cosy chat with lawyer friends over brandy and cigars at the end of a good dinner."

Mr Egan quoted Lord Irvine from an article he wrote in The Guardian, March 4th, 1992 -

"There is growing dissatisfaction with the outdated, secretive and elitist arrangements for the appointment of judges and composition of the judiciary ... There can be no argument against a shake-up of the judicial appointments system."

Judge hails from Toton

NEWLY-appointed Judge for the Midland and Oxford Circuit, Judge Keith Matthewman, QC., is very much "a local boy."

Educated at Long Eaton Grammar School and University College, London, he was called to the Bar in 1960 and entered practice in 1962.

He took silk in 1979 and, later in the same year, was appointed a Recorder — also on the Midland and Oxford Circuit, which covers Nottinghamshire, Derbyshire, Lincolnshire and Leicestershire.

Judge Matthewman, who is well-known as an advocate on the circuit, is married, with one son. He lives at Toton and "Who's Who" lists his recreations as gardening and cine photography.

This was three months before Derry Irvine was named as the Shadow Lord Chancellor by his best friend and fellow Scot, John Smith on 18.7.92, when he replaced Neil Kinnock as leader of the Labour Party after its fourth straight election defeat.

Regardless of the appointments' system, failure to become a judge was never once considered by Keith. Achieving his ambition at the relatively young age of 47 was a forgone conclusion, having been in Silk four years and at the Bar for 21 years, four years of which as a Recorder.

I was beginning to confuse 'Keith's boss', the Lord Chancellor of Great Britain, with the Lord Chief Justice. The former who sits on the Woolsack as the Speaker of the House of Lords, is currently Lord Irvine of Lairg. It is a political appointment and therefore not a job for life. As 'Sir Humphrey Appleby' used to say in the BBC's 'Yes Minister' - 'The Prime Minister giveth and the Prime Minister taketh away!'

End of a good era

FOR local reporters who cover the courts regularly, the appointment of Judge Keith Matthewman QC, 47, will mean the end of an era.

Among a number of counsel who appear frequently at Nottingham Crown Court — most of them helpful and co-operative — Mr Matthewman, as he was until recent days, has always been one of the most helpful.

In fact, whenever a newcomer was being briefed and Mr Matthewman was seen to be concerned in a case which was likely to pose problems, the not-infrequent advice was: "Oh, it's Mr Matthewman — you can always ask him" — and there would be sighs of relief all round.

One of his great gifts — in a field where reporters are not notably gifted — was his ability to grasp financial facts.

Not only grasp them — but transmit them in comprehensible form.

When it came to cases of fraud and deception, he always had a knack of getting to the root of the matter — outlining the salient points, discarding the frills and saying confidently to some bemused reporter: "But you won't want all that."

So, although there must be rejoicing for the new judge's elevation, there will inevitably be some regrets.

Perhaps, as he skilfully sums up and unravels the tangled web that is the basis of almost all cases centred on money matters, he will spare a thought for the days when he could act as a unversal interpreter.

Latest appointments include: Mr Paul Vivian Baker QC, and Mr Keith Matthewman, QC, to be circuit judges. The Lord Chancellor will assign Mr Baker to the South-eastern circuit and Mr Matthewman to the Midland and Oxford circuit. Dr Sidney Cotson, to be a member of the University Grants Committee.

● *NEWLY-APPOINTED Judge for the Midland and Oxford Circuit, Judge Keith Matthewman, QC — pictured with his wife Jane — lives at Toton.*

He was educated at Long Eaton Grammar School and University College, London. He was called to the Bar in 1960 and entered practice in 1962.

He took silk in 1979 and later the same year was appointed a Recorder — also on the Midland and Oxford Circuit, which covers Nottinghamshire, Derbyshire, Lincolnshire and Leicestershire.

Judge Matthewman, who is married with one son, lists his recreations in "Who's Who" as gardening and cine photography.

Derry Irvine (remembered for the £300-a-roll wallpaper extravagance) is a very different character from the down to earth and unpretentious Keith Matthewman who said to me in our first conversation *'Narvel, what's all this 'Sir'? My name is Keith.'* In Mr Egan's book, a barrister tells us about an incident in Hong Kong during the late 1980's shortly after Irvine had received his peerage -

The Daily Telegraph, Tuesday, March 22, 1983

CIRCUIT JUDGES

Mr Paul Vivian Baker, QC, 59, and Mr Keith Matthewman, QC, 47, have been appointed Circuit Judges. Mr Baker is being assigned to the South Eastern Circuit and Mr Matthewman to the Midland and Oxford Circuit.

*"Derry was sitting down having tea in the Mandarin Hotel and I came with my solicitor for tea. He went over to Derry and said - 'Oh Mr Irvine, how nice to see you! And Derry said - **Lord** Irvine! It was almost laughable, really. The poor guy was terribly shocked."*

The present Lord Chief Justice, Lord Woolf, is the head of the Court of Appeal, which is a permanent legal appointment.

So what made Keith Matthewman become a judge: prestige? power? money? In her July 1994 BBC World Service interview with Judge Matthewman, Rosalind English reflected upon this point -

"Senior barristers drop their most lucrative practices at the merest whiff of appointment to the Bench; solicitors have fought tooth and nail for decades for eligibility to become judges. Which is odd because becoming a judge means losing your independence and joining the civil service, usually taking a drop in income and, above all,

230

surrendering the cut and thrust of the forensic battlefield for the sober role of umpire."

Keith gave his best response to those considerations in a different interview five years later to Jeremy Evans on Radio Nottingham -
"All barristers are basically ambitious people. The idea of being up there, running a court, as opposed to being down there, being run - appealed to me. Let the truth be spoken - we are arrogant! Every barrister knows that the judge in his court is all powerful. In your court you are God and that's the way it's got to be! If the court is to be run properly, then you've got to be completely and utterly in charge of everything which goes on."

Privately, Keith admitted to me that he enjoyed power, but was quick to link power with responsibility -
"A judge has awesome power which has to be used properly, fairly and judicially. Awesome power to take away a prisoner's freedom which could cost him his job, his livelihood, his house, his loved ones. And it's no use worrying about it afterwards ... a worried judge is a bad judge. If you went home and cried into your pillow you'd never do the job. You don't do the job unless you're capable of doing it. You need to have self-confidence, self-assurance and move on to the next case."

Judge Matthewman summed up his job in similar terms to Mr Evans -
"You don't go to the Bar or the Bench unless you're a particular sort of person who is not easily upset, whose emotions are not pulled, tangled and jangled. Facts are for the jury. You tell or rehearse the facts to the jury, explain the law and get it right. Everything is in your hands so it's got to be right."

Keith told me that becoming a judge had a dramatic effect on his social life.
"Sad, but inevitable, you become isolated and drift away from the barristers you've known. I'm up there, and they are below, so they tend to think you've become a different species, a higher species, no longer 'one of the boys'."

Some of those barristers who were once 'below' and appeared before Judge Matthewman have since become High Court Judges. In 1992 there was a lengthy, well publicised, fraud trial at the Nottingham Crown Court in which Anthony Hughes QC successfully prosecuted a Birmingham solicitor (see page 219). Judge Matthewman gave the prisoner five years and today, Mr Hughes is Mr Justice Hughes the Junior Presiding Judge of the Midland and Oxford Circuit.

When Keith was sitting at Derby Crown Court, John Goldring QC was before him defending the son of the famous TV personality Eric Morley who organised the Miss World competition. A case which made the national headlines. Another time at the Nottingham Crown Court, Mr Goldring was defending a man accused of negligence in connection with a light aircraft propeller injury. Judge Matthewman fined the defendant £2000 and ordered him to pay £8000 costs which caused him to become so enraged that, later, he came back to the building with a fishing bag! Since there is scant opportunity to fish at the Nottingham Crown Court, the suspicious security guards inspected the contents of the bag to find that it concealed an air rifle. The furious man, frustrated and denied permission to enter made threats against Judge Matthewman and promptly left!

Quite naturally this was very distressing for Jane, feeling vulnerable at home with a young Adrian. The police suggested a police guard or an alarm button for protection. Keith declined both these measures on the grounds that a genuinely dangerous man is unlikely to proclaim publicly his intention to harm one of Her Majesties judges.

Fortunately nothing happened to Keith, or indeed to the defending barrister Mr Goldring QC, who, incidentally, is today, Mr Justice Goldring.

Similar high drama once occurred at Derby Crown Court. Just before Judge Matthewman was about to sentence, the prisoner asked his counsel Peter Joyce, now Peter Joyce QC, if he may speak directly to the judge. Permission was granted -

"May it please Your Honour. I've spent all dinner-time in church praying for Your Honour. I do want to mend my ways so please don't send me to prison.

At the conclusion of this emotional appeal, Judge Matthewman delivered to the defendant exactly the same prison sentence upon which he had decided just before the heartfelt appeal. This produced a sudden and dramatic personality change in the dock. He spat out -

*"You f***ing bastard!! Rot in Hell!!"*

Obscene abuse was accompanied by violence. The court policeman suffered a broken arm when he lunged out to help the dock officer struggling to restrain the maddened prisoner. For his safety, Judge Matthewman was asked to leave the court which, reluctantly, he did.

This incident reminded me of a comment made by Judge Benson regarding the endless debate on appropriate and correct sentencing -

"For everybody who likes a sentence, there'll be somebody who doesn't like it - very often the person who receives it!"

As recently as May 10th, 2001 a young criminal, who had robbed a disabled man outside a Nottingham night club, took violent exception to the sentence of three years passed by Judge John Hopkin. Suddenly he jumped out of the dock and leapt over several court benches to (unsuccessfully) intimidate Judge Hopkin, a former rugby player. The Nottingham Evening Post of 11.5.01 asked Keith for a comment -

"This is a situation which is becoming too serious to be ignored. With the present lack of discipline and general yobbish behaviour now current in society, and too acceptable to many people, judges have become vulnerable."

We are told these attacks on judges are very rare, but in January 2001 courtroom security made national headlines when Her Honour Judge Ann Goddard QC, at the Central Criminal Court (The Old Bailey) was repeatedly punched by a disgruntled prisoner who had leaped out of the dock. No doubt with many other colleagues, Keith wrote to her a letter of support and commiseration. In The Nottingham Evening Post 14.4.99, Judge Matthewman was the first to criticise the removal of the permanent police presence (with its useful panic button) at the Nottingham Crown Court on economic grounds - *'Disappointing, indeed inexplicable.'* Judge Hopkin said the Police Liaison Department had been useful in dealing with *'stroppy individuals'* and its sudden absence attracted an anxious comment from Nottinghamshire Victim Support about increased witness intimidation.

In preparing for this biography, Keith gave me a pile of personal letters, most commending and some critical. A surprising number of positive letters are from serving or former prisoners who comment on the imposed sentence, such as this one -

"... nobody likes to be sentenced by you because your sentences are tough, but they do like to be tried by you because your trials are fair."

Brent Bond sustained a severed jugular vein, a mutilated ear and serious deep, permanently scarring facial wounds when he was attacked in 1999 by a man wielding a machete. The victim also suffered two strokes due to loss of blood pressure and is now permanently blind in one eye. Judge Matthewman took the view that 13 years in jail was the appropriate sentence. Others took the view that this punishment was too lenient. The attacker had a different view and successfully appealed. The sentence was reduced to ten years by the Court of Appeal.

Day after day, week after week and year after year, Keith has had to face and deal with the harrowing experiences and reality of real life horrors which, fortunately, most of the rest of us only see on television or read about in the newspapers. But each day he would be able to leave this high drama and return to the warmth, love and comfort of his home and family.

The difference between murder, rape, grievous bodily harm, the occasional machete attack and the odd domestic drama back in Keith's own home - was dramatic in itself. Such a crisis occurred some 20 years ago when he arrived at the house one day to find a distraught Adrian: his precious and much loved two pet tortoises, Tilly and Touché, had escaped from their garden pen. Nothing was heard of them until days later when a neighbour complained that something had been happily munching, causing demolition and utter ruin to his cherished, prize winning lettuces. After civil apologies all round and the safe return of Tilly and Touché, Keith went back to the Nottingham Crown Court to deal with more of the 'mad, bad and the desperate'.

Returning to those barristers who appeared before Judge Matthewman and have now moved on to higher office, good examples would be Brian Appleby QC, Richard Benson and Richard Curtis QC who is now a High Court Judge. Keith was fairly new to the Bench at that time and recalls the following fraud case as 'interesting and enjoyable', but not, of course, for the three defendants who were accused of stealing coal from Vic Hallam at Langley Mill.

They were defended by Mr Curtis and prosecuted by Mr Appleby as a Leader and his Junior, Mr Benson. During the course of this case it was rather unusual, but necessary for the whole court, judge, barristers, clerks, the accused and the jury to travel from Nottingham and visit the actual site at Langley Mill to view the scene. The intriguing assembly of a Crown Court right outside the adjacent factory stirred up a great deal of curiosity in the workers who strained, squashed up and 'rubber-necked' through the open windows to witness this bizarre gathering. And then it happened! Over to the Judge -

"For reasons which I still don't understand to this day, suddenly, they all broke out into a horrendous loud chorus, shouting and singing - 'They're guilty! They're guilty!' Not something we had anticipated."

In these circumstances it was necessary to abort this field trip, indeed abort the whole trial because Judge Matthewman had to dismiss the jury since they may have been influenced by this immature and loutish outburst. Keith once told me 'a worried judge is a bad judge': I think it can be added 'an angry judge is a dangerous judge'. This was certainly so for the two factory owners who were responsible for the conduct of employees during work time on their property. Keith had a responsibility to the public purse and a great deal of time and money had been wasted by this appalling charade. The whole case had to start again and a new jury sworn in costing thousands of pounds.

Back at the Nottingham Crown Court in his seat of power, Judge Matthewman issued orders that a senior police officer should go forth unto Langley Mill with an edict of judicial displeasure! An ultimatum was delivered to the effect that, in due course, the whole court would once again progress to Langley Mill to inspect the scene and if the two factory owners could not control the disruptive behaviour of their workers, two factory owners would speedily find themselves behind bars!

To be fair, the gentlemen concerned were mortified, totally unaware of the original incident and profusely apologetic. The second visit took place successfully in utter silence, no faces to be seen at any of the closed windows and, to be absolutely sure, private guards were placed all around the factory!

There was a time when Keith had the reputation of being 'The Fraud Judge'. He presided over several well known cases and a lengthy one in particular lasting several months is recalled as -

" ... *one of the most fascinating fraud cases I have ever tried - a battle to be savoured, a battle to remember!*"

It was another example of a barrister appearing before Judge Matthewman who has now been promoted. Rex Tedd QC was defending and Leading. He is today the Leader of the Bar Midland and Oxford Circuit. His opponent prosecuting was David Farrer -

"*David was like a tiger! A sight and sound for sore eyes and ears when in full flight - nothing got past him. He cross-examined with a measured ferocity and always got his point across.*

Rex, an equally excellent barrister, was a different character and employed a more gentle approach - but rock solid in persuading witness to agree with what he was suggesting to them."

This was a big case with a number of other counsel, leaders and juniors. About half way through the trial, Rex Tedd persuaded Judge Matthewman that some of the counts of the indictment against his client should be withdrawn with an instruction to the jury find the defendant not guilty. At the end of this long process the jury retired to their deliberations and found the prisoner not guilty on all the remaining counts.

So much for facts, but it is the skill and talent of the legal personalities which made such an impression on Judge Matthewman -

"*I've been extremely lucky and privileged to listen to some of the superb barristers who came before me.*"

Chapter 24
The Parole Board

"Protecting the public and reintegrating prisoners into the community through a just, open and efficient process."

This is the slogan of the Parole Board which was printed at the foot of a letter sent to Keith Matthewman, [dated 13.3.01] from its Chairman, David Hatch. It spoke of the Government's attempt to modernise the criminal justice system in a publication called 'Criminal Justice: The Way Ahead', a reminder that The Law, never written in stone, is fluid, ever changing and reacting to new circumstances. Over the last five years sentencing has become a very complicated part of criminal law and judges have had to keep up with the ever increasing bureaucracy caused by these statutory and somewhat stressful changes. As a former teacher I know all too well about that side of the job! Keith has called sentencing 'a nightmare and a mess'. He wrote a full page article for the Daily Express on the last day of August in 1997, entitled 'Free our judges to punish the guilty'. The following was sub-headlined as his most significant comment -

"A legalistic quagmire has been created in which natural justice has been swamped."

Mr Hatch's letter contained bad and good news. Half of serious offenders will re-offend and be re-convicted within two years of release. For 'high risk' serious offenders that figure increases to 82%.

Depressing reading, but here is the good news - 96% of prisoners released by the Parole Board do not offend while out on parole licence.

Overleaf is an invitation from Michael Howard [28.6.96] to Judge Matthewman to join the Parole Board.

Keith has great respect for Michael Howard -

"He recognised that unless you punish criminals properly, they will have no respect for the law. He transformed the whole attitude of the Home Office and a large number of politicians.

QUEEN ANNE'S GATE LONDON SW1H 9AT

2 8 JUN 1996

Dear Judge

I am writing to ask you whether you would be willing to serve as a member of the Parole Board. In considering this invitation, you may wish to study the leaflet attached to this letter which gives details of the parole scheme, the functions of the Parole Board, and the fees payable. The Chairman of the Board is Lord Belstead.

Members of the Board have invariably found the duties both rewarding and challenging. I very much hope you are willing to help with this important work in the treatment of offenders and protection of the public by accepting appointment to the Board. If so, I should like your appointment to take effect from 1 July 1996 for a period of two years.

Training will take place soon after your appointment; the Parole Board will contact you about this shortly.

MICHAEL HOWARD

Parole role

JUDGE Keith Matthewman, a senior judge who sits at Nottingham Crown Court, has been appointed a member of the Parole Board. The appointment is at the invitation of Home Secretary Michael Howard and is for two years. Judge Matthewman, 60, said: "This will be a new challenge and I am looking forward to it." He was educated at Long Eaton Grammar School and University College, London.

Saturday July 13, 1996 **Evening Post**

When I was at the Bar, clients always asked - 'Can you get me off with probation, Mr Matthewman?' The one thing they feared was being sent to prison. They'd do anything to avoid it. People don't seem to understand that; especially those who have never met a criminal in their lives. Only barristers and solicitors go down into the cells and see the whining wickedness of many criminals who deserve punishment but who can't stand the thought of being sent to prison. They know perfectly well what they've done to their victims and have little conscience. Rather like that sadistic killer in the film 'Dirty Harry' who said to Clint Eastwood - 'I have my rights': this just after the criminal had buried alive and suffocated an innocent young girl. Far too many weak schoolteachers, probation officers and social workers seem to be on the side of the criminal."

On the same theme in his retirement speech Keith spoke of a conversation he once had with an angry London taxi driver whose friend and fellow driver had been knifed. The assailant was sentenced to four years in prison, but this was reduced to two years by the High Court.

"I really felt for this taxi driver, who, incidentally, had no idea who I was. I could not defend this appalling reduction of sentence. Until High Court Judges get their wives or daughters raped, or their sons beaten up and mugged, or their homes burgled - they will never know what it's like to be a victim and will keep on reducing my sentences."

However he does have faith in the Parole Board and allows that some criminals feel remorse for what they have done. Sean Akins was intrigued with the mysterious workings of the Parole Board and felt that the public would be interested in this particular aspect of Keith's work - hence this chapter.

The Parole Board deals with applications from all prisoners who have been sentenced to four years or more who ask to be moved to open conditions like Sudbury [Category D] or released from prison completely before serving the full term of their original sentence. Lifers are divided into two groups. Mandatory lifers have received a life sentence for committing murder. Discretionary lifers have committed a serious offence such as manslaughter for which the maximum penalty is life in jail. The task of Keith and his team is to look at the representations they make in the form of reports from prison officers, probation officers, psychologists, psychiatrists, hostel workers etc. In the case of mandatory lifers, the Parole Board makes a recommendation to the Home Secretary that they are too dangerous, or perhaps safe to move to open conditions, or even safe to be released. The Home Secretary would have to make the final decision. In the case of a discretionary lifer, the Parole Board makes the final decision.

During the hearing, the panel sit at a table. The venue is inside the prison itself in the case of a discretionary lifer. The Chairman is a retired or serving judge placed in the centre. A psychiatric member sits on his right and an independent member to his left. Independent members come from various backgrounds of professionals who may be serving or retired such as - psychologists, probation officers, principal probation officers, magistrates, chief constables, prison governors, professors of law, miscellaneous academics and other people who have been dealing with crime and criminals. As Keith put it -

*"In fact all who we used to call 'the good and the great' - all who, in spite of what you read in the press, make up their **own** minds following the regulations and using their own common-sense. We are **not** told what to do by the Home Secretary. Some time back it was said that a well known prisoner was not released because the Parole Board did as they were told by the Home Secretary. I can tell you categorically this was not the case - since **I** was on the panel of that Parole Board which refused leave for that famous gangster to be released into the community. The Secretary of State indicates his view in discretionary lifer cases but this is not in any way binding on the Board. It is taken into consideration in just the same way as the views set out in the dossier of views of the members of the Panel acting completely independently."*

Opposite Keith sits the prisoner himself who is usually a discretionary lifer. Most mandatory lifer hearings take place in the absence of the prisoner. The prisoner is flanked by his legal representative to his left [a solicitor or barrister] and the Secretary of State's representative [normally a senior prison officer] to his right. At the head of the table sits the Panel Secretary who is responsible for the administrative duties during the hearing. Opposite the Secretary sits the particular witness (there may be several) giving evidence about the prisoner.

Now into retirement, Keith continues to enjoy his very interesting work on the Parole Board.

Opinion

Evening Post *Thursday August 28, 1997*

Time to make punishment fit the crime

"IF YOU are old enough to commit the crime, you are old enough to take the punishment."

Judge Keith Mattthewman was paraphrasing the opinions of ordinary, sensible, decent, law-abiding Nottingham folk.

He couldn't have put it more accurately.

Fortunately for the Hyson Green youth on the other side of Judge Mattthewman's courtroom, Parliament believes it knows better.

Never mind the circumstances of the case — burglary at a deaf student's flat, followed by a vicious assault on the security guard who tried to arrest him.

Never mind the youth's lack of remorse and apparent contempt for authority — he failed to surrender on bail to the magistrates' court and thrice missed an interview with a social worker.

And never mind the wisdom of the judge who weighed it all up — and decided the correct sentence should be five to six years' custody.

The judge's hands were tied by Parliament. The maximum sentence he could give to a juvenile offender in these circumstances was just two years.

That is a pathetically inadequate penalty.

Judge Mattthewman is right. The law must be changed to allow courts to impose punishments to fit the crime.

The police know it, too.

And so does the public.

When will the politicians do something about it?

ON behalf of my wife, neighbours, relatives, friends and myself, thoughts regarding soft laws and Judge Keith Mattthewman QC, are set out as follows.

Any law which does not allow judges to impose punishments to fit the crime is an ass of the highest order, and must be changed immediately without excuses, denials or the like.

A slow burning anger and feeling of resentment simmers among the populace, against the wets and wimps who make these laws.

Redress

Politicians must act now to redress the situation.

Crime and violence is of paramount importance in its suppression.

The upholding of the law and the fitting punishment of offenders has to be.

It's up to you, Parliament. Act now!

R. S. HOPKINSON
Stanhope Crescent
Arnold

We all agree with the judge

I AND all my family and friends think that Judge Keith Mattthewman should have all the power necessary to impose much stiffer sentences and reveal the names of suspects irrespective of age.

If they're old enough to commit the crime, they're old enough to do the time.

R. THORNTON (Mrs)
K. PALLENDER
C. THORNTON
J. THORNTON
J. GLOVER (Mr and Mrs)
R. SEAKIRK
D. PEARCE
M. EVANS
M. FORKINGS

It is about time a lot of hands were "untied" such as those of the police, teachers, and other authorities.

J. ROGERS
Haswell Road
Bulwell

NEP 4.9.97.

Bring back the 'cat'

I HAVE never written a letter to a newspaper before, but I do in regards of the small sentence for a youth who deserves a severe punishment.

When I was in my teens, there were two youths who were given three strokes of the cat-of-nine tails.

They did not hurt anyone, but stole some money. It's getting worse.

Bring the 'cat' back then see — they won't be back for more.

C. WILKINSON
Cross Street
Arnold

Chapter 25
Praise from the Post

Praise not just from the Nottingham Evening Post, but also the national press, the people, other judges and members of the Bar. Keith Matthewman has had many letters from the public expressing support for his tough line on sentencing and sympathy for victims, but The Post has consistently reflected Nottinghamshire public opinion with front page headlines during the 1980's, 1990's and now into this new Millennium. On March 15th 1989, Post Comment led with - 'JUDGE SETS SHINING EXAMPLE'.

"Let's applaud Judge Keith Matthewman. The comments he made yesterday shine out like a beacon of common sense. He spoke for the common man when he said that violence in Nottingham will only stop when attackers realise that they will be properly punished. We agree. A potential offender, whether driven by drink or bravado will think twice if he knows that his liberty is in jeopardy. He has done the citizens of Nottingham a great service through his no-nonsense approach. Society pays judges to make tough decisions and this week His Honour Judge Keith Matthewman, QC did not shirk from that responsibility and duty. In so doing he took a significant step towards ridding the streets of this city of the violence which has long since reached totally unacceptable proportions."

In August 1997 a 15 year old from Hyson Green burgled the home of a deaf student while he slept. When a security guard tried to arrest him the thief bit into his cheek before hitting him in the face causing serious injury to his eyes and nose. On a front page headline - 'JUDGE'S FURY' - The Nottingham Evening Post 28.8.97, Keith Matthewman pointed out that a sentence of five to six years in custody would have been appropriate, but Parliament had prevented him from imposing more than two years in a young offender institution.

The Nottingham Evening Post Crown Court reporter Judy Cullimore spoke to me of her first experience with the *'God-like figure'* on the Bench. The man who had the awesome power to -
" ... determine whether a defendant walked free from court or was escorted to the cells below to serve a prison sentence after

pleading guilty to a crime. I first met Judge Matthewman when my colleague, John Seymour and I went to a leaving party for an usher. Several judges were standing around, but in their civvies they look quite different from the familiar characters we're use to seeing in court. There we were, drinks in hand, feeling slightly uncomfortable, when a man approached us. This man was wearing a warm friendly smile -

'Hello, I'm Keith Matthewman. I often see you in my courtroom. It's a pleasure to meet you both.'

The three of us spent the next fifteen minutes chatting together. I was forcibly struck by how genuinely interested Judge Matthewman was in the work of a court reporter and how totally down-to-earth, in touch with the real world and totally lacking in pomposity he was - qualities shared by many of his fellow judges at the Nottingham Crown Court.

A few weeks later, making my way out of court, the Clerk approached me -

'His Honour would like a word with you. Will you step into his chambers, please.'

My mouth went dry and my stomach began churning! Oh, God! A court reporter's worst nightmare. I've dropped a clanger in one of my reports and I'm being summoned to the presence for a telling-off. With trembling legs, I followed the Clerk and was ushered into the inner-sanctum to be greeted with a cheery -

'Come in and sit down, Judy. There's nothing wrong, so don't look so worried. As we have a bit of a hiatus in the trial I thought you might like a cup of coffee and a chat. Judges can get very lonely, believe it or not.'

That cup of coffee was to be one of many over the years. As a member of a profession held in mistrust by many people, I was grateful to be trusted enough by Judge Matthewman (and many of his colleagues, court staff and my friends in the Probation Service) for them to relax with me and exchange news and gossip, without fearing I would rush off shouting - **HOLD THE FRONT PAGE!***"*

Much praise was spoken on the morning of December 22nd, 2000 in Nottingham Crown Court when several judges and barristers analysed the past career of Judge Matthewman to celebrate the event of his retirement. John Milmo QC -

"Keith was one of those who if I knew I was to be against him, extra careful preparation was the order of the day if I was not to be out-gunned and out-flanked, but I could never - and I never have - complained of any unfairness either from Keith Matthewman as an opponent or His Honour Judge Matthewman on the Bench.

When he took Silk, I was led by him on a number of occasions. Both as a Junior and, in Silk, he taught me much, not only by what he said (he did not set out to educate) but by what he did and he was an example to all his younger colleagues who, if they were wise, learnt from him.

Those involved in the criminal process look for a just judge, a fair judge, able to see both sides and, in the old phrase, without fear or favour, affectation or ill will and those who have been privileged to appear before him will well know that in Judge Matthewman, they may not have had the speediest trial in the land, no Speedy Gonzales he, but what they do know is that they did have a just judge, a fair judge and perhaps the fundamental attribute of a criminal judge is an ability to distinguish not just between the innocent and the guilty, but to make a much more difficult judgement between guilty defendants and to be able to distinguish between the professional criminal and the one-off.

It was one of Judge Matthewman's strengths that he had that ability. The first time-defendant, who was going through a difficult period, but fell to temptation could expect to receive a modest sentence recognising his lack of any criminal sophistication and that's what he/she got.

But God help the professional criminal! He asked for it, he got it and the public for whom, as I said, the courts exist, knew that. That's why he was held in such high respect by the public of Nottingham. In his court, villains could expect courtesy, an even-handed approach during a trial, but on conviction - an exemplary sentence."

Chapter 26
Keith Matthewman: The Paradox

To conclude, let us consider Keith Matthewman the paradox. How do we reconcile the youthful, idealistic, left wing socialist with the image of the steely, unsparing, battle-hardened judge of recent years?

Give it a little thought and the answer is deceptively simple. Inside the traditional judge, still intact, resides that same idealistic young man of the early 1960's. In a strictly political sense, Keith may have left the 'far left' of his youth, but has carried with him into his autumnal years the very best of socialist philosophical values - a deep sense of social justice, a disapproval of blood sports, a penchant for class equality, a loathing of racism and enthusiastic tolerance for minority groups. He has no time for the artificial, the pretentious or the pompous.

In the blurb, on the back cover of this book, of all the terrible crimes listed, there is one missing which is not technically a crime - disrespect. This I fear the most - disrespect. I have seen it creep into my professional and personal experience little by little, insidiously eroding the quality of all our lives. Perhaps this is why Judge Matthewman is the hero of so many in this region. He has been prepared to use his position, power and prestige to confront this growing menace. He has been prepared to speak out and attack the increasing tolerance of the yob culture. He had not been afraid to say that fear of punishment is missing: the same fear which used to keep us all much safer half a century ago.

Let us give the last word to Judy Cullimore. She was speaking to me about Keith's sense of fun, occasions when he would lighten the atmosphere with quick quips and wry comments which caused Court 5 to 'rock with laughter'. There were other times when he would be serious and talk about keeping TV cameras out of court and the need to retain dignity - 'It will be a sorry day when wigs and gowns are scrapped.'

"I remember him bemoaning the fact that the new court buildings bore a resemblance to a 'three star hotel' unlike the old Shire Hall which -

'Looked and felt a building with a dignified presence, where justice was dispensed.'

Having said that, he grinned at me.

'Don't quote me. It will make me sound like the archetypal old fuddy-duddy judge who is the favourite butt of jokes in the media.'

Fuddy-duddy? I don't think so Your Honour. I look back with gratitude and affection at the way you smoothed my path and made my time as Crown Court reporter for the Nottingham Evening Post such an enjoyable and memorable period of my career as a journalist.

Judy Rose (formerly Cullimore)

Bircotes,
Doncaster.
DN11
1-12-88

Your Honour,

Now that my Probation Order
has reached its end, I would like
to thank you for giving me the
opportunity to prove that I can
lead an honest life.

I appreciate the trust placed
in me by you and your making
me aware of the consequences
should I misplace that trust.

I hope my success will
mean that you will feel able
to take a similar risk with
others in my position.

The most satisfying thing
is that I have been able to
get my younger son out of the
care of the local authority

Yours sincerely,

John

Judge Matthewman QC.

I have completed recently my first period
of jury service, an experience I found
to be interesting, emotional & sad
but I want to thank you for your
kindness, consideration & courtesy shown
to the jury — a ray of comfort in
what I consider to be unforgettable moments
in my life.

Yours sincerely,

Dorothy M Marshall

Matthewman Annals

1936/0 - Keith Matthewman was born on January 8th to Frank Matthewman and his wife Elizabeth who lived at 200 Sheffield Road, Birdwell, near Barnsley. January 20 - Death of George V. August 26th - World's first regular television transmission from Alexandra Palace in London. December 11th - Abdication speech of Edward VIII and the ascension of George VI.

1937/1 - May 12th - Coronation of George VI. May 28th the 'phlegmatic' Stanley Baldwin resigned and Neville Chamberlain became the new PM. August 8th - Birth of Raymond Matthewman.

1938/2 - The Matthewmans moved south to 17 Marton Road in Chilwell, Nottinghamshire.

1939/3 - September 3rd - Neville Chamberlain made his famous broadcast announcing the start of World War Two. Frank Matthewman joined the army.

1940/4 - May 10th - In an atmosphere of crisis, Chamberlain resigned and Churchill the new PM offered '... *nothing but blood, toil, tears and sweat.*'

1941/5 - Keith started at Meadow Lane Infants School, Chilwell.

1943/7 - November 19th - Frank Matthewman was promoted to Lieutenant.

1945/9 - April 30th - Hitler shot himself. July - Labour landslide victory, Clement Atlee became the new PM. End of the war. Keith joined the cubs.

1947/11 - September - Keith started at the Long Eaton Grammar School.

1949/13 - Keith had a paper round and delivered for the Co-op Butcher at Chilwell. September - Geoffrey Prime was appointed as the new French Master at Long Eaton Grammar School.

1950/14 - February - Labour won again with a cut majority.

1951/15 - Significant visit of Keith to the Shire Hall in the Sheriff's Gallery and his decision to go to the Bar. October - Election victory for the Conservatives. Churchill was the PM again at the age of 77.

1952/16 - February 6th - Death of George VI. Lieutenant Frank Matthewman had his first short story 'Murder for a Living' published in the Nottinghamshire Guardian. September - Keith entered the Lower Sixth Form. December - Keith gained 'O' Levels in English Language and Maths. December 11th - Lord Goddard sentenced 19 year old Derek Bentley to death.

1953/17 - March 25th - Death of Queen Mary. June 2nd - Coronation of Queen Elizabeth. Keith gained 'O' Level in Latin and appeared in 'She Stoops to Conquer' and 'The Dark Lady of the Sonnets'. September - Keith entered the Upper Sixth Form.

1954/18 - January - Keith became Hon. Secretary for the Debating Society and in June gained 'A' Levels in English Literature, History and French. July - Jane Maxwell the Athletics Captain for Derwent House won the 100 and 150 yard race on Sports Day. Keith's first job: testing tanks. October - Keith started University College London to read law and became a scoutmaster at Bethnal Green.

1955/19 - January - Keith moved to South Kensington to share a flat with Anthony Scrivener and John Rhind. April 5th - At the age of 80, Churchill resigned and Sir Anthony Eden became the new PM. May 25th - Eden won the General Election. July - Keith took a vacation job at a high class store in the West End. July 13th - Ruth Ellis was the last woman in England to be hanged.

1956/20 - June - Keith worked as a sandwich-board man and later took a vacation job at Frigid Foods in Cleethorpes. July 26th - Suez Crisis. November 19th - Keith took part in the Trafalgar Square Suez demonstration.

1957/21 - January - Eden resigned and the Queen sent for Harold Macmillan, not as expected, Rab Butler. July - Keith graduated from University College London and, for a few months, worked as a salesman for Jubbly Soft drinks. Macmillan told the nation - *'You've never had it so good!'*. Thomas Maxwell, Jane's father died aged 57. Lieutenant Frank Matthewman retired from the REME workshops and bought a grocers shop at 215 Cromford Road, Aldercar. Keith joined them in September and attended his 'Call Up' medical for National Service.

1958/22 - September - Keith moved into a small flat at Ilford and started teaching at Barking Secondary Modern School near London.

1959/23 - January - Keith started his private study for the Bar Exams and moved back to help out in the Aldercar shop in July. August - Keith joined the Labour Party. October - the PM, 'Supermac' won the third consecutive Conservative election.

1960/24 - Keith saw Jane Maxwell at Geoff Kingscott's record parties; was 'Called to the Bar' at Middle Temple, London; elected as a Labour Councillor on the Heanor Urban District Council and appointed to a post at William Howitt Secondary Modern School in May.

1961/25 - July - Keith left his teaching position and started his new job in the Rolls Royce International Division Licensing Department.

1962/26 - January - A significant chance meeting with Brian Smedley at the Bull's Head in Breaston in which Keith was invited to apply for a pupillage in Denis Cowley's Chambers. Consequently he joined chambers in Nottingham on April 3rd under pupil master Tom Heald. October 20th - Keith married Jane and they set up home at 22 Redland Drive, Chilwell.

1963/27 - October - Macmillan resigned and Lord Home was the new PM. November - Assassination of President Kennedy.

1964/28 - October - Councillor Matthewman was asked, but declined to stand as the Member for the Ilkeston Constituency in the General Election. Labour won with Harold Wilson as the new PM after the 'thirteen wasted years'. Lieutenant Frank Matthewman and his wife Elizabeth retired from the shop and moved to 16 Carlton Road, Long Eaton.

1966/30 - July - Jane left her teaching job. September 1st - Lieutenant Frank Matthewman heard his short story 'To Fittings and Labour' read on the BBC Light Programme.

1968/32 - April 8th - Birth of Adrian Matthewman. The beginnings of prosperity at the Bar and Keith had a large house built at Toton.

1970/34 - June - The Conservatives won the General Election and Edward Heath was the new PM. Successful barristers were hit by a top tax rate of 91.25% on income above £15,000.

1972/36 - Courts Act which ended the Quarter Sessions and the Assizes. July - Willy Bach became a pupil at 24 The Ropewalk.

1973/37 - Britain went on a three day week due to paralysing strikes.

1974/38 - March - The General Election was almost a draw - *'Who rules Britain now?'* Harold Wilson formed a government with no real power.   83% taxation took its toll and the Matthewman's annual holiday was at Wollaton Hall!   Second election in October returned Labour with a tiny minority. December - Average wage settlements hit a record of 26% and inflation was 20%.

1975/39 - February - Miners accepted a pay rise of 35%. April - Unemployment topped one million. May - The pound fell like a stone losing a quarter of its value. July - Inflation hit a record 26%. Mr Wilson announced a maximum six pound per week pay rise with a total freeze on all incomes above £8,500.

1976/40 - Death of Lieutenant Frank Matthewman aged 76. March 16th - Harold Wilson suddenly resigned and James Callaghan was the new PM.

1977/41 - Keith became a Deputy Circuit Judge, now called an Assistant Recorder.

1979/43 - 'Winter of Discontent' - Industrial chaos caused electoral damage to the Labour Government. Keith took Silk and became a Recorder on the Midland and Oxford Circuit. June - Margaret Thatcher won the General Election.

1980/44 - November 10th - Michael Foot became the new leader of the Labour Party now in opposition.

1981/45 - Geoffrey Hoon was interviewed by Keith Matthewman at 24 The Ropewalk in Nottingham. January - 'Gang of Four' broke away from the Labour party and launched the new Social Democratic Party.

1983/47 - March 28th - Keith Matthewman was appointed a Circuit Judge on the Midland and Oxford Circuit. July - Mrs Thatcher won a landslide victory. October 2nd - Neil Kinnock became the new Labour leader.

1984/48 - Judge Matthewman became a Member of the Committee of Circuit Judges.

1986/50 - Death of Elizabeth Matthewman. Judge Matthewman became a Member of the Nottinghamshire Probation Committee.

1987/51 - July - Margaret Thatcher was elected to a third term with a massive majority.

1990/54 - November 22nd - Mrs Thatcher resigned and John Major became the new PM.

1991/55 - January - 'Desert Storm' launched the Gulf War. The new Criminal Justice Act was criticised by Judge Matthewman in a Radio Trent interview.

1992/56 - Judge Matthewman appeared in an award winning documentary - 'Caution - Our Hands Are Tied'. April - John Major was returned as the PM as the Conservatives won their fourth consecutive victory.

1993/57 - April 16th - Judge Matthewman made twelve appearances on Central TV's 'Crime Stalker'. Judge Matthewman was appointed a President of Mental Health Review Tribunals.

1996/60 - Judge Matthewman was appointed to the Parole Board.

1997/61 - May - After 18 years, Labour was returned to power under Tony Blair.

2001/65 - January - Judge Matthewman retired. September 11th - On this grim Tuesday morning, thousands of innocent people were murdered by faceless fanatics who attacked, suddenly, out of the skies of New York and Washington DC. Having been educated in the United States and having spent thirteen years of my life in that good country, I feel it is appropriate to take this opportunity (a few days before going to print) to give condolences to the many bereaved.

Since Judge Matthewman has spent most of his professional life fighting crime and, as with all law-abiding citizens, rightly appalled at this particular horrific crime on such a mammoth scale, he joins me in expressing heartfelt sympathy for the many victims and their families.

Acknowledgements

The author would like to thank the following for kindly
giving up their time and providing valuable information.

Michael Auty, Lord Bach of Lutterworth, Frank Bacon, Ex Chief
Constable Colin F. Bailey QPM, His Honour Judge Richard Benson,
Keith Beresford, Dame Margaret Booth DBE, Dr Richard Brumpton,
Julie Dunn of Channel 4 Television, Terry Durand, His Honour ARM
(Bob) Ellis, Carol Harper, His Honour Thomas R. Heald, Nita Higham
nee Matthewman, Jean Hodgkinson nee Merricks, Ex Chief
Superintendent Michael F. Holford QPM, FBIM, The Rt. Hon.
Geoffrey Hoon MP, Colin Lane, Captain Adrian Matthewman, Colin
Morley, Mike Morley of Central Television, Mark Patterson of The
Nottingham Evening Post, Bob Pembleton, Geoffrey Prime, Ann
Roberts nee Thorpe, Judy Rose nee Cullimore of The Nottingham
Evening Post, Anthony Scrivener QC, Bill Shaw of Shaw's Heritage
Services, Dennis Skinner MP, Sir Brian Smedley, Michael Trotman
and Dorothy Wincott nee Frost.

Special thanks to Graham Glen the Editor of The Nottingham Evening
Post for kind permission to reproduce extracts. The Ilkeston Local
Studies Library, Matlock Local Studies and Heritage Library were also
helpful.

Cover photographs - Alan Thompson LBIPP LMPA

Most of all many thanks to Keith and Jane Matthewman.

People in this Book

Mr Allen, Ellen Akins, George Akins, Sean Akins, Mr Justice Alliott, Mr Allton, His Honour Judge Brian Appleby QC, Rhona Angel, Ernest Ashley, Brenda Ashton, Mr Atkinson and Michael Auty.

Lord Bach, Frank Bacon, Lord Baden-Powell, Ex Chief Constable Colin F. Bailey QPM, Miss Balantyne, Stanley Baldwin, Fred Barras, Councillor W Belfield, Patrick Bennett QC, His Honour Judge Richard Benson, Derek Bentley, Keith Beresford, Rt. Hon. Lord Bingham, Sheila Birch, Derek Bird, Brent Bond, Dame Margaret Booth DBE, Melvyn Bragg, Lord Brandon of Oakbrook, Maurice Brentnall, Lord Bridge of Harwick, Trish Briggs, Paul Britton, Miss Brooks, Dr Carole Brown, Geoffrey Brown, Marian Bryson, James Bulger and Maud Buxcey.

Mr Calton, Ian Carmichael, Sue Carpenter, Mrs Nancy Carswell, Henry Cecil, Neville Chamberlain, Bernard Chapman, Graham Chapman, Dame Agatha Christie, Michael Churm, Freda Cirillo nee Brentnall, David Clarke, Rt. Hon. Kenneth Clarke QC, MP, Cynthia Clements, Cyril Clifford, Kenneth Coats MEP, Ian Cobain, Miss Cockerell, Mr Cocking, Jillian Colclough, Doris Cook, Pat Cook, Denis Cowley QC, Tom Courtenay, Kenneth Creffield, Joyce Crofts, Peter Crofts, Mr Crompton, Dan Crompton, Andrew Culf, Dorothy Cullen, Richard Culpin, Dr Andrew Cunningham and Mr Justice Curtis.

Rachel Davey, His Honour Judge Ian Davidson QC, Sue Davis, Dawson, John Deave, Pat Dennis, Charles Dickens, Mr Dillingham, Lord Diplock, Tom Dineen, Julie Dunn of Channel 4, Terry Durand and Ian Dury,

Sir Anthony Eden, Sergei Eisenstein, His Honour ARM (Bob) Ellis, Lord Elwyn-Jones, Rosalind English of the BBC World Service, Jeremy Evans of Radio Nottingham, M. Evans, Willie Everard, Don and Phil Everly.

Lord Justice Farquharson, David Farrer QC, Lynn Ferguson of Channel 4, Jim Ferraby, Raymond Fletcher MP, His Honour Judge Flint MP, Keith Floyd, M. Forkings, Frederick Forsyth CBE and David Friend.

Pat Gamble, Frances Gibb, Alan Gilbert, Anne Gilbert, Mr and Mrs J. Glover, Mr Justice Glyn-Jones, Nicholas Godber, Lord Goddard, Mr Justice Goldring, Mr Greenhalgh, Pauline Greensmith and Tony Gregory.

Simon Harrison, Bob Hales, Brenda Hales, Colin Hallam, Paul Hallam, His Honour Judge Andrew Hamilton, James Hanratty, Carol Harper, Peter Harrison, Councillor Mrs P Hart, William Hartnell, David Hatch, Paula Havard, Ray Hawkins, Kath Haywood, His Honour Thomas Heald, Nora Healy, Mr Hendrix, Miss Anne Henshaw, Lord Hewart, Alan Hibbert, Nita Higham nee Matthewman, Barry Hines, Jean Hodgkinson nee Merricks, Ex Chief Superintendent Michael F. Holford QPM, Derek Hollingsworth, Ray Hollingsworth, Les Hooley, Marina Hooley, Rt. Hon. Geoffrey Hoon MP, His Honour Judge John Hopkin, R.S. Hopkinson, Horace, Rt. Hon. Michael Howard QC, MP, 'Tubby' Hudson, Mr Justice Hughes, Mr Justice Hunt, Louise Hunt, Mr Hunter and Geoff Hunter.

His Honour Judge Richard Inglis and Lord Irvine.

Rt. Hon. Michael Jack MP, Lord Chief Justice Jeffreys, Mr Johnson, Calder Jose, Bill Joss, Peter Joyce QC, Mr Justice Jowitt and Lord Justice Judge.

Rose Kearns, His Honour Judge Tom Kellock QC, Lord Keith of Kinkel, Jasmine Kendall, Geoff Kingscott and Derek Knight.

Colin Lane, Myrtle Lane, Lord Chief Justice Lane, Albert Lang, Bill Leafe, Jim Leafe, Councillor A. Lee, Bernard Levin, Humphry Lewis, Brian Longbottom, Gordon Lucas, Maria Lunn, Roy Lynk and Howard Lyon.

Lord Mackay, Pat Malcolm, Maurice McCourt, Maxine McCoy, Mr Justice McCullough, Brendan McGrath, Ian MacGregor, Sue MacGregor, Julie McGuinness, Ian McLaren QC, Miss Mary McLening, Jonathan McLeod, Jim McNamara, Miles Malleson, Dorothy Marshall, Tony Martin, Al Martino, Groucho Marx, Miss Constance A Mason, Captain Adrian Matthewman, Elizabeth Matthewman, Lieutenant Frank Matthewman, Jane Matthewman, Marion Matthewman, Raymond Matthewman, Liz Maxwell, Richard Maxwell QC, Thomas Maxwell, Rt. Hon. John Major MP, Mr Justice May, Dave Mellors, Stanley Mellors, Derrick Midgeley, John Milmo QC, Evelyn Mitchell, Leslie Mitchell, Peter Moffat, Ted Moore, Pat Morgan, Colin Morley, Eric Morley, Mike Morley and Mr Morton.

Colonel Nasser, Ted Newberry, Mr Justice Nield and Margaret Niland.

George Oliver MP, Terry Oliver, His Honour Judge James Orrell and Mr Ossuski.

Albert Pacey, K. Pallender, John Panton, Mark Patterson, Richard Payne, Miss Peaches, Alf Pearce, D. Pearce, Michael Pearce,

Bob Pembleton, George Pembleton, Jane Pembleton, David Pettefar, Melanie Phillips, Frank Pickles, His Honour James Pickles, His Honour Judge Christopher Pitchers, Mr Alan Priestley, Mr Pritchard, Professor Alan Prichard, Geoffrey Prime and Patrick Philip Prothero.

Glenys Radford, Ken Radford, District Judge Graham Richards, Stephanie Richmond, John Rhind, Peter Rhodes, Stephanie Richmond, John Rigby, Dave Rippon, Johnny Rippon, Ann Roberts nee Thorpe, Barbara Roberts, F.E. Roberts, Mr Robinson, Mark Rodgers, J. Rogers, Erwin Rommel, Judy Rose nee Cullimore, Mr Justice Rougier and Dame Margaret Rutherford.

Mr Sanders, Mr Saville, Arthur Scargill, Paul Scarrott, Anthony Scrivener QC, R. Seakirk, Jeff Seamer, Nick Seaton the chairman of the Campaign for Real Education, Ray Sewell, Paul Sharpley, Bill Shaw, Alan Sillitoe, Miss Silk, Councillor WT Slack, Michael Skidmore, Dennis Skinner MP, Noel Sisson, Sir Brian Smedley, Edward Smith, Harold Smith, Harry Smith, Leonard Smith, Mary Smith, Mike Smith, Shaun Smith, Winifred Molly Smith, David Spence, Pete Spence, Jo Stafford, John Stalker, John Stobart, Rt. Hon. Jack Straw MP and Frank Swain.

Margaret Taft, Rex Tedd QC, Rita Tew, Baroness Thatcher, Geoffrey Thibeault, Dr Thompson, Sharon Thompson, C. Thornton, J. Thornton, R. Thornton, J.L. Telleray, Mr Townshend, Peter Turner and Terry Turner.

Lord Varley.

Dilys Walden, David Walker, Neil Walker, Mike Walvin, John Warren QC, P.W. Watson, Derek Weekes, Andrew Widdowson, His Honour Judge David Wilcox, C Wilkinson, James Williamson, Rt. Hon Harold Wilson, Dorothy Wincott nee Frost, Lord Woolf, Mike Woodhouse, His Honour Judge Brian Woods, Mr Wright, Mrs Wright nee Deacon and Bert Wynn.

Bibliography

Cater Walsh & Co   *Official Court Reporters*

R.J. Cootes   *Britain Since 1700.*

Drive Publications Limited   *Illustrated Guide to Britain.*

Julie McGuinness and Jeremy Evans   *The Century Speaks, Voices of*
                                          Nottinghamshire on BBC
                                          Radio Nottingham. Tempus
                                          Publishing Ltd 1999.

Dorling Kindersley   *Chronicles of the 20th Century*

Dominic Egan   *Irvine,   Politically   Correct?*
                                          Mainstream Publishing.

Local History Society   *Heanor Street Names (1977)*
                                          Life in Old Heanor (1983)
                                          Heanor - Then and Now
                                          (1987)

Reader's Digest,   *Yesterday's Britain.*

Carol Ellis QC and
Hillary Jellie Barrister at Law.   *The Weekly Law Reports.*

About the Author

Narvel Annable's first book "Miss Calder's Children" (1997) described his early post war schooldays in Belper, a quaint Derbyshire mill town. His second book "Heanor Schooldays" (1998) was also autobiographical covering his unhappiness in a grim, Dickensian, Church of England junior school from 1955 to 1958. Adolescence and the move to William Howitt Secondary Modern School in September 1958 was a dramatic improvement, graphically retold in the second half of the social history.

In 1963 he emigrated to the United States and arrived in Detroit on the day before the assassination of President Kennedy. The next seven years saw him in a variety of jobs which included labourer, lathe hand, bank messenger and camera salesman. In 1975 he graduated from Eastern Michigan University (magna cum laude) and taught history for a year at St Bridget High School in Detroit.

In 1976 he returned to Derbyshire to help organise and launch 'Heritage Education Year 1977' at Sudbury Hall. From 1978 to 1995 he taught history at a large comprehensive school which gradually became more progressive. Mr Annable criticises these changes in some detail in his first two books. Seizing retirement at the earliest opportunity, he started to write historical and educational articles for the local press and has spoken several times on BBC Radio Derby. "Death on the Derwent" - A Murder Mystery set in Belper 1949, his third book and first novel was published in 1999. His fourth book "A Judge Too Far" - A Biography of His Honour Judge Keith Matthewman QC of the Nottingham Crown Court was published in 2001.

Inspired by 'Heanor Schooldays', Mr Annable is currently working on his second novel - "Lost Lad" A Mystery set in Derbyshire in 1960.

By the same author ...

"Death on the Derwent"

A Murder Mystery set in Belper 1949

ISBN 0 9530419 2 1

Join the formidable schoolmistress Miss Florence Calder and her small cantankerous hunchbacked sister Miss Madge, as they detect and attempt to unmask a clever murderer in the leafy, ivy-clad, quaint and quieter Belper of 1949.

This entertaining blend of fact and fiction, set against the skilfully described background of spectacular Derbyshire scenery, is both an intriguing 'whodunit' and also a local history. Atmospheric narrative will take you around the nooks and crannies of the old mill town, in both bright sunshine and also in menacing thick fog.

It is complete with a body in a boat, psychic phenomena in the candle lit haunted halls of the rambling old Bridge House School, a seance, a conjuring trick and all ending in a surprise.

Some hilarious, colourful and quirky characters spanning the social divide from the past poverty of Cowhill, to the opulence of Bridge Hill, combine with suspense and dramatic tension to produce a thoroughly enjoyable thriller. 204 pages.

"So who has done it? Well Narvel has, but he'll keep you guessing right up to the final breath."

John Holmes, BBC Radio Derby.

"A remarkable murder mystery novel ... gives a new twist to the whodunit genre ... a skilful mixture of fact and fiction ... strong historical interest ... complications and twists, red herrings and false trails. Mr Annable has got himself a real-life, ready-made character in Miss Florence Calder. This could be - should be - the start of a series of Miss Calder novels."

Geoff Hammerton, The Derby Evening Telegraph 17.12.99.

"Peopled with distinctive characters ... meritorious for the descriptive detail. A well produced book. Worth reading a second time or more, fully to appreciate the construction of this ingenious novel."

Margaret Beardsley, The Belper News 23.02.00

"Great characters!" **Bob Attewell, The Belper Express 13.01.00**

"I loved the rich and qualitative language, the machinations, twists and turns of the plot. I was empathetic with the characters as they desperately tried to unravel the mystery Mr Annable had so brilliantly created."

Terry Ladlow, 'Terivision Productions', Wetwang, Driffield, East Yorkshire 22.03.00

"Simon Tonks is the silly village fool who ends up as a servant to the Calders, Claud Hoadley is the pompous Belper man-turned-snob, who teaches elocution so that the townspeople can 'better themselves', and Aubrey Pod is a pushy Mr Toad of Toad Hall - style character who is full of himself."

Paul Imrie, 'Talk of the Town', The Derby Evening Telegraph 23.11.99.

"Interesting and amusing." **Marla Addison, Peak Times 10.12.99.**

"Death on the Derwent" can be obtained directly from the author by sending a cheque for £6.95 plus £1.50 for post and packaging to -
44 Dovedale Crescent, Belper, Derby DE56 1HJ.

Also by the same author ...

"Heanor Schooldays"
A Social History

ISBN 0 9530419 1 3

This book deals with the last hundred years but majors on the Author's personal experience of the 1950's and 1960's in which he recreates the optimistic social atmosphere of teenagers enjoying the popular culture of the day. You will also gain insight into the gritty, unpretentious, honest character of Heanor folk.

It is a graphic colourful and emotional journey from the depths of despair to the heights of happiness. Along the way Narvel Annable honours the memory of teachers, headmasters and headmistresses, who have shaped and influenced the lives of countless Heanorians. Disquiet is expressed as discredited modern teaching methods are contrasted to the successful tried and trusted methods of past years.

Forty-five photographs and fifteen documents will rekindle memories. The work is supported by a foreword from His Honour Judge Keith Matthewman, QC, and contains first hand accounts from many contributors including the one time local lad, The Rt. Hon. Kenneth Clarke, QC, MP, the former Chancellor of the Exchequer from 1993 to 1997. 205 pages.

"I was enthralled. A cracking collection of tales."

John Holmes, BBC Radio Derby.

Described on November 5th 1998 in the **Ripley and Heanor News** and the **Belper News** as -

"Vivid and detailed memories of a 1950's childhood. Sensitively written, Narvel explores the vagaries of the educational system which helped to develop his character and prepare him for adulthood. This is an important snapshot of social history, and the author brings it to life with recollections of strict discipline, bullying and extreme forms of punishment. A roller-coaster of emotions."

Pauline Oldrini

"Heanor Schooldays" was also reviewed on December 4th 1998 in **The Derby Evening Telegraph** -

"Mr Annable mixes anecdotes with comment to provide an important record of changes made in education as seen from the sides of both pupil and teacher."

Geoff Hammerton

Heanor Schooldays" was on the 1998 list of 'Recommended Publication' by the **Campaign for Real Education** at 18 Westlands Grove, Stockton Lane, York YO3 0EF.

"Heanor Schooldays" received the following foreword from **His Honour Judge Keith Matthewman QC** -

"Narvel Annable has managed to do what most authors never could; that is, to make a book about the details of his schooldays a thoroughly enjoyable read.

In his unique style he gives us a history of people and institutions. He gives us his views on education, past and present, and we are treated to a fascinating glimpse of a school-life in the fifties and sixties, complete with all its sorrows and joys.

You do not have to remember those days to enjoy this book: you do not have to be an educationalist to enjoy this book: but if you are in either group, or both, you will enjoy it all the more - and so will your children."

"Heanor Schooldays" can be obtained directly from the author by sending a cheque for £8.95 plus £1.50 for post and packaging to -
44 Dovedale Crescent, Belper, Derbyshire DE56 1HJ.

Look out for Narvel Annable's next whodunit novel -

Lost Lad

A Mystery set in Derbyshire 1960

In the glorious summer of 1960, six pals from William Howitt Secondary Modern School in the small mining town of Heanor decide to cycle up into the high Derbyshire hills.

They have a great time and everything goes well - until they cycle out of the tiny grey limestone village of Litton, along a high wind-swept narrow country lane and speedily descend the 650ft steep drop into the deep, but beautiful wooded ravine which is called Miller's Dale. Six boys were happily racing down the hill, but only five reach the bottom!

In the following hours, the boys make a thorough search for their friend - in vain. Eventually the police make a time consuming, careful, professional search - in vain. Where is the lost lad?

Forty years pass and one of the original pals who has spent most of his adult life abroad, returns to Derbyshire, attends a school reunion in Heanor and decides to re-open the search.

An odyssey which takes many twists and turns around the lives of five different men, some of whom can hardly recognise each other after four decades. An investigation which turns other lives upside-down. A quest which eventually comes to a dramatic and stunning conclusion when we finally learn the devastating truth about - the 'Lost Lad'.